The West Speaks

THE WEST SPEAKS

INTERVIEWS BY JERRY GORDON

Copyright © Jerry Gordon, 2012

All rights reserved. No part of this book may be reproduced in any form or by any means, electronic or mechanical, without permission in writing from the publisher except by reviewers who may quote brief passages in their reviews.

Published by New English Review Press
a subsidiary of World Encounter Institute
PO Box 158397
Nashville, Tennessee 37215

Printed in the United States of America

Cover Design by Kendra Adams
Photos left to right, top to bottom, Kenneth Timmerman, Geert Wilders, Bat Ye'or, Nina Shea, Richard L. Rubenstein and Kurt Westergaard

ISBN 978-0-578-09993-4

First Edition

NEW ENGLISH REVIEW PRESS
newenglishreview.org

To Jean-Ellen, my life companion and editorial partner, without whose critical support I would not have been able to reach a wide and growing readership in the *New English Review*.

To my supportive children, Harold, Illisa, Leslie, and granddaughters, Arielle, Amanda, Elana and Lindsay.

To Rebecca Bynum, my abiding colleague and publisher of the *New English Review*, who conceived of this project.

"If I am not for myself, then who will be for me? And if I am only for myself, then what am I? And if not now, when?"

- Rabbi Hillel

CONTENTS

Preface ix

1) Arieh Eldad 13

2) Jonathan Housman 30

3) Kurt Westergaard 39

4) Geert Wilders 45

5) Erick Stakelbaeck 53

6) Richard L. Rubenstein 71

7) Sam Solomon 84

8) Lars Vilks 91

9) David Yerushalmi 99

10) Charles Jacobs 113

11) Kenneth Timmerman 121

12) Robert Wistrich 136

13) Lars Hedegaard 143

14) David Beamer _____ 153

15) Bat Ye'or _____ 161

16) Nina Shea _____ 176

17) Elisabeth Sabaditsch-Wolff _____ 193

18) Ibn Warraq _____ 204

19) Mark Durie _____ 215

Epilogue _____ 229

PREFACE

On September 11, 2001, Islamic terrorists, well educated young men – Saudi, Egyptian, and Yemeni nationals - hijacked four airliners (American Airlines Flight 11 and United Flight 175 from Boston's Logan airport, American Airlines Flight 77 from Dulles airport and United Airlines Flight 93 from Newark Airport). With captive passengers aboard, they flew into the Twin Towers of the World Trade Center in Manhattan and the Pentagon in Arlington, Virginia. Brave actions of the 40 passengers and crew aboard Flight 93 led to the first counter-attack within thirty minutes of the sky-jacking. The Flight 93 passengers overcame the Islamic terrorists diverting the aircraft from its ultimate target, the Capital building in Washington, crashing into a field in Shanksville, Pennsylvania instead. These 19 Muslim terrorists killed more people than the Japanese sneak attack on Pearl Harbor on December 7, 1941 - over 3,000. They didn't discriminate in their mindless slaughter whether their victims were Christians, Jews, fellow Muslims, Buddhists or Hindus. Economic losses from the unprovoked attack ran into the billions. Trauma touched hundreds of millions in America and around the globe. The names Osama bin Laden and Ayman al-Zawahiri of al Qaeda became front page news. On May 2, 2011, US Navy Seal Team Six killed Osama bin Laden in a firefight in Pakistan. Khalid Sheikh Mohammed, the alleged mastermind of 9/11, had been captured previously. He confessed under duress and subsequently has been in detention at Guantanamo Bay awaiting prosecution at a military tribunal.

The country on 9/11 was suddenly adrift in the wake of this disastrous Pearl Harbor of the 21st Century. In the years that followed 9/11, our country's military found itself enmeshed in the long war against the network of Islamic jihad terror groups in Afghanistan, Iraq and world-wide, costing thousands of casualties and billions of dollars to prosecute. Over seventeen thousand Islamic terror attacks have occurred, since 9/11. Hundreds of thousands have died or been horribly injured from these jihad attacks. Attacks like those made by Indonesian Islamists at a crowded Bali nightspot frequented by Australians on October 12, 2002 by Moroccan Al Qaeda affiliates on commuter trains in Madrid on March 11, 2004, by native born British Muslims on the bus and underground system in London on July 7, 2005 and by Pakistani terrorist in Mumbai on November 26, 2008.

Muslim young people, we suddenly learned, are being indoctrinated in fundamentalist Islam in mosques and madrassas throughout the world's Muslim community of believers - the ummah. These believers are collectively engaged in a jihad, or struggle, to remove all obstacles to the spread and ultimate dominance of Islam. One of these obstacles is the Constitution of the United States of America. This effort is being financed with billions of petro-dollars from Saudi Arabia and the Gulf Emirates. Terms like Londonistan and Eurabia are now commonly used to describe the Islamization and infiltration of the U.K. and the E.U. by Muslim advocacy groups demanding enclaves ruled by Islamic Shariah law.

In the aftermath of this onslaught of Islamic terrorism against the West, a virtual international confederation of counter-jihad advocates arose to expose the Grand Jihad of the core Islamic doctrine: a totalitarian creed disguised with a thin veneer of religious practices seeking world domination by supplanting the Judeo-Christian values that undergird Western liberal democracy. Hebrew University Professor of Islamic and Chinese History Raphael Israeli delineated the conflict during a series of lectures in America in early 2012. He contrasted the sovereignty of the people, the bedrock of our Western concept of representative democracy with the uncreated inviolable words of the Islamic god, Allah, and his divine prophet Mohammed in the Qur'an. The Qur'an brooks neither criticism, nor grants precious individual rights of liberty and freedom as it is *"inshallah,"* the will of Allah, which prevails. According to Israeli there are no negotiations possible under Islam. Unbelievers confronting conquering jihadist Islam have three choices: death, conversion or subjugation under Shariah law; a system that Islamic scholar Bat Ye'or has called dhimmitude.

Dhimmitude is a system of laws and cultural practices directed at depriving conquered unbelievers of basic freedoms in exchange for payment of *jizya*, which is a poll tax and a form of extortion paid for being left alive in a subjugated state. It has been called a form of ritualized barbarity. Under Shariah, as propounded in the rulings of the four major schools of Islamic law, free speech is criminalized as blasphemy and the right to leave Islam by choice, apostasy, is punishable by death. Women are despised as evil, forced to adopt clothing to make them invisible and subject to death by stoning for the merest human feelings. Children, both boys and girls, are victims of pedophilia. Islam erupted in a paroxysm of hatred against the protected (under dhimmitude) "people of the book," Jews and Christians. The Jews who scoffed at the rants of the "prophet" Mohammed in the Arabian city of Yathrib, later renamed Medina, found themselves slaughtered, their women raped and children enslaved. Jews and Christians have been demonized with hatred under Islam over the millennia. Christians were victimized and marginalized in lands in which they and minority Jews once dominated. Subjected to intimidation, pressures to convert, deprived of property under the oppressive system of dhimmitude, Christian lands were converted into Muslim realms and the survivors forced to flee to diasporas in the West. Where once church bells tolled, the muezzin's call now rings out calling the majority Muslims to prayer five times daily. Islam, which means submission in Arabic, now represents more than 1.4 billion people. It is currently engaged in furthering its penetration of the West through a Grand Jihad based on subterfuge, manipulation of host country laws and infiltration of governments.

Against this inexorable onslaught are the watchers on the ramparts of the West. Like modern day Jeremiahs, they are unloved for issuing a warning of what could eventuate by acquiescing to the demands of the virtual Caliphate. A Caliphate made up of 57 Muslim nations (including the Palestinian Authority) funded by the Saudi-backed Organization of Islamic Cooperation. These watchers have seen vain hopes of the West dashed - hopes that Muslim minorities might assimilate, as did non-Muslim immigrants before them. Instead, these Muslim immigrants are demanding adoption of Shariah law and courts along with self rule. Shariah doctrine clearly rejects basic civil and human rights laws.

This collection of interviews, originally published in the *New English Review,* displays the courage of those who have spoken up in the media, the councils of government, and have been tried for the right to criticize the totalitarian doctrine of Islam. Some have been acquitted, but others have been convicted and fined. These courageous men and women, defenders of liberty and freedom, cover several continents: America, Australia, Europe and Asia. They include both Jewish and Christian theologians, Muslim apostates, members of parliament, journalists, Islamic scholars, artists, editorial cartoonists, historians, housewives, international human rights lawyers, parents of 9/11 victims and physicians. They are citizens of Australia, Austria, the Netherlands, Denmark, Israel, Sweden, the United Kingdom and the United States.

These interviews, while presented in chronological order have been updated to reflect recent developments for each personality interviewed.

All those interviewed, as the title of this collection implies, speak fearlessly as advocates for the West, for Western values of free speech, liberty, freedom and human rights as memorialized in both unwritten and written constitutions, common law and the UN Universal Declaration of Human Rights.

Pensacola
February 2012

1
ARIEH ELDAD
NOVEMBER 2008

Israeli Knesset Member, Dr. Arieh Eldad, is a nationalist gadfly among the country's politicians. He is a member of the Moledet party list of the minority National Union faction that favors the willing transfer of "Palestinian" Arab refugees from the disputed territories of Judea and Samaria to the de facto Palestine: Jordan. With more than 70% of Jordan's population composed of Palestinian Arabs, Eldad considers that the real "two state solution." Jordan has plenty of territory to absorb their fellow Arabs now languishing in the squalid UNWRA camps in Samaria, Judea and Gaza. Eldad and others in his party argue that international investment in agricultural production, water, energy, urban and jobs development in Jordan is required to help facilitate absorption.

This has not made Dr. Eldad, a world ranked plastic surgeon and reserve Brig. General in the IDF Medical Corps by profession, a welcome party in the current discussions between the Kadima government and PA President Mahmoud Abbas leading to a possible "peace agreement." Neither would secretary of State Condoleezza Rice in the waning days of the Bush Administration look with interest on Dr. Eldad's suggestions. The agreement under discussion is virtually in tatters given the prospects for a general election in Israel. Eldad is pleased with this outcome, as it stifles any "shelf agreements" from being concluded.

Eldad, however, has a more expansive agenda. He organized a gathering of world parliamentarians in Jerusalem in December, 2008 on "Facing Jihad." He considers Israel the "canary in the mines of radical

Islam," something his fellow Israelis would rather not think about. He brought courageous Dutch parliamentarian, Geert Wilders, to show his controversial film "Fitna" (strife or chaos in Arabic) and legislators from Belgium, Denmark, France, Italy, the U.K. and America to formulate a declaration against Islamization among Western democracies. Eldad deems it crucially important for Israelis to become educated about the nuances of this existential threat that seeks to extinguish the Jewish state as well as other non-Muslim nations. Eldad has traveled to conferences in Brussels and America to confer with anti-jihadists and in the process create an alliance to oppose the Grand Jihad. In Manhattan in late September, while attending a Stonegate Institute conference featuring Wilders, he took time to speak at a protest rally against Iranian President Mahmoud Ahmadinejad outside the Grand Hyatt Hotel, where the latter was attending an interfaith Iftar dinner during Ramadan.

Eldad's late father, Dr. Israel Eldad was a nationalist philosopher, teacher and leader in the pre-state, Lehi resistance group. He was a Revisionist in the mold of Ze'ev Jabotinsky. Dr. Eldad is frequently complimented after public talks when people come up to him and tell him that he reminds them of his father.

Eldad has excoriated Israel's government leaders for the debacles of the unilateral withdrawal from the Gush Katif settlements in Gaza in 2005 and for the failure to defeat Hezbollah in the Second Lebanon War in 2006. He was injured in the massive protest and clash at the Judean hilltop settlement of Amona in February, 2006, when more than 5,000 Israeli police and IDF troops confronted 4,000 protesters. As a result of his injuries at the protest, he was not able to return to his profession as a plastic surgeon and head of the program at the Hadassah Ein Kerem Hospital in Jerusalem.

Eldad had been a vocal critic of many public figures through his weekly columns in leading Israeli newspapers, *Yediot Aharonot* and *Ma'ariv*. When the editors were changed, his jeremiads against corruption in government and Israeli society were silenced. He has frequently debated with the extreme left-wing former Labor Justice Minister, Yossi Beilin. Beilin is considered the father of the failed Oslo Accords and Geneva Agreements.

In this wide ranging interview with Dr. Eldad, you will gain some insights into his Zionist nationalism, the necessity for Israeli political reform and the military defeat of Iran's proxies, both Hezbollah and Hamas. The creation of an enduring alliance of Western politicians to combat the Grand Jihad poised to engulf their countries and the State of

Israel is a significant element in his efforts.

Gordon: Your father, the late Israel Eldad was a heroic independence fighter, educator and opposition leader in Lohamei Herut Yisrael (Fighters for the Freedom of Israel) or Lehi. What can you tell us about him and his influence on you as a member of the Knesset?

Eldad: My Father, Prof. Israel Eldad, was a rare combination of a rabbinical scholar, philosopher, and underground leader in the pre-State of Israel era. He was a teacher, a trenchant idealist, but also a person full of humor and love: love of his family, his people, and the Jewish Homeland, Israel.

Orthodox Jews often refer to their fathers as "my father, my teacher." This is a very apt description of my father. He taught me the Torah and to play chess. He taught me history and what lay in the future. He taught me not to be afraid to be in the minority of prevailing opinions and always to be cautious when praised by rivals. He taught me that the Jewish people can only rely on themselves. He taught me to put my personal interest after my nation's interest, and to always seek out where I can serve my country in the most effective ways. When I was a child he took me to the fields to watch the ants. When I grew older he took me on the Ninth of Av (that sorrowful commemoration of the destruction of the First and Second Temples in 586 B.C.E. and 70 C.E and the Jewish Republic in 135 C.E.) to the Israel Museum. We stood before the statue of the Roman Emperor Hadrian, who smashed the last rebellion of Bar Kochba at the fortress of Betar in Judea. My father would look into his eyes and ask him:" Nu? (Well?), where are you and where are we?"

Israel Eldad was not only a great father and a teacher. He was a prolific author of many important books. These works include: *About the Torah* (*Hegionot Mikra*), memoires of his years in the Revisionist Movement of Ze'ev Jabotinsky and the LEHI underground – *The First Tithe* (recently translated into English by Ze'ev Golan); the "Jewish Revolution" – which I was privileged to publish the second edition of recently; his lectures about the poet Uri Zvi Greenberg that I edited with my eldest daughter Karni; four volumes of articles entitled *Chronicles – the news of the past*; and eight volumes of translations of the German Philosopher Frederic Nietzsche.

My father's writings provide me with a veritable encyclopedia and fount of wisdom. When I need answers to define our current situation, speak in a synagogue on Shabbat, or teach in a pre-military preparatory school, his thoughts provide answers. He taught me well and left me a living legacy of what is to be done. My best compliment is when people approach me after a talk and say: "You remind me of your father."

Gordon: As a National Union opposition leader in the Knesset, you have espoused a doctrine of "willing transfer" with regard to "Palestinian" Arab communities in Judea and Samaria. Dissident Israeli Arab citizens and even Arab Members of the Knesset (M.K.) have engaged in sedition and support of the terror groups Hezbollah and Hamas opposing Israel's existence as a Jewish state. Could you explain what "willing transfer" entails and give some examples of internal Arab sedition?

Eldad: Humanitarian resettlement of Arab refugees is neither original with me nor is it new. Arab refugees are not under the responsibility of the United Nations High Commissioner for Refugees, but instead are controlled by a special agency designated only for Palestinians. – The UN Refugee Works Relief Administration or UNWRA. 50-70 million refugees have been resettled since the end of World War II. More than four million Palestinians are the only ones still in these UNWRA refugee camps. Because the UNWRA camps are virtually administered by Palestinians, these UNWRA refugees, now in the third generation in 60 years, have been taught incitement to hate against Israel and Jews, all thanks to funding of nearly a half billion dollar annually donated by taxpayers in the West. How bad are these UNWRA Camps? An average refugee family in the camp at Balata, near Nablus, has an annual income of $700 and lives in appalling conditions. I am convinced that these people must be resettled, preferably in Jordan. Jordan is effectively, Palestine. 70% of the Jordanian population are Palestinians. This is the de facto fulfillment of "the two state solution." If a large scale international program was created to bring water, energy, housing and jobs to a designated area in Jordan a willing transfer could happen. Within a few years we would be able to resettle 2-3 million refugees in Jordan.

This plan will not solve the problem of Arab Israeli citizens who oppose the state of Israel as a Jewish state. They do not want individual rights. They want national minority rights in Israel. They demand that Israel become a Bi-National state. They are not satisfied with Jordan as the Palestinian state. They want a third state for Palestinians only. Effectively what they are seeking is a 'Judenrein' (Jew free in German) state in Gaza, Judea and Samaria. They seek to undermine the State of Israel and reject it as a Jewish state. They want to eliminate Israel so that Jews will not have a state of their own in the world. They want to change the national Anthem "Ha'tikva" to something else that they can identify with, change the flag, and erase "the law of return" that grants Israeli citizenship to every Jew who makes Aliyah. In other words they are the enemies within the Jewish state of Israel.

Gordon: You have been the leader in the formation of a new party in Israel, Ha'tikva (the "hope"). Why did you and others in Israel feel that a new secular nationalist party was required? What is the timetable for Ha'tikva implementation before the next Knesset General Election?

Eldad: I am a Member of the Knesset (Israel Parliament) for Moledet ("homeland" in Hebrew) which is part of the National Union party faction. Moledet was established by the late Minister of Tourism, Rechavam (Gandi) Zeevi, who was murdered by Arab terrorists in Jerusalem on October 17, 2001. Moledet embraces the idea of willing population transfer as an integral part of a comprehensive plan to achieve real peace between the Jews and the Arabs. It promotes the view that Jordan is Palestine. Moledet is neither a religious or secular party in the Knesset. It is a party for the entire national wing in Israel. After Gandi was murdered, Rabbi Benni Elon took over leadership of Moledet. It gradually merged with religious parties (Tequma, Ahi and NRP) and the National Union became a de facto religious party. Israelis who are secular and do not wear a Kippa (male Jewish head covering) did not vote for the National Union. They voted Likud. These secular nationalists were alienated by former PM Ariel Sharon when the settlements of Gush Katif in Gaza and North Samaria were uprooted. Israel Beiteinu, M.K. Avigdor Lieberman's Russian émigré party in the Knesset also advocates the division of Jerusalem and creation of a Palestinian State. Effectively, these secular nationalists had no place to go and many simply stayed home. The National Union stands at a cross road. The Knesset faction could become a united, non-sectarian party by going to the voters and asking them in primaries to elect their representatives to the Knesset. Or the faction could become a religious-only party, with a nominating committee of Rabbis' and public figures to decide who will represent it. If National Union can preserve the original spirit of Moledet I will stay. If it becomes a de facto and de jure religious party, then I will go with the newly formed Ha'tikva party list, to attract the non- religious voters in the nationalist camp. This would assure them that they can vote for a true ideological party. Only in Israel can such a split enlarge the power of the right wing nationalist camp.

Gordon: You are a world ranked plastic surgeon, Reserve Brig. General in the IDF Medical Corps, as well as an Israeli opposition Knesset member. How has that professional background influenced your membership on Knesset Committees regarding Israel's national security and counter-terrorism policies?

Eldad: I am an active member of the Labor, Welfare and Health committee of the Knesset and the chairman of sub-committees on various health issues.
My legislative efforts leverage my professional background and experience, as both a burn wound surgeon and as an IDF Commander in the Medical Corps. Unfortunately, my expertise as a plastic surgeon does not help me in the fields of national security policy making and foreign affairs. Sometimes I feel that a psychiatrist could do a better job. The decisions of the current leaders of Israel cannot be explained by any other modality in medicine.

Gordon: There was an incident at a Beersheba Hospital involving a Palestinian woman terrorist who had received skin transplant treatments authorized by you. Could you describe that incident and what it illustrates about Israeli humanitarianism versus fanatic Islamic Jihadism?

Eldad: I was instrumental in establishing the Israeli National Skin Bank, which is the largest in the world. The National Skin Bank stores skin for every day needs as well as for war time or mass casualty situations. This skin bank is hosted at the Hadassah Ein Kerem University hospital in Jerusalem where I was the chairman of plastic surgery. This is how I was asked to supply skin for an Arab woman from Gaza, who was hospitalized in Soroka Hospital in Beersheba after her family burned her. Usually, such atrocities happen among Arab families when the women are suspected of having an affair. We supplied all the needed Homografts for her treatment. She was successfully treated by my friend and colleague Prof. Lior Rosenberg, and discharged to return to Gaza. She was invited for regular follow up visits to the outpatient clinic in Beersheba. One day she was caught at a border crossing wearing a suicide belt. She meant to explode herself in the outpatient clinic of the hospital where they saved her life. It seems that her family promised her that if she did that, they would forgive her.

This is only one example of the war between Jews and Muslims in the Land of Israel. It is not a territorial conflict. This is a civilizational conflict.

Gordon: As a Knesset opposition party leader you have criticized and protested against the Sharon/Olmert governments on their unilateral withdrawal from the Gush Katif settlements in Gaza in August, 2005. Why did you oppose the Gaza disengagement? How has that retreat made Israel less secure and more vulnerable to Hamas and Palestinian Islamic Jihad terrorist rocket and missile attacks?

Eldad: People did not open their eyes and see what inevitably happened in Israel after the unilateral disengagement from Gush Katif in Gaza and Northern Samaria in August, 2005. The IDF Chief of Staff, General Moshe Ya'alon said such a step would be a huge boost for Hamas terrorism. The people of Israel trusted Sharon, but neither he nor they heeded these warnings. My colleagues and I from the National Union warned about the looming catastrophe. We warned that Hamas would take over and turn Gaza into the largest terror base in the Middle East. The government did not listen. They accused us of being "Messianic" and blamed us because we wanted the Settlements in Gush Katif to stay forever. That was true. We believe that the land of Israel belongs to the people of Israel and that Jews have the right to live everywhere in this land. But the combination of hatred from the Left in Israel against the settlers and trust in Ariel Sharon, as "Mr. Security," was lethal. The public did not question the logic of the plan. Sharon never tried to prove how this was going to improve our security situation. Gaza fell into the hands of Hamas turning it into a huge 'terrorstan.' Once this had occurred, the failed and corrupt Kadima government of Olmert did not dare go back and destroy Hamas. They knew that reentering Gaza would prove that they were wrong to withdraw. Sharon insisted on going back to the last centimeter of the old "Green Line" (the 1949 Armistice line referred to as the "Auschwitz line" by the late Abba Eban, Israel's veteran Foreign Minister). This set an unfortunate precedent for any future agreement with the Palestinians: uprooting of Jewish settlements and ethnic cleansing of Jews in the region. Arabs are allowed in Israel, while Jews are not allowed in the areas of the Palestinian Authority. This anti Zionist step undermines the very basis for Jewish settlement in the land of Israel. We have yet to pay the full price for this crime.

Gordon: You were injured in the Amona settlement protest in February, 2006. How did that affect your professional career? Did the protest demonstrate resolve against further unilateral withdrawals from disputed territories in Judea and Samaria?

Eldad: During the terrible evacuation of Gush Katif in August, 2005 no real resistance to the police or the IDF occurred. The deportees wept, hugged and danced with the soldiers. They climbed into buses only to see their homes, where they lived for 30 years, destroyed in minutes. For many settlers it was not only the destruction of their dreams and homes, they also lost their trust in Israeli political leadership.

The Israeli Supreme Court on February 1, 2006 ordered the destruction of nine houses built without permission in the Judean hill top settlement of Amona. PM Olmert of Kadima had been in office only a few weeks. He wanted to show the hated settlers that he was a strong leader. The settlers, in turn, wanted to wipe away the stain of the non-resistance in the face of the Gush Katif expulsion of the preceding August. The collision was inevitable. More than five thousand Israeli Police, Israeli Border Police, and IDF soldiers faced 4,000 protesters. Within the first moments of the clash, I was brutally attacked by policemen who knew that I was a member of the Knesset and had immunity. However, they had orders "to teach us a lesson." One of the policemen named Ibrahim Rihal, held my right hand, and twisted my thumb until he tore the ligaments. I lost consciousness. Operated on after a few days, the torn ligaments were sutured. However, I remain with 10% permanent disability. This does not prevent me from voting in the Knesset. However, I do not know if I will be able to perform surgery, if and when I try to go back to my profession following my service in the Knesset. At the end of the clash that fateful day in Amona there were 250 settlers and 60 policemen in hospitals. Nine houses were destroyed. A parliamentary committee was formed to investigate the events at Amona. But a new standard of resistance was achieved. No government in Israel will take for granted that they can evacuate a settlement and destroy it. They know very well that the next time they try it; they may have to kill some of us first. They know that no government in Israel will survive such brutality. The fact that the government avoids any attempt to forcibly evacuate settler outposts after Amona is the direct result of that very traumatic day.

Gordon: Given your membership on Knesset Security and Defense Committees, why, in your opinion, did Israel fail to win the Second Lebanon War against Hezbollah in 2006? Has the IDF overcome deficiencies in unit training, material and equipment cited in the Winograd Commission report? Can Israel cope with another possible conflict on its Northern border with Lebanon?

Eldad: Israel failed to win the war against Hezbollah in August, 2006 because it had a cabal of incompetents. We had an incompetent crook as Prime Minister, Olmert, with no military understanding. We had a Defense Minister Peretz, who was a union activist clown. We had an IDF Chief Of Staff (COS), Halutz, who was a pilot who did not understand how win a ground war against Islamic guerrillas. This tragic combination was the result of the criminal decision of Ariel Sharon who nominated his yes-man, IDF COS Halutz, in order to perform the unilateral disengagement from Gaza a year earlier. I asked PM Sharon, in Knesset defense committee deliberations, if Halutz was nominated because of corrupt political reasons to command the IDF in a real war. Sharon mocked me, lowered his glasses, looked me over and said: "I see you are worried, Doctor …Do not worry, and I am here." Another criminal decision by Olmert was nominating, as Minister of Defence, Peretz, who did not have a clue about security and military issues. He did so even though Peretz asked to be the Minister of Finance. However corrupt Olmert wanted that cabinet post for his good friend Hirshzon (now facing trial on the accusation that he has stolen millions from the public and could possible spend years in jail, if convicted). The third corruptive element was the pattern of behavior of the IDF general staff. They all knew that the way that Olmert, Peretz, and Halutz conducted the Second Lebanon War led to military failure. They were careerists. They did not want to risk their personal careers. There was not one among them who was ready to resign publicly to tell the people of Israel the truth about the way the war was conducted.

There are many myths about the low level of training of the reserve units of the IDF. It is true that this level was very poor. But the regular excuse was: "No money for training." It is true that budget cuts were made in the years before the war, and the military needed an additional million training days annually. But one should not be confused by these arguments. The IDF spent 4.5 million training days to prepare the army for the Gaza disengagement. 50,000 soldiers and policemen were trained to evacuate the settlers, including "mental preparation." The government of Israel spent what was needed to fight a real war in

Lebanon on the futile training of the IDF to evacuate Jewish Israeli citizens from Gaza. An action that enabled Hamas to build a terror state.

Since the Second Lebanon War, IDF reserve units have been trained, and the country has rid itself of the corrupt and incompetent triumvirate that led Israel during the debacle. Yet, there are more lessons to learn, and unfortunately the wrong conclusions were taken by the current political leadership. They think that the next time a conflict with Hezbollah or Hamas occurs that they can avoid war. They did that in the case of the continuous Kassem and Katyusha rocket bombardments from Gaza on Israeli towns in both the western Negev and the south of the country. The government of Israel allowed a cease fire that gave Hamas the freedom to arm, train, build weapons and ammunition depots. Unfortunately, this will lead to needless loss of IDF soldiers' lives in the inevitable re-occupation of the area in order to destroy the Hamas terror infrastructure. The IDF is better now. The military plans are ready. However, there are no effective leaders to command the IDF. What Israel needs urgently is capable and effective leadership.

Gordon: In light of the virtual veto power that Hezbollah has over the Lebanese government of PM Fuad Saniora and the failure of UNSC 1701 to prevent the restocking of tens of thousands of rockets and missiles threatening Northern and Central Israel, what can the next Israeli government do to combat this threat?

Eldad: The only way to remove the threat of the Iranian proxy Hezbollah in Lebanon is a large military operation equivalent to the First Lebanon War in 1982. This will be an essential step before any attack on Iranian nuclear weapons development facilities. Israel should understand that if we decide to attack Iran and remove the nuclear threat, we will be attacked from Lebanon, Gaza strip, and, perhaps, Syria. Thus, the first step in the attack against Iran should be a pre-emptive strike against Hezbollah and Hamas. The timing of the war against Hezbollah should be coordinated with the plans against Iran.

Gordon: The Western Negev town of Sderot has been under daily siege from Palestinian Islamic Jihad Kassem rockets for over seven years. Why has the Sharon-Olmert government tolerated this? What could be done to destroy terrorist rocket factories and firing teams?

Eldad: Israel policy towards the Kassem bombardment from Gaza on Sderot and the western Negev is the tragic story of mainstream Zionism. From the very beginning there was a conflict among Zionist leaders about the true nature of this national movement. There were those who claimed that Zionism was born to solve the "trouble of the Jews," and therefore the State of Israel was created to be the "safe shelter." The lessons that I have learnt from my father were that Zionism should be a double edged sword of a freedom movement: to liberate the Jewish people from the Diaspora and to liberate the land of Israel from any foreign rule. Unfortunately, mainstream Zionists shaped the State of Israel as it is today. They emphasized the basic needs of citizens for food and shelter, but not the aspirations of the Jewish people who sought independence, sovereignty, and the liberation of our ancestral homeland. When the political leaders of Israel run for re-election, they believe that they must promise its citizens peace. Peace and not redemption, peace and not liberation of the land of Israel from the Arab occupation that started in the 7th century. Peace and not fulfilment of our destiny as a nation. They reflect the refugee state of mind. So they endeavour to mollify voters with a short-term cease fire rather than victory over enemies. This led the political leaders of Israel to embark on the "Land for Peace" formula. Even when reality proved that giving land to the enemy only leads to more bloodshed and there was no peace partner. They were afraid that if they admit they were totally wrong, the citizens of Israel would kick them out of office. The price for the State of Israel to exist as a Jewish State was too heavy for these leaders. They were Chamberlains, not Churchills. They did not have the deeper roots in the land of Israel that the religious Zionists have. If it is only a shelter the political leaders can decide if the country needs to be bigger or smaller. They can decide if the shelter needs to include Gush Katif, Sderot in the western Negev or only around Tel Aviv. That is why they were ready to give up Gush Katif. They are ready to give up Judea, Samaria, and the Golan and divide Jerusalem. That is why the Kassem and Katyusha rockets fell on our land from Gaza. This attack on our sovereignty did not lead to an all-out war against the enemy who dared to attack us.

Gordon: This year, Hamas received shipments of Katyusha rockets from Iran and launched those against major Southern Israeli population center of Ashkelon. The IDF failed in an attempt to create a security belt in Northern Gaza to destroy these Hamas rocket launching sites and supplies. What should the Israeli government and the IDF have done to intercept and destroy the rockets, arms and munitions coming into Gaza from Iran to counter this threat to Israel's Southern border?

Eldad: There is only one answer to the challenge of the jihad from Gaza: a military one. Israel should create a five kilometer wide corridor in the south of the Gaza strip to separate it from the Sinai Peninsula. It should reoccupy the northern part of Gaza in order to rebuild three settlements that were destroyed during the unilateral Gush Katif disengagement, and annex these areas into the State of Israel. This would tell the Arabs that they will pay permanently for any further attack through our building new settlements and acquiring more land. The IDF should enter the Gaza Strip to eradicate Hamas. The concept that we can run away from terror and the terrorists will let us live quietly, has failed. We have to understand that there is a price to pay if we want to be an independent Jewish State. It is still a lower price then what we will have to pay as Dhimmis living at the mercy of the Islamic terror.

Gordon: Young IDF Sgt. Gilad Shalit was kidnapped in June, 2006 by Palestinian terrorists in Gaza. Why have the Olmert government and the IDF failed to seek his release from a Hamas dungeon and what could be done to accomplish it?

Eldad: Olmert, his government, and previous ones in Israel were not courageous enough and surrendered to terrorist demands. The spirit of Entebbe (the rescue of nearly 100 Jewish hostages in July, 1976 in Uganda by IDF commandos) is no longer the spirit of our current leaders. The only answer to the kidnapping of Sgt. Gilad Shalit would be an ultimatum to Hamas that Israel will kill one Hamas commander in Gaza every day until Shalit is back home. Only if they knew that Israel was not going to release terrorists and murderers as a prize for kidnapping, would they release captives like Shalit.

Gordon: Iran's nuclear threat to Israel's existence looms large as a concern for you and other MK's in Israel. Does Israel have the military and strategic capabilities to carry out a unilateral pre-emptive attack on key Iranian nuclear facilities?

Eldad: Yes.

Gordon: We have written about the Syrian bio-warfare threat. Does Israel have programs and resources to defend its citizens against this non-conventional threat?

Eldad: We can defend ourselves beyond the protective means and medicine. But, the best defence is deterrence.

Gordon: You have been a relentless critic of the corruption in the Olmert government. With the recent indictments of PM Olmert and the Kadima party leadership vote, do you believe that the ruling coalition can survive? Will there be a call for general elections to form a new Knesset in the spring of 2009?

Eldad: Internal corruption is an existential threat to Israel. The lessons that I have learnt in the case of former PM Ariel Sharon taught me that one should not accept a corrupt Prime Minister in Israel even when he builds settlements. You never know when he will flip and change his ideology under threat. The crisis of leadership in Israel is reflected in Kadima due to the weakness of other major players in the political arena. Labor can only lose from a general election, while Shas is always for sale to any coalition party leader. That is why I am afraid we may see another Kadima Government that could be formed by Livni. The coalition will exist thanks to the utmost weakness of its partners.

Gordon: Why is corruption so pervasive in the Israel political system and what can be done to reform it?

Eldad: Some deep reforms are needed in the political system in Israel. I believe that at least half the MK's should be directly elected by their constituents. An important step should be the conduct of open primaries for all parties, to elect leaders and the list of candidates for the next Knesset. There should be strengthening of the National Police and separate the Attorney General from being the legal advisor for the government. These are essential steps in the struggle against the corruption in the political system in Israel.

Gordon: What is "protektsia" – the system of graft – and why is it so prevalent in Israeli politics?

Eldad: "Protektsia" was the system developed by the Labor Socialist parties in Israel to assure that they would keep the government in their hands forever. The system was adopted by Likud, Shas and other parties when they were in the government. The reforms advocated against corruption are relevant because "Protektsia" is just another form of corruption.

Gordon: Why in your opinion haven't Israeli citizens done more than complain about political corruption?

Eldad: We are doing much more than just complaining about corruption. We have rid ourselves of a corrupt PM, his Minister of Finance, a previous Minister of Justice, Commissioner of National Police and many others. I am sure the situation now is better than it was a few years ago.

Gordon: You have been a weekly columnist for major Israeli newspapers *Ma'ariv* and *Yediot Aharonot*. That has afforded you an opportunity to air your views to the general public. What have been the reactions of readers to your commentary?

Eldad: *Yediot Aharonot* and *Ma'ariv* were important media outlets for me. I could see the reactions in talkbacks and through the echoes in the media. My weekly commentary was so influential that people who were worried that the words that I wrote would harm them politically did everything they could to silence me. When *Yediot Aharonot* changed its chief editor, I could no longer write for them. Then I moved to *Ma'ariv*. When *Ma'ariv* changed editors, among his first actions was stopping my weekly column.

Gordon: The Israel Broadcasting Authority has a virtual monopoly on TV news in the country. What should be done to break this monopoly so that a wider set of views can be aired?

Eldad: In order to break the government electronic media monopoly we will have to stop the special tax collected from citizens to keep Channel 1 and Kol Israel (Radio) alive. Then we will have to "open the air" to anyone who wants to broadcast. This way we will have Channel 7 Radio (and perhaps television as well) that were closed by the Supreme Court because they were telling the truth. The formal reason given by the Supreme Court was, of course, that they did not have the permits needed to broadcast. However, no such steps were taken against the left wing "Voice of Peace" when they broadcast from a ship off the coast of

Israel. We will have to attract investors to open new TV channels. 55% of Israelis define themselves as "right wing" so they deserve a broadcasting station that will reflect their opinions.

Gordon: You have undertaken a program to reach out to the future generation of Israelis through a series of debates in the public high school system. Has this aided in conveying the Zionist ethos and your views to audiences of young impressionable minds?

Eldad: In a series of debates against Meretz leader Yossi Beilin in Israeli secular schools, I presented the plan "Jordan is Palestine – Resettlement of Arab refugees and No to Palestinian state west of the Jordan river." Beilin presented his "Geneva Plan" – the two state solution. After each debate the students voted. In 30 out of 32 high schools, I won.

Gordon: You have opposed any peace plan with the Palestinians that entails a division of Jerusalem and cession of disputed territories in Judea and Samaria. Given current government deliberations with PA President Mahmoud Abbas, how will such arrangements impact the territorial integrity of Israel? Will they fail to achieve approval in either a Knesset vote or a mandated national referendum?

Eldad: Olmert's and Livni's plans are suicide for Israel. His public statements created an impossible situation for anyone who tries to offer a lower price. Olmert or Livni will not be able to perform on their plans. The current situation is that such plans do not have a majority in the Knesset. Not because the MK's are very strong but because even those who want to give every inch of Judea and Samaria, Golan and Jerusalem, to our enemies do not have a relevant partner. It is obvious that if Israel withdraws from Judea and Samaria a Hamas State will be created within less than 72 hours. There is an urgent need to have a National Referendum as a condition to any land concessions. In this way we will be able to deter the corrupt and weak MK's.

Gordon: The Olmert government through the intermediaries of the Turkish and French governments has engaged in discussions with the Syrian government of Bashir Assad about a possible peace agreement that would entail cession of the Golan. You oppose such discussions. How do you end these initiatives?

Eldad: The "initiatives" to give the Golan to Syria can be stopped if we change the Kadima government in general elections. In the event that Livni can create a coalition government, a big if, given Shas's alleged demand not to divide Jerusalem, we have to try to put it down and go for elections. Another important barrier is the national referendum that will be needed to approve any proposed shelf agreement. Unfortunately, a lot of damage has already been done by the Kadima government.

Gordon: You have announced a meeting in Jerusalem in December with Israeli and EU parliamentarians to develop a plan to combat Islamofascism. What do you anticipate will be the outcome of this Jerusalem Conference? Was this the result of your attendance at the Brussels anti-jihadist conference last year? Why aren't the Israeli and most Western governments more concerned about the threat of Islamofascism and the advance of radical Islam? After all, Israel is the "canary in the mine" of radical Islam.

Eldad: The current leaders of Israel are not interested in the struggle against global jihad and the Islamization of Europe. It contradicts their thesis that if only we can solve "a territorial conflict" with the Palestinians we will have peace. But this is not a local territorial conflict. Rather, it is a local symptom of a global disease. As the conflict is a religious war, territorial concessions are irrelevant. The "Facing Jihad" conference in Jerusalem, December 14-15, 2008, will be a Lawmaker Summit involving parliamentarians and legislators from Denmark, Holland, Belgium, Italy, UK, Switzerland, America and other countries. We will work in Jerusalem on various legislative initiatives to combat the spread of Islam in the world. The second half of the meeting will be educational: teaching Israelis the real nature of the conflict and what our enemy really wants. It is true that many Europeans still believe in appeasement of the Muslims as the way to act in the hope that the problem will disappear. However, more and more Western political leaders are not ready to sit still and do nothing. Among the agenda items for the Jerusalem "Facing Jihad" conference will be: 1) screening the film "Fitna" by the Dutch MP Geert Wilders; 2) drafting and promulgating the "Jerusalem Declaration" to condemn all forms of Anti-Semitism and Racism; 3) recognition of the State of Israel as a Jewish State; 4) rejection of the "two State Solution"; and, 5) a declaration to fight Islamization of the free world. Israel, the canary in the mine of radical Islam will have found new allies at the conclusion of the conference.

Gordon: How do you see the future of Israel as an independent Jewish state in the Middle East?

Eldad: We must reintroduce the truth that the land of Israel belongs to the people of Israel. Israelis must have the same commitment to the land of Israel that every citizen in the world feels towards their homeland. We must recognize the State of Israel as a Jewish State, not only a state of Jews. With God's help we will overcome all challenges. The Arabs are not the problem. It is the Jews that we have to change.

* * *

Dr. Arieh Eldad is no longer a gadfly without portfolio. Interest in "Jordan is Palestine" has become a matter of serious consideration by Israeli and other policy experts in the wake of the collapse of the Israeli Palestinian Authority peace discussions and the rise of the Arab Spring in the winter of 2011-2012. He has been embroiled in debates on the issue with King Abdullah II of Jordan and his fellow Knesset members.

Eldad in late November 2011 said, "The discussion is relevant and more urgent than ever. The shocks and upheavals in the Middle East will not pass Jordan by."

Jordan's King Abdullah II, responding to comments by Eldad, told reporters "the Jordanian option is an illusion. Jordan is Jordan, and Palestine is Palestine."

Eldad retorted, "It is better Abdullah announce today that Jordan is the national homeland for the Palestinians – or else seek asylum in London."

Eldad's plan calls for "two states on two sides of the Jordan River." He contends that Jordanians would prefer Israel on its borders rather than Hamas, a reference to possible Hamas take over of the Palestinian Authority. His plan calls for natural resource and economic development coupled with resettlement of Palestinian refugees.

Could it be that the time for consideration of Eldad's plan has come given King Abdullah's dalliance with the Muslim Brotherhood's Islamic Action Front in the Jordanian Parliament?

2
JONATHAN HAUSMAN
MARCH 2009

Wednesday, February 25, 2009, an audience of Christians and Jews attended an event featuring Dutch parliamentarian, Geert Wilders, at Congregation Ahavath Torah in Stoughton, Massachusetts. That afternoon, Rabbi Jonathan Hausman spiritual leader of Ahavath Torah, was feted, called a "hero" and given an ovation at a Republican Jewish Coalition New England Chapter luncheon. Many anti-jihad activists were in the audience, among them, Charles Jacobs, founder of the American Anti-Slavery Group, Andrew Bostom, author of *The Legacy of Jihad* and *The Legacy of Islamic Antisemitism*, and Professor Dennis Hale of Boston College. Hausman had also contacted Jeff Jacoby, *Boston Globe* columnist who interviewed Wilders, and helped to arrange a radio interview with talk show host Michael Graham. Rabbi Hausman had been the sparkplug behind organizing the event in Stoughton.

The Wilders tour began Monday with luncheons and private dinners in Manhattan, and appearances on *FoxNews* Glen Beck's "War Room" and the "O'Reilly Factor." Wilders was in Washington the prior Thursday at an event on Capitol Hill organized by Sen. Jon Kyl (R-AZ) and sponsored by the International Free Press Society and the Center for Security Policy. Friday, Wilders held a public news conference at the National Press Club. Later he was recognized at the CPAC convention.

We contacted Rabbi Hausman to find out why he is such an exception in the American rabbinate. Rabbi Hausman understands the dark inner core of political Islam and its threat to our US Constitution and

Western Judeo-Christian values. Unfortunately, too many in the American rabbinate have become the equivalent of the dhimmi. They have frequently been involved in outreach to Muslim clerics in interfaith dialogues and defended Muslim Brotherhood fronts.

We delved into Rabbi Hausman's background to find out what propelled him to organize these events for Wilders.

Gordon: Rabbi Hausman, tell us about your background, where you grew up, family political affiliation and your education both here in the US and the Middle East.

Hausman: I was raised in the greater Bridgeport, Connecticut area. My four grandparents were immigrants to the US. My father's folks, whom I did not know, came from Austria-Hungary. My paternal grandfather was from a small town outside of Krakow, Poland and my grandmother from somewhere near Vienna. My mother's folks I knew quite well as both died when I was an adult. They both came from Czarist Russia, near the Ukrainian city of Vinnitsa. All arrived in the US by 1908 and were hardworking people. Interestingly all were registered Republicans once obtaining US citizenship. Only one grandfather voted for FDR and that was only once. Otherwise, no FDR votes were cast… a rarity amongst Jews of that generation. All of my grandparents believed in personal responsibility, hard work, limited government and limited government intrusion into the lives of the citizenry, and support for what we would call First Amendment rights including freedom of speech and the establishment clause. Coming from Central and Eastern Europe, they knew first hand the depredations of an intertwined political-religious government and the harm it caused the citizenry in general, Jews specifically. My parents were Depression and World War II era people. Raised at that time they apprehended the lessons of appeasement in order to avoid battle (intellectual and military). As a child, I remember vividly many political and historical discussions amongst, between and with my parents and grandparents dealing with significant issues of the day (e.g. civil rights, political candidacies, Israel, Europe, Vietnam, Jewish identity and learning). As a result, I was raised to become conscious of events of historical significance swirling around us. I also developed a keen and passionate identity as an American and as a Jew.

Not only were my grandparents Jewish Republicans, but so were my parents. They manifested a strong belief in limited government, strong defense, were fairly moderate vis a vis social issues and held a belief that American national culture had a positive influence on and mission in the world. They believed and passed on to my brothers and me the view that the US had nothing for which to apologize regarding her role as a Western democracy and force for good in the world. Mind you, neither of my folks maintained that the US was perfect. Rather, they maintained that the US was historically unique. My father fought against totalitarian fascism in the US Army during World War II, was proud of his service, always made sure that we understood the sacrifice for freedom asked of his generation and that such freedoms had to be nurtured and protected assiduously. "If you want to be free, you have to fight for it," my father used to say.

My father and maternal grandfather saw strength in the multivaried textures of the US, but always believed in and inculcated in us a distinctly national ethos of thankfulness for the unique gifts that this country offers. My Uncle Ziggy used to say "remember, despite any differences, Americans are all the same. Our differences give this country resilience. A monochrome country does no one any good."

My folks were hard workers who, along with my maternal grandparents, stressed reading and education. My brothers and I all became readers. All of us have acquired at least two degrees each from universities.

I always had a passion for philosophy, history, politics, religion, Judaism and languages. As a result, I obtained a BA in Judaic Studies, an MA in International Affairs focusing on the Middle East, eventually a JD and finally some time in yeshiva studying for the Rabbinate. I spent time traveling and working in Israel (I speak Hebrew) and some time traveling and some significant time studying in Egypt (I speak Arabic). I also spent some time in Ramallah, West Bank.

Egypt was an interesting experience as I was there before and during the Camp David process. I was never a left of center fellow in terms of my political philosophy and appreciation of history, trends, etc. However, I saw in 1970s Egypt a country teaching its youth to hate Jews, America, women's rights, general education, democratic values, and democracy. I saw the activity of the Muslim Brotherhood up close and personal. I saw the abject poverty of and dissociative treatment of the Coptic Church and its adherents. I wouldn't say that it was an eye opener for me, but it was probably the most formative educational experience in my life. I remember returning to the US and telling my father "there will never be peace. If there is to be a hint of it, Sadat better live for 20 years minimally." He was assassinated some 2½ years later.

Gordon: What gave rise to your concerns about the threat of Islamization here in the US?

Hausman: I've always been aware historically that Islam is a triumphalism, supersessionist and supremacist way of life. Islam, in my mind, is not solely a religious philosophy, but a total and complete political-religious polity. As such, Islam directs every aspect of a person's life with no tolerance or respect given anyone who will not "submit" to the will of Allah. If you will not submit, there are all sorts of consequences (e.g. special taxes, restrictions in terms of livelihoods and construction of houses of worship, other reminders of one's second class and inferior status, jihad). The prevalence of doctrinal issues such as taqqiyya, da'wa, jihad combined with Islam's bloody past and present are sanguine reminders that no Reformation has occurred.

It was evident in the fervent military expansion of Islam's border until the defeat at the battle of Tours in the 8th century, the defeat of the Ottoman Turks at the gates of Vienna in the 17th century, the US experience with the Barbary pirates in the late 18th and early 19th century, the Islamic conquests of historically Buddhist Afghanistan, and the Moghul warring in the Indian subcontinent for the past 200 years. When an American maintains that 9/11 was our first contact with Islamic expansionary fervor, jihad, fascism and totalitarianism, I shudder at the paucity of historical understanding. It wasn't the first…what about "to the shores of Tripoli," the Iranian takeover of the US embassy in 1979, the Marine Corps barracks destruction in Lebanon in 1983, the first attempt to destroy the World Trade Center in 1993. I only name a few historical incidents.

This is not to say that all Muslims are inherently evil or murderous. However, 10% of 1.3 billion adherents is quite a lot of people to subscribe to this side of Islamic political life and subdue the non-participatory.

Gordon: You have endeavored to educate your congregation about the Islamic precepts and anti-Semitism. How did you do this?

Hausman: I write about these issues from the perspective of Jewish survival and American political life. I use our synagogue bulletin; send articles on my personal list serve to members of the synagogue for further distribution, table talk, bringing in speakers informed to a much greater degree than I regarding these subjects (some of whom are at the fulcrum of activism). I also helped to establish a pro-Israel activist list serve, am involved with a number of other list serves concerning Israel and freedom issues. I am also intimately involved in outreach by way of organizations such as Christians United for Israel, Christians and Jews United for Israel, Jewish Policy Institute and I do a tad of public speaking. This list is illustrative and by no means exhaustive. I do not consider myself an activist. I just want to be informed and do my job…nothing special.

Gordon: When did you first become informed about Geert Wilders and when did you make contact with him?

Hausman: I have to laugh! I read his remarks delivered in Jerusalem on December 18, 2008. His lecture made the internet rounds. I responded to one set of e-mails (from a couple of activist and scholarly friends of mine) writing "Geez, we should bring this guy to Boston." An internet search engine is a wonderful tool. With the help of a friend, I made contact with his scheduler.

I was not sure if Mr. Wilders would actually have been able to speak, though I did write with that express intention and invitation. I found out that he had a Boston meeting during the day. Shortly before I traveled to Israel, a friend and I arrange an interview with talk radio host, Michael Graham. Another friend of mine and I made contact with Jeff Jacoby. It was while in Israel recently that I received a note from the same scheduler (who works for the International Free Press Society) of the commitment to speak at my synagogue.

I distinctly did not want a circus atmosphere at the synagogue the evening during which Geert Wilders spoke. Therefore, I determined and gave strict instructions to those helping me not to engage in a thorough publicity blitz. We posted this opportunity to four pro-Israel list serves, a couple of blogs, to the New England Republican Jewish Coalition list serve, and one announcement in the local Jewish weekly. As the Middle East Forum Law Project was a co-sponsor, I am certain that these good people spread the word as well. No TV or radio outlets were notified, to the disappointment and/or chagrin of a few attendees. However, I had my reasons. The most important reason was to have Wilders speak in front of people and allow these people to witness an historic figure, one who functions at the crux of important events. Better that the attendees have opportunities to ask questions than the press.

Gordon: What support did you have from your congregation and the general community in sponsoring the Wilders presentation at your synagogue?

Hausman: Due to Wilders notoriety, there was some concern amongst the congregation. However, I owe my synagogue President a debt of gratitude. She argued the issues of freedom of speech and the civilizational context in which we presently find ourselves. I argued from Jerusalem as I was leading a congregational mission to Israel at the time. Our local police department was terrific. A security plan was easily assembled.

All the general community knew was the Wilders would be speaking. We basically had 18 days to arrange his schedule in Boston, make interview appointments, arrange for limousines, some food, and arrange flights from Boston to his subsequent destination. We had 11 days to arrange the talk at my synagogue as it was the last piece of the puzzle, but Geert really wanted to appear. Scheduling was tight, but well worth it.

Gordon: What was the significance of Jeff Jacoby's Boston Globe interview of Wilders?

Hausman: Jeff is an incredibly talented opinion columnist. His analyses are trenchant, cogent, and well-researched. He has national reach and readership. Jacoby offered an opportunity for Wilders to speak without the observable bias of many opinion journalists who appear regularly in most major newspapers today.

Gordon: You attended an event Wednesday afternoon at the Harvard Club in Boston for Wilders, who organized that?

Hausman: I attended a Republican Jewish Coalition (RJC) luncheon in the afternoon. During the introduction of RJC members active in New England, my name was mentioned by Harris Vederman as one of the significant players in the region. He noted that I have opened my shul to RJC programs regularly since becoming involved and announced the Wilders program. I received an ovation and was asked if the event was open, to which I responded open to everyone. Steve Leventhal and I facilitated Wilders appointments with RJC headquarters people in Washington, DC. Steve is the RJC New England Communications Director…and a good one at that.

Gordon: What was the composition of the audience at your synagogue and what elements of Wilders presentation were particularly engrossing for you and those who attended?

Hausman: The audience was mixed, some congregants, majority non-congregants, Jews and non-Jews (it was Ash Wednesday and many foreheads carried the mark of church attendance that day), activists and non-activists, people who heard of or seen Wilders previously (on YouTube, for example) and those who had not, those who were skeptical regarding Wilders positions and those who agreed with Wilders. Everyone was respectful.

We began with a request from the International Free Press Society – a showing of *Fitna*. I introduced the film by reminding people of the Barbary Piracy early in our country's infancy, Churchill's analogy of the Qur'an to Mein Kampf and said "you are about to watch a 15 minute film that could quite possibly place a man in jail for 2 years."

When the film was over, I had just begun my introduction for Wilders when the place exploded with applause as he came to the podium. It was quite a moment. A standing ovation! To watch him begin to grin as he saw that an ordinary crowd of people understood his battle for freedom and liberty in protecting and defending Judeo-Christian values and civilization, his love of his native Holland's freedoms that are under assault solely from a restive and increasingly radicalized Muslim population and his affinity for Jews and Israel was something to behold. He spoke passionately of his kinship with Jews, his over 20 visits of varying lengths and reasons to Israel, his having lived in Israel for over two years earlier in his life. He emphasized that his feelings for Jews and Israel and his relationships with Jews and Israel make him anathema to the right and the left, an odd alliance he remarked. "Neither the far right nor the far left can claim me nor want me, and I denounce both," was his comment.

Personally, I focused on what is happening in Holland and elsewhere in Europe, and it is deeply disturbing: Islamic clerics and Muslim political organizations are openly, indeed brazenly, attempting to impose Shari'a law on Muslims and non-Muslims alike, using violence and the threat of violence to get their way. In the face of these provocations, the people who should be defending the liberal traditions of western democracy run and hide, leaving the field to terrorists and those who sympathize with and enable them. At the risk of his life and his freedom, Geert Wilders has tried to expose this danger, and to warn Americans that what has happened in Europe could happen here. Indeed, as he pointed out on Wednesday, it is happening here. "Lawfare" is an increasingly used tool for the Islamist agenda in the US. My colleague, Professor Dennis Hale of Boston College, was one of several people sued for defamation for pointing out the connections between the leaders of the Islamic Society of Boston (ISB) and such terrorist organizations as the Muslim Brotherhood, Hamas, and al-Qaeda. These were not fanciful charges based on rumor or innuendo. They were based on documentary evidence, and as that evidence accumulated, the ISB (the Roxbury Mosque) was forced to drop its lawsuit. However, they remain free to teach the next generation of Boston Muslims, the same hateful ideology that has forced Geert Wilders to travel with bodyguards.

I cannot speak for other attendees as their reactions will be relative. The man has courage. He is the true hero in this saga. The rest of us just play our respective parts.

Gordon: What do you think will happen in the wake of Wilders' Boston visit and your support of it vis a vis the Boston Jewish leadership and communal outreach groups?

Hausman: I am not sure that I can answer the question directly. We unfortunately live in an age where dissent - unless it's from the radical left or from third-world movements (no matter how authoritarian) - is considered unacceptable, and those who dissent are marginalized and ostracized.

I would hope that our elected or self-appointed leaders would learn to appreciate history instead of acting upon motivations, however well-intended, that put us in danger. Dialogue only achieves results if the language of discourse is the same as well as the underlying motivations. You can't say one thing in English and maintain the diametrically opposite in Arabic so that only the Arabic speakers know what you intend.

Only recently has our local Jewish Community Relations Council stopped dialogue with the Muslim American Society. Why did it take so long for this action? I have colleagues who maintain memberships in all sorts of groups that promote dialogue, etc. I tell my daughter, the information is in front of your nose. You simply have to read it.

I am not sure anything will change. Ostriches will be ostriches.

Gordon: In summing up, why do you think Wilders and his experience combating Islamization in Europe is relevant to Americans?

Hausman: People like Wilders are always controversial, and they are never perfect. Yet, imagine if such a person had come to this country from Germany in 1934, to warn us about an unimaginable horror being prepared for Europe's Jews. How many people would have dismissed such warnings as alarmist propaganda? How many would have accused the messenger of being a warmonger (they said this about Churchill for much milder warnings)? But imagine how we would now honor the memory of such a messenger, and of those who gave him the space and the time to tell his story? My mother is 80 years old. She remarked that she never thought that she would bear witness to 1935 a second time in her life.

I would gladly bring this program again without changing anything about the experience and refute those who would try to stigmatize the courage of a Geert Wilders or those who allow him a forum from which to speak. Voltaire said: "I disapprove of what you say, but I will defend to the death your right to say it." Personally, when history has its say, I would rather be on the side of Churchill and not Chamberlain.

* * *

Rabbi Jonathan Hausman has become a singular spokesman for views contrary to those of the mainstream, liberal rabbinate in the US. He focuses on matters like criticism of Muslim Jewish interreligious dialogue, Islamic Shariah law versus Jewish Halacha law and outreach to Christian Evangelical Zionists. He has established an adult lecture series at Congregation Ahavath Torah that has attracted notable speakers. Among them are Andrew McCarthy, author of *The Grand Jihad*, Bat Ye'or and her husband David Littman, columnist Mark Steyn, Dr. Mark Durie, Prof. Raphael Israeli, and Gen. William "Jerry" Boykin. He has also become a much sought after speaker in his own right.

3
KURT WESTERGAARD
OCTOBER 2009

Kurt Westergaard, the genial, but controversial Danish cartoonist who drew the "cartoon that shook the Muslim world," had just finished a whirlwind North American Tour sponsored by the Danish and International Free Press Societies. The tour was occasioned by the fourth anniversary of the publication of his famous Mohammed cartoon with a turban shaped like a bomb along with 11 others by the Danish newspaper, *Jyllands-Posten* (*JP*). Mr. Westergaard has had a long association with *JP* as one of Denmark's premier satiric cartoonists. His appearances on this tour included events at Princeton and Yale Universities, a closed luncheon at the Manhattan Institute, a dinner with the Hudson Institute briefing council, TV and newspaper interviews with the *National Post* in Toronto among others. We had facilitated the Manhattan Institute event and posted commentary and interviews about Mr. Westergaard's appearances at Princeton and Yale. We were fortunate to have caught up with him through the auspices of a colleague, Bjorn Larsen, and held this interview just prior to his departure for Denmark.

Gordon: How long have you been associated with *JP* as a satiric cartoonist?

Westergaard: About 28 years.

Gordon: What is the story behind your "rouge et noir costume" that has become your emblematic uniform?

Westergaard: It is my gimmick, the colors of anarchism, black and red. The red trousers stimulate my legs.

Gordon: The Danish Constitution guarantees free speech. How important is that to you as both a Dane and satiric cartoonist?

Westergaard: It is very important. There is no living as a cartoonist without it. Every dynamic democracy needs freedom of speech.

Gordon: What was the basic theme or message you wanted to convey in your Mohammed cartoon?

Westergaard: It was to show Islamic terrorists who use parts of the holy book [Qur'an] as an inspiration to kill others. I was right. The drawing came to me, and as a result they wanted to kill me.

Gordon: What can you tell us about the Imams who publicized the *JP* cartoons in the Muslim world?

Westergaard: The Danish imams wanted support. The imams knew that they are important and can decide on behalf of their god what actions to take. The Bible in Genesis talks about man created in God's image not the other way around.

Gordon: What was your first reaction to the destruction of Danish embassies, properties and deaths that occurred in Muslim countries in the wake of the Mohammed cartoons?

Westergaard: I was shocked. But did I feel responsible? No. The riots were staged by local machines in Muslim countries that diverted attention away from their people's deplorable status. I am sorry about people being killed, but it was not my responsibility.

Gordon: Why do you think you were singled out for intense reaction by Muslims?

Westergaard: I believe that it was graphic elements of the cartoon which struck hard - the anarchist bomb and the Arabic inscription on the turban.

Gordon: You did an interview in September, 2006 on TV2 Denmark with Kasem Ahmad, spokesperson of the Islamic Council. What were your thoughts when he abruptly walked out, while being filmed? What message were you trying to convey and what was your reaction?

Westergaard: It was the most scary situation I have encountered. We started talking peacefully, on a couch, Ramadan had finished and we started to eat. Then he wanted another apology from me. I said no. The guy started yelling about my paper, and that Jewish/American dark forces owned the paper. He wanted to stop the broadcast. The news staff did not want to obey him. It all scared me. This man is highly intelligent, and educated as an engineer. I do not understand him. I wanted to talk to him, but never managed to establish contact again

Gordon: Kasem Ahmad in February, 2008 protested against freedom of speech in Denmark with Hizb ut Tahir leader Fadi Abulatif and called for extermination of Jews using Koranic verses. How did you and other Danes react to that?

Westergaard: We react very strongly against antisemitism by radical Muslims. Our history shows we care. We saved many Danish Jews in WWII. We sent them across the straits to freedom in Sweden

Gordon: When the Danish Security and Intelligence Service (P.E.T.) in February, 2008 arrested three men, a Dane and two Tunisians, in a plot to murder you, what happened to you and your family?

Westergaard: We were heading to Paris for a weekend trip, when this story broke. But, instead, we had to be evacuated, late at night, to a safe house. We then had to move continuously among 8 to 10 safe houses for a while. We were pissed, angry. I was doing my job and now I was threatened, | wanted to strike back.

Gordon: For three years you and your wife were under protective security 24/7 by P.E.T., what did they do to safeguard you, how did your family adjust and when did the nightmare end?

Westergaard: The nightmare has not ended. Nevertheless, the

PET people are there and are close good friends. They gave us 24/7 protection. We could call on them and they would respond. We have a good relationship.

Gordon: Despite your being in protective custody, you have been unstinting in speaking out and giving interviews to the press and media. What motivated you to do that?

Westergaard: My temperament. I refused to hide. This was also good therapy for me. By the way, my family is multi-ethnic, multi-religious, multi-lingual. We have nice kids with marriages across a number of backgrounds that have produced wonderful grandchildren. This is a real example of how it CAN work

Gordon: In 2008 you drew another cartoon, this time depicting a burka clad pregnant Muslim woman with a belly shaped like a bomb. That became a poster for the Danish Free Press Society. What was the message behind that cartoon?

Westergaard: It was about the troubling demographic developments in Denmark and Europe, the high birthrate among Muslims and being outnumbered by them.

Gordon: You have said repeatedly that you have no regrets about having penned your Mohammed cartoon, and yet others including the *JP* editors and even members of the Danish government have apologized. Why didn't you apologize?

Westergaard: Why should I apologize? I was just doing my job. My tradition is what I followed, so I have nothing to apologize for.

Gordon: Given the threats against your life from radical Muslims, what are your views about Islam and Muslims in your native Denmark and Europe?

Westergaard: They came with nothing. We gave them everything to get started; money, homes, schools. The welfare state also provided free schooling. They have more freedom than they ever had where they came from. We simply want them to respect our democratic traditions.

Gordon: Dutch politician Geert Wilders is an advocate for an EU Free Speech law. Do you support him in this effort and why do you think protection of freedom of speech is important?

Westergaard: Democracy cannot work without free speech. We tried the appeasement in the 30's. We tried to stop, in 1933, making cartoons that were against Hitler and Nazi Germany. We shut down until 1940 and Germany occupied us anyway. It was a bitter failure and a lesson learned.

Gordon: You drew cartoons for a book by your friend Lars Hedegaard, columnist for the *JP* and head of the Danish Free Press Society. What themes did you convey?

Westergaard: I support Lars. He writes, I draw. His book contains some of his sharpest columns.

Gordon: You are just concluding a North American visit to the U.S. and Canada on the occasion of the fourth anniversary of the *JP* publication of the Mohammed cartoons. Who sponsored the tour? Where did you appear and what were the reactions of the audiences and media?

Westergaard: The FPS in Denmark and the IFPS in both Canada and the US sponsored my trip. I appeared at Princeton and Yale Universities, the Manhattan Institute and the Hudson Institute. In general, the responses were good, but there were also protests.

Gordon: What message do you want Americans and Canadians to remember from this tour?

Westergaard: If you want to do something about freedom of speech, then the only choice is USE IT, exercise it.

* * *

Kurt Westergaard survived two attempts on his life. The most serious one involved an attack on his residence in January of 2010 by an axe-wielding Somali Muslim allegedly affiliated with the Somali Muslim terrorist group, Al-Shabaab. His assailant was found guilty of an attempt to perform an act of terrorism and attempted murder by an unanimous jury and convicted in February of 2011 in a Danish court. He was sentenced to nine years in prison and will be expelled from Denmark permanently upon his release.

Westergaard was given the Sappho Award by the Free Press Society of Denmark (headed by Lars Hedegaard) and inscribed to a "journalist who combines excellence in his work with courage and a refusal to compromise." German Chancellor Amgela Merkel presented him with the M100 Media Award for his "contributions to freedom of opinion."

Security concerns for Westergaard's safety still affect his travels. Westergaard and his wife were sent home to Denmark in September of 2011 for security reasons, preventing them from attending a press conference in Oslo for the publication on a children's book for which he had done the illustrations. The Norwegian Police Security Service commented, "Westergaard lives with a death threat hanging over him and is a vulnerable person."

4
GEERT WILDERS
NOVEMBER 2009

October of 2009 was a tumultuous time for Geert Wilders, leader of the Dutch Freedom Party (PVV) in the Hague Parliament. Dutch public opinion polls show Wilders and the PVV in the lead position in any future Parliamentary election. The PVV is currently the leading Dutch party in the European Parliament. What sets Wilders apart from most EU political leaders is his ringing support of America and Israel. He considers Israel as fighting for all of us given its embattled position in the Middle East. As he says in his speeches: "we all are Israel."

His courageous stand against encroaching Islamization in his native Holland and the EU was emboldened by a 2009 decision of the British Immigration Tribunal that overturned the previous decision by disgraced former U.K. Home Secretary, Jacquie Smith. Smith had barred Wilders' entry at London's Heathrow Airport in February of 2009 on the specious grounds that his presence at a private showing of his controversial film *Fitna* at the House of Lords arranged by Lord Malcolm Pearson and Baroness Carolyn Cox would somehow disrupt, "community harmony."

Wilders' British lawyer who argued his case successfully before the Immigration Tribunal is a former Muslim who left Islam. Wilders returned to the House of Lords venue in March of 2010 to show *Fitna*. Wilders has shown his film in the US Capitol Building in Washington, DC and to audiences across America in California, Florida and New York. In November of 2009, he traveled to Prague to show *Fitna* in the

Senate of the Czech Republic.

Wilders took a well deserved victory lap in London and at a press conference arranged by Lord Pearson re-affirmed that free speech in Western democracies is a paramount bedrock value.

Wilders then sprinted for the US following the London meetings for a full week of appearances in both Philadelphia and New York. These included events at Temple University and the Union League Club in Philadelphia organized by the David Horowitz Freedom Center. In New York, Wilders spoke at the Harvard Club which was arranged by the Hudson Institute and at Columbia University (CU) and sponsored by the CU College Republicans and a faculty group, the CU Chapter of Scholars for Peace in the Middle East.

Controversy concerning his appearances in both venues in America persisted. At Temple University attempts were made by the Muslim Students Association to force administrators to cancel the event on the grounds that Wilders' criticism of Islam causes "disruption of community harmony" – the same rationale used to bar Wilders from Britain that was overturned by the British court system. Criticism of religion is considered protected speech under the US Constitution's First Amendment provisions. Fortunately, the courage of a campus sponsoring group, Temple Purpose, to press ahead on free speech grounds enabled Wilders' appearance. In the wake of his appearance at Columbia University, the student newspaper *The Spectator*, published an opinion piece, "Wild, Wild Wilders," by Adel Elsohly, the graduate student adviser to the local Muslim Students Association chapter. Elsohly wrote: "Today we call on everyone, not as Muslims, members of a cultural group or a University, but as humans, to ask him - or herself with all sincerity: Don't we all deserve freedom from fear?"

Essentially, Elsohly was arguing that "freedom from fear" trumps freedom of speech. It was left to a prominent American apostate, Mohamed Asghar, co-founder of Former Muslims United, to rebut this logic and in the process defend Wilders' views on the threat of Islamization:

> I agree that all humans deserve freedom from fear, including the one that emanates from a religion, called Islam. It calls upon its adherents to kill all those who do not believe in Allah, Muhammad and the Day of Judgment. Consequently, most non-Muslims, who have understood Islam and its teaching, remain in constant fear of being executed by its followers, whenever the former find themselves among the latter.

To put into practice what Muslims preach and claim about the mankind's right to be free from fear; can we ask the Muslims to remove from the Quran those passages, which require them to kill the Non-Believers and to convert them to Islam by persuasion or force, or to eliminate them from the face of the earth?

Gordon: What was your professional background before you entered Dutch politics?

Wilders: I worked for the Dutch social insurance agency before I entered politics, where I first worked as a speechwriter for the liberal People's Party for Freedom and Democracy. In 1997, I was elected in the city council of Utrecht, one of the larger cities in the Netherlands.

Gordon: How long have you been a member of The Hague Parliament?

Wilders: I have been a member of the Dutch Parliament for more than 11 years now.

Gordon: When do you form the Freedom Party?

Wilders: I left the liberal People's Party for Freedom and Democracy in 2004, due to many irreconcilable differences, amongst which was the party's position on Turkish accession to the European Union, to form my own party.

Gordon: How extensive have been your travels to Israel and the Middle East? Did that experience lead to your defense of Israel?

Wilders: As a young man, I traveled extensively through the Middle East, including Iran, and lived in Israel for two years. Israel is a beacon of light in an area - the Middle East - that is pitch black everywhere else. Israel is a Western democracy, while Syria, Saudi Arabia, Iran and Egypt are medieval dictatorships. The so-called 'Middle East conflict' is not about land at all. It is a conflict about ideologies; a battle between Islam and freedom. It is not about some land in Gaza or in Judea and Samaria. It is about Jihad. To Islam the whole of Israel is occupied territory. Islam forces Israel to fight and Israel is not just fighting for itself. Israel is fighting for all of us, for the entire West. Israel is fighting the jihad that is meant for all of us. So we should all defend Israel. We all are Israel.

Gordon: What knowledge did you acquire from your readings and travels about Islam and its doctrine towards unbelievers?

Wilders: Islam is a totalitarian ideology, a doctrine of hate, and it is not difficult to find in the Quran what Muslims are expected to do with unbelievers: they are to be killed. Just look at Surah 4 verse 56, or Surah 47 verse 4, to name a few.

Gordon: What were the transforming events in Holland and the EU that led you to take a stand against Islamization?

Wilders: The encroachment of Islam on everyday life in the Netherlands and Europe is very significant. Mosques and burqas are popping up everywhere you look, gays and women are regularly harassed on the streets of our main cities. That creeping Islamization is what we have to fear most, because every mosque, every Islamic school, every burqa is regarded by many Muslims as a building block towards a larger goal, towards domination. In order to preserve our freedom, our democratic society and our civil rights, it is vital that we stop the Islamization immediately.

Gordon: You have espoused bans on the Quranic canon as "hate texts." How has that been received by the Dutch non-Muslim and Muslim populations?

Wilders: My Freedom Party was the winner in the recent elections for the European Parliament. Right now, in the polls, we in fact are leading. If there would be elections in the Netherlands tomorrow, I could very well become the next Prime Minister.

Gordon: Why do you advocate restrictions on Muslim immigration in both Holland and the EU?

Wilders: We have to stop the mass immigration from Muslim countries simply because more Islam means less freedom.

Gordon: Why did you produce the film, Fitna?

Wilders: I felt I had the moral duty to educate people about Islam and the Islamization of Europe. The duty to make clear to everyone that the Koran stands at the heart of what some people call terrorism but is in reality Jihad. I wanted to show that the problems of Islam are at the core of Islam, and do not belong to its fringes. I have warned against the dangers of the Koran and Islam in numerous interviews, opinion articles, speeches and of course parliamentary debates, but pictures often say more than words. That is why I made *Fitna*.

Gordon: Were you surprised by the intense reactions of Dutch Muslims and Muslims throughout the umma to the film?

Wilders: Actually, the reactions of Muslims, in particular Muslims in the Netherlands, were relatively mild. It was mainly cultural relativists that threw a fit over it. Also, there were some Muslims protesting in Afghanistan, Pakistan and Indonesia who were burning dolls depicting me and shouting terrible things.

Gordon: Why has a court in the Kingdom of Jordan issued a warrant for your arrest?

Wilders: Because of *Fitna*, Jordan threatens to prosecute me for blasphemy, demeaning Islam and slandering the Prophet Muhammad; violations of the Jordanian Penal Code, even though the alleged violations did not even occur in Jordan. As you know, Jordan is a non-democratic country, without an independent or impartial judicial system and without a strongly developed civil society. Jordan's attempt to prosecute me is an infringement on the sovereignty of my country, the Netherlands. It is an infringement on freedom of speech. Jordan's attempt is in fact a hostile act towards freedom itself.

Gordon: You have been under 24/7 protection by the Queen's Royal Protective Service in Holland for over four years. What triggered it and how has it disrupted your family and everyday life?

Wilders: My critical view on Islam has resulted in the loss of my personal freedom. Following the arrest of extremist Islamists who were planning to assassinate me I have been put under 24-hour police protection and have been for almost five years now. I have to stay in safe houses, army barracks and even prison cells because this is the only way in which the Dutch authorities can protect me. Everything I do and everyone I meet is monitored closely. As a result of this, my wife and I no longer have any privacy.

Gordon: What can you tell us about the decisions of the Amsterdam Appeals and Dutch Supreme Court cases that effectively criminalized your free speech?

Wilders: The Amsterdam Appeals Court gave a decision which I believe was politically motivated. I hope and trust that the court of law that will handle my court-case will be more sensible and throw the charges out like they should be.

Gordon: Why in your opinion did the British Immigration Tribunal recently overturn former Home Minister Jacquie Smith's ban on you entering the U.K.?

Wilders: They ruled that the decision of the British Home Secretary to ban me was unjust, illegal and a violation of freedom of speech. The ban was a ridiculous and politically motivated decision by the British government and thankfully the British judges have proven to be a lot wiser than the government.

Gordon: What was the reception you received upon arrival in Britain from those supportive of your right to speak freely versus British Muslims who wanted to stifle it?

Wilders: A Muslim mob demonstrated outside, shouting: "Freedom go to hell," "Shariah for the Netherlands," "Enemy of Islam Geert Wilders deserves capital punishment" and "Islam will dominate the world." But most people I met that day were happy that the preposterous ban was overturned and I was able to travel to the UK.

Gordon: The Freedom party is highly popular in opinion polls of Dutch voters. Is that a reflection of their approval of the party's agenda and your views?

Wilders: Of course it is! Many people in the Netherlands are fed up with the ongoing Islamization of our country, and the cowardice of the political elite that is squandering our liberties in favor of Islam, for the sake of their utopian ideas of cultural relativism.

Gordon: Given your recent European Parliamentary election victory, do you anticipate taking up the several positions you have won? If not, why not?

Wilders: We already have. Our MEP's are already hard at work exposing the outrageous workings of the European Parliament. Only last week, they refused a very large portion of the needlessly high allowance for expenses they are entitled to because they refuse to waste the taxpayer's money.

Gordon: Do you anticipate that Dutch elections might be held prior to 2011? Given your leading position in polls of likely voters in Holland, could you form a ruling coalition government?

Wilders: I truly hope that the elections will be held prior to 2011. The sooner we can get rid of this appalling cabinet, the better. And judging by the current polls, a lot of voters agree with me.

Gordon: You are a great admirer of the individual free speech rights guaranteed under the First Amendment of the US Constitution. You have advocated the development of an EU law guaranteeing free speech rights in member countries. Why do you think that is an important form of protection given the current legal environment that bars criticizing a religion like Islam and Sharia law?

Wilders: Let me make something very clear: Islam is NOT a religion as such. Islam is more of a totalitarian ideology that poses as a religion. It is comparable to other totalitarian ideologies like Communism and Nazism. And if you say this, you are prosecuted like I'm being prosecuted in the Netherlands. So it is very important that we reiterate the importance of the right to free speech. After all, it is one of the building blocks of our Western society.

Gordon: From your recent trips to America, how concerned are you about the rise of Islamization here?

Wilders: Although the Islamization in America isn't as widespread as in Europe, it is a genuine threat. America is facing a stealth Jihad, an

Islamic attempt to introduce Sharia law bit by bit. There are a growing number of examples of Islamization in the United States, for instance Muslim cab drivers at Minneapolis airport refusing over five thousand passengers because they were carrying alcohol; Muslim students demanding separate housing on university campuses; Muslim women demanding separate hours in gyms and swimming pools. I could go on and on. Also, the recent changes in policy of the American government do not bode well for the future. The United States recently joined Egypt in sponsoring an anti-free speech resolution in the UN Human Rights Council. The Obama-administration and Europe supported a resolution to recognize exceptions to free speech for any negative religious stereotyping. This appeasement of the non-free Arab world is the beginning of the end. It is erosion of free speech and of the First Amendment. This UN resolution is an absolute disgrace. But fortunately, a growing number of Americans take notice of what is happening and are aware that if things continue like this, America will have the same problems as we are currently faced with in Europe.

* * *

Geert Wilders has seen both his and his party's fortunes rise since our interview with him. He was acquitted on June 23, 2011 by an Amsterdam Appeals Court of all charges of "incitement to hatred and discrimination" in an action brought against him by leftist and Muslim opponents. The Dutch Freedom Party (PVV) finished third in the 2010 election winning 24 seats (15% of the 150 seats) in The Hague Parliament. Wilders elected not to become a junior member of the ruling coalition of Dutch PM Rutte of the Christian Democratic Appeal (CDA) and its partner, the VVD. Instead, he chose to exercise political suasion through negotiation of key issues regarding Islamization in Holland. He remains steadfast in support of Israel and the Jewish people and is an advocate for Israeli MK Eldad's peace plan of "Jordan is Palestine." In January 2012, Wilders called on the Dutch government to issue an official apology to survivors and their families for its "passivity" in the face of Nazi murders of 100,000 Dutch Jews during the Holocaust. Wilders' forthcoming book about "the true nature of Islam and world opposition to Islamization" is scheduled to be published in the US in April of 2012.

5
ERICK STAKELBECK
NOVEMBER 2009

Erick Stakelbeck is the on-air commentator on terrorism and national security affairs for the Christian Broadcasting Network (CBN). Stakelbeck is one of the few who, by dint of education and experience, knows the threat of Islamization in America and Israel. He didn't start out his journalistic career after graduating college in the late 1990's with that in mind. Prior to the watershed 9/11 date, Stakelbeck, a Philadelphia native, former high school and college basketball player, was bent on a sportswriting career and ended up covering the NBA for a publication in New York.

After awhile he found sports reporting less than fulfilling. After 9/11 he set out to learn more about radical Islam through in-depth research and eventually ploughed through the Qur'anic canon. His family background (his father was a U.S. Airborne veteran) and longtime interest in foreign affairs and the Middle East were motivating factors. Through David Horowitz, he first realized his dream of writing on Islamic terrorism at *FrontPageMagazine*. Subsequently, he joined Steve Emerson's Investigative Project on Terrorism and authored opinion pieces for a wide array of publications: *The Wall Street Journal, Jerusalem Post, Washington Times* and *National Review Online* among them. He also began appearing on Fox News, CNN and other television networks as a terrorism analyst. When he was offered the chance to go on-air and report on terrorism and national security for CBN full time, he jumped at the chance.

Stakelbeck has his own program on CBN: "Stakelbeck on Terror." He focuses on the growth of homegrown terrorism; the world wide Sunni al Qaeda network; the "stealth jihad" of Muslim Brotherhood fronts like the Council on American Islamic Relations (CAIR), Islamic Society of North America (ISNA), Muslim American Society (MAS); Saudi influence in the US; the wars in Iraq and Afghanistan; Iranian support of terrorist groups like Hezbollah, Hamas and the Palestinian Islamic Jihad; and the threat of nuclear Iran to Israel and US interests in the Middle East.

Stakelbeck is decidedly pro-Israel. He periodically talks to general audiences on behalf of the American Israel Public Affairs Committee (AIPAC), Christians United For Israel (CUFI) and other pro-Israel organizations.

Gordon: What was your journalism background before you became a CBN terrorism correspondent in the Washington Bureau?

Stakelbeck: I've had quite a ride since graduating from Holy Family University in Philadelphia--my hometown--in 1999. They say beginning writers should write about what they know. Being a former high school and college basketball player and hoops junkie, my immediate inclination was to follow the bouncing ball. My first full-time journalism gig was as a sportswriter, covering sports for a local chain of newspapers based in suburban Philly. At the same time, I was freelancing for some national basketball publications, interviewing college and NBA players. I got my big break with one of them in 2000 and moved to New York City to work as an assistant editor and staff writer, covering the NBA. I soon found that while I loved sports, writing about today's athletes felt very unfulfilling, especially with so many pressing, life-or-death issues going on in the world which increasingly commanded my interest.

Like most Americans, I was outraged, angered, saddened, dismayed--you name it--in the aftermath of 9/11. I felt a burning desire to do something to help in the fight against these Islamist barbarians at the gates--a fight that was clearly shaping up as a struggle for the very existence of America and Western civilization. I immediately began consuming every book, DVD, white paper--you name it—that I could get my hands on about Islam, the Middle East and terrorism. As Sun Tzu said: "know your enemy." I had already had a lifelong interest in these topics, courtesy of my father, who was a former member of the U.S. 101st Airborne Divison and a student of military history. So things fell into place very quickly. I read and re-read the Koran and Hadiths. I also read the Bible from cover to cover for the first time.

After an intensive year of study, I decided that I wanted to put my journalistic talents to use and begin writing about these topics. I had been a longtime admirer of political pundit and conservative activist David Horowitz, who has written so eloquently and bravely about his transition from radical Leftist to one of the towering intellectual figures of the American Right. I contacted David, introduced myself and sent along a few clips, asking if I could publish something on his popular website, *FrontpageMagazine.com* (FPM). David, to my eternal gratitude, agreed to give me a shot. I was soon turning out columns about Islamic radicalism, terrorism and campus radicalism for FPM. Even better, David hired me as a researcher for his book, *Campus Support for Terrorism*.

While working for David, I met terrorism expert Steve Emerson, whose groundbreaking work on homegrown jihad I had long admired. Steve had noticed my work at FPM and liked what he saw. He offered me a job as a senior writer at his Washington, D.C. think tank, The Investigative Project on Terrorism. I spent almost two years working for Steve, writing columns and longer pieces for *The Washington Times, New York Post, Jerusalem Post* and *National Review Online*, among others. The topics ranged from Iran and Syria to Al Qaeda to CAIR and beyond. Learning under an accomplished investigative journalist and terrorism expert like Steve was, in a word, invaluable. While working for Steve, I was also able to build up my contacts and begin doing TV and radio appearances for Fox News, CNN and others. I soon discovered that I liked the wide platform TV provided. I saw an opportunity to reach a larger and more diverse audience on air than I would through my print columns and articles. The more people that would learn about the imminent threats we were facing, the better. That is how I looked at it.

So when I learned that CBN was looking for an on-air correspondent to work out of their Washington, D.C. bureau, covering terrorism and national security, I was seriously interested. I had always loved CBN's hard-hitting, un-PC work on radical Islam and foreign policy issues, and also its strong pro-Israel stance. It seemed like a perfect match when I took the job, and it has turned out to be exactly that. As you can see, I have been very fortunate to have had some great mentors in this field and have been blessed with some incredible opportunities. Not bad for a guy from Northeast Philly!

Gordon: How long have you been the CBN terrorism correspondent?

Stakelbeck: Since May 2005: about four-and-a-half years.

Gordon: How do you develop the stories that you report?

Stakelbeck: Number one, I am constantly reading the latest news on terrorism, national security and the Middle East. I spend a good deal of time talking to contacts and picking their brains as well. There have been times when contacts have alerted me to a compelling story or helped put me in touch with a great interview subject. In my research, I try to look for patterns and trends that are emerging. For instance, since we have had an explosion of homegrown terrorist plots on U.S. soil since May; my work has been heavily focused on that over the past six months. I also look for important stories that no one else is covering, or that are not being covered in any kind of depth by the mainstream media. I always find that "culture clash" stories are interesting in that regard. Examples are stories I have done recently on Somali Muslim immigrants moving to small town, rural America and Hamas supporters setting up shop in the heart of Middle America: Columbus, Ohio. I am very blessed that the CBN News team trusts my instincts and gives me a great deal of creative freedom to pursue stories that I believe all Americans need to know about.

Gordon: How broad is the range of your reporting? Domestic, International or both?

Stakelbeck: The range of my reporting is pretty broad and covers both domestic and international security. I focus on a few things. Number one, Al Qaeda and the worldwide Sunni Jihadist movement. Number two, homegrown terror threats, homeland security news, and the "stealth jihad" waged by Muslim Brotherhood affiliated groups like CAIR and ISNA and also the Saudis. Third, the wars in Afghanistan/Pakistan and Iraq. Fourth, the broader Middle East, with a particular focus on the Iran/Syria/Hezbollah/Hamas axis. Lastly, any issues affecting Israel's security and global antisemitism. I have also reported on North Korea, Russia and Venezuela and their nefarious activities. It's a full plate but I love every second of it.

Gordon: What in your experience have been significant changes in Federal government counter-terrorism policies over the past several years?

Stakelbeck: The collapse of "The Wall" that began under the Clinton administration and existed until 9/11 gave a big boost to our counterterrorism efforts. This wall of separation, insanely, prevented the foreign intelligence (CIA) and domestic criminal investigative (FBI) communities from sharing information about terrorism-related investigations. That barrier is gone today, and while there is still a good amount of inter-agency rivalry and squabbling, all sides have forged a more united front in the war against radical Islam. On the negative side, the Obama administration, unfortunately, has made the disastrous decision to close Guantanamo Bay prison and potentially house hundreds of hardened Islamic jihadists on U.S. soil. Even worse is the administration's morale-crushing move to seek the possible prosecution of brave CIA officers who do the unpleasant but necessary work that saves American lives. Interestingly enough - and much to the hard Left's chagrin - the Obama administration has actually retained most of President Bush's highly effective anti-terrorist policies, from the Patriot Act to rendition to drone missile strikes in the tribal regions of Pakistan. But any positive moves the current administration has made have largely been negated by the extremely dangerous decisions on Gitmo and CIA interrogators. There is also the matter of how to define our enemy, from an "official" government standpoint. I was critical of the Bush administration when it dropped terms like "Islamic terrorism," "jihadist" and "radical Islamist" from its lexicon in favor of terms like "violent extremist" to define our enemy. The Obama team has taken this politically correct, intellectually dishonest strategy even further, with Department of Homeland Security Secretary Janet Napolitano going so far as to describe acts of Islamic terror, comically, as "man made disasters." Let us be honest with the American people about who exactly we are fighting, what our enemies believe and what they seek.

Gordon: From your contact with senior officials in the counterterrorism and intelligence communities, do they understand the threat of Islamization both here and abroad? If not, why not?

Stakelbeck: The average field agent definitely "gets it" when it comes to radical Islam and jihad. Many of the bureaucrats at the top of these agencies, unfortunately, do not. Yes, they fully understand the basic fact that radical Islamists want to kill us. But some of them haven't the foggiest idea about Islamic history, doctrine or eschatology beyond the politically correct, misleading platitudes supplied by CAIR and other American Islamist "civil rights" organizations. These groups are, in reality, offshoots of the Jihadist Muslim Brotherhood movement, which was the precursor of Al Qaeda and Hamas. Despite their radical pedigrees, CAIR and their ilk have been able to curry favor with the F.B.I. and law enforcement agencies over the years, even conducting "sensitivity training" for agents. In such forums, jihad--which has historically meant violent military conquest in the name of Islam--has been recast as mere "spiritual struggle." For example, going to work and raising your kids could be your own personal Jihad. This is pure bunk and fatally misleading. But it is the kind of dangerous nonsense that has been able to creep into our law enforcement and intelligence communities, thanks to well-meaning but misguided "outreach" efforts by the FBI's hierarchy, among others. The Bureau, to its credit, has cut ties with CAIR, at least for the moment, due to the group's links to Hamas fundraisers. But it continues its "outreach" to other American Islamist groups unabated. I'll wager that since 9/11, under both the Bush and Obama administrations, far too few officials have taken the initiative to go out and learn about our Islamist enemy--read the Koran or Hadiths or study Islamic doctrine and history. What a far cry from the days when Ronald Reagan was devouring every book he could get his hands on about Marxism and Communism during the Cold War. Again: know your enemy.

Gordon: David Gaubatz and Paul Sperry in their new book *Muslim Mafia* uncovered plans of Muslim Brotherhood front groups such as CAIR, the ISNA, MPAC, and MAS to penetrate the Congress and the Obama Administration to further their Islamist agenda and overturn our Constitution. How dangerous do you believe that threat is and what can be done about it?

Stakelbeck: I attended a press conference in October at the U.S. Capitol where four Republican members of Congress (led by Sue Myrick, one elected official who definitely understands the jihadist threat) called for a full Department of Justice (DOJ) investigation into CAIR's activities, not to mention an IRS investigation into the group's non-profit status. These lawmakers were moved to act after reading eye-opening documentation laid out in *Muslim Mafia*, which includes evidence that CAIR is seeking to place interns in Congressional offices in an attempt to exert greater influence on Capitol Hill. As I stated earlier, I believe the threat posed by CAIR and its fellow Muslim Brotherhood fronts like MAS and ISNA is severe - one glance at the now infamous

1991 Muslim Brotherhood memorandum that was revealed in the Holy Land Foundation terror fundraising trial tells us that. According to this memo, all American Brotherhood members "must understand their work in America is a kind of grand jihad in eliminating and destroying the Western civilization from within, and sabotaging its miserable house by their hands and the hands of believers so that it is eliminated and God's religion is made victorious over all other religions." It's obvious from this memo that any group with ties to the Brotherhood--like CAIR, ISNA and MAS-- is no friend of the U.S. As a result, they should be denied any and all access to the halls of power (starting with the White House, Capitol Hill, the intelligence community and the Pentagon) and be subject to full DOJ investigations. That includes a close look at their sources of funding, much of which comes from overseas.

Gordon: You uncovered new details about Daniel Boyd, the alleged ringleader of a homegrown terrorist cell in Raleigh, North Carolina. Tell us about your investigative work there.

Stakelbeck: Our CBN News team, along with my friend and colleague, terrorism expert, Daveed Gartenstein-Ross, was able to uncover new details about Boyd that had been previously unreported. Boyd's case had so many fascinating elements and was a great case study in homegrown jihad. It had a little bit of everything. Think about it: Boyd was a white convert to Islam who had trained overseas in Afghanistan/Pakistan. He then returned to the U.S. with newfound fighting skills, and the hunger for violent jihad had never left him. In his mind, how could he ever go back to a normal, quiet life after that? He craved jihad. Raised and educated in the U.S., he was able to ingratiate himself into American society and deceive his non-Muslim neighbors. Boyd also possessed a trait which virtually every homegrown jihadist I have investigated shared: a virulent hatred for Israel and Jews. He actually attempted to enter Israel in 2007, with plans to travel to Gaza and link up with jihadists there. Luckily, the Israelis did not let him enter the country. In addition, Boyd hated the U.S. military, as evidenced by his desire to attack American military bases. Lastly, Boyd was, by all accounts, a very charismatic, forceful figure who was able to attract impressionable young people in his local Muslim community with his radical message. Even some of his young, non-Muslim neighbors looked to him as an "advice giver," according to one that we spoke to. So, this case had many of the classic homegrown jihad traits.

We were able to uncover revealing details about Boyd (he had stolen from a local business, had poor relations with his employer, etc.) simply by knocking on doors in and around Raleigh and asking questions. Considering that some of his neighbors--even after the release of the damning indictment against him--still maintain Boyd's innocence, acquiring a full portrait of the man was essential. I feel we were able to get one: and it wasn't pretty. He may have had his well-meaning, infidel neighbors fooled, but local Muslims knew all too well about Boyd's extremist views and lust for armed jihad. I spoke at length, off-the-record, to a local Muslim leader in Raleigh who knew Boyd and his family well. This Muslim leader said that "nothing in [Boyd's] indictment surprises me. He talked about jihad all the time," adding that Boyd often bragged about his time spent fighting in Afghanistan during the late 1980's and was a pied piper type among young people.

This Muslim added that more people should have spoken out about Boyd, noting, sadly, that Islamic communities in the U.S. have become much too insular and isolated—they've circled the wagons, so to speak. This is a crucial and troubling point. Although it is important to note here that a Muslim informant apparently aided the feds in their investigation of Boyd.

Gordon: In your view, how dangerous is the homegrown terrorist threat?

Stakelbeck: I believe that if we do have another terror attack on American soil in the near future, it will most likely come from a homegrown cell or individual that does not need guidance from Al Qaeda. In other words, young American Muslims inspired by Al Qaeda, but radicalized on the Web or at the local mosque. It does not take a brain surgeon to walk into a crowded shopping mall, yell, "Allahu Akhbar" and begin firing at random. We actually did see an act of Islamic terror here back in May, when a Muslim convert shot and killed a U.S. military recruiter in Arkansas. In fact, since May, we have seen no less than seven major terrorist plots broken up on U.S. soil. And that isn't even including the Arkansas shooting or the continuing pipeline of Somali-Americans going back to their home country to join the Al-Qaeda linked Al-Shabaab group. This is a dizzying array of plots—including the biggest since 9/11, by the Najibullah Zazi cell in New York/Denver—showing that the homegrown threat is worsening. These plots are occurring in some of the most out-of-the-way places where you would never expect

Islamic terrorists to set up shop: Raleigh, North Carolina, Springfield, Illinois. Rural Arkansas. These terror cells aren't just popping up in New York City or LA: immigration gateway cities. These are often in quiet suburban communities, even rural areas.

We have, thankfully, thus far been able to avoid another attack due to superior law enforcement and intelligence work, and a little bit of luck.

Gordon: You've reported on the assimilation problems of Somali Muslims in American communities. Why has this immigrant community produced homegrown terrorists who become jihadis in Somalia and further, what should our government do to screen radical Muslim immigrants from coming to America?

Stakelbeck: I think the biggest problem with the Somali community in the U.S. is the lack of assimilation that you mentioned. I have covered and followed the Somali Muslim communities in several cities: Columbus, Ohio, Minneapolis, Minnesota, even in rural Tennessee. And the current running through every one of these communities is a failure to assimilate. Somalia hasn't even had a functioning central government for the past 20 years. It's a hotbed for warlordism, jihadism and banditry. It's just a very nasty place, one of the most dangerous, most backward places in the world. So to take people from this kind of situation and bring them to a major metropolitan area in the United States is frequently a recipe for disaster.

I have interviewed several Somali American Muslims, who have come here, gotten a taste of U.S. society and Western civilization, and have immediately withdrawn. The government helps them get on their feet for the first few months, but then they are essentially on their own. Many people in these Somali-American Muslim communities are becoming very isolated. They are not making an attempt to reach out and become a part of the American fabric. When you have a situation like this, with a self-isolating, immigrant Muslim community whose religious and cultural norms are alien to most Americans, the people in that community are more susceptible to radicalism. When they feel isolated and alienated from society, from the culture-at-large, what do they lean on? What they know. And what do they know? Oftentimes, they lean on Islam. Some Somalis feel like they don't have any prospects, that they don't belong here or fit in. If they come under the sway of a radical Imam who can convince them, "Hey, the West, the U.S., is your enemy, and you should destroy this country from within," then, unfortunately, some can be susceptible to that message. We see it in the Somali community here and we see it in other immigrant Muslim communities, not only in the U.S. but throughout the West. Minneapolis is a good case study. There is one particular mosque that a number of Somali Muslims attended who then went back to Somalia to wage jihad and join an al-Qaeda-linked group. Investigators believe that they likely fell under the sway of radical teachings at that mosque.

Gordon: Why, in your view, did the Obama administration appoint Leon Panetta as CIA director? Has he exhibited independent judgment over the terrorist interrogation issue that embroiled Congress this summer?

Stakelbeck: The choice of Panetta was a head scratcher for me. President Obama had talked during his campaign about breaking from the past. He said was going to put a new face on Washington. Then he turns around and picks Leon Panetta, a guy who is a longtime D.C. insider and former adviser to Bill Clinton as his CIA director. Prior to Panetta taking this post, he did not have a strong intelligence background. I talked to Pete Hoekstra, a Republican Congressman who is very involved in intelligence matters--one of the best on these issues. He told me--surprisingly--a week after the Panetta pick, that he liked it. He said he thought Panetta's diverse experiences in Congress and as an adviser to President Clinton were a positive. Hoekstra pointed out that Panetta was privy to high-level intelligence briefings during the Clinton years. He also liked the fact that Panetta wasn't a member of the intel community, wasn't an intel "insider," and would bring an outside perspective to the CIA.

All that may be true. But what we've seen so far is that Panetta really hasn't been out in front, hasn't been very public at all, and has basically been undermined at every turn by the Obama administration. There are reports that he and Eric Holder, the Attorney General, have had screaming matches in the White House over Holder's insistence on possibly prosecuting CIA interrogators. As a result, the morale of the CIA has never been lower. Panetta realizes this and just how devastating these prosecutions would be for the agency. The end result of what the administration is doing will weaken the CIA. There were actually rumors a few months ago that Panetta might step down. I tend to think he won't step down because he is a loyal Democrat who wouldn't want to cause a public fuss and embarrass Obama. But if he did step down, I wouldn't be shocked, just because he's been undermined so badly in public by this administration.

Gordon: Why did the Obama administration endeavor to appoint acknowledged critics of Israel, like Charles Freeman with past Saudi connections, to the National Intelligence Council and ex-Republican Senator Chuck Hagel as foreign intelligence advisor?

Stakelbeck: I think it has become obvious that for some reason, the Obama administration enjoys offending and insulting supporters of Israel. After the Freeman appointment, I tried to give them the benefit of the doubt. Even though Freeman's long history of anti-Israel demagoguery, Saudi ties and unabashed Arabism was readily accessible via a simple Google search. But in the months since the Freeman fiasco we have seen a steady stream of anti-Israel appointees and choices for awards from this administration. We had Mary Robinson, who oversaw the UN Conference on Racism in 2001 in Durban, South Africa, which descended into an anti-Israel, anti-Semitic hatefest that the U.S. and Israel literally walked out of. Yet the Obama administration turns around and gives her the highest civilian honor you can receive in the United States--the Medal of Freedom--for her work towards women's rights. They certainly knew of Desmond Tutu's anti-Israel views, yet he received the same award, along with Robinson. At a time when seemingly the entire world - even previously reliable allies like Turkey - is turning against Israel, this is particularly inexcusable. Now you have Chuck Hagel, a harsh critic of Israel for years, being named to an advisory post in the administration. You had Jim Jones, the President's National Security Advisor, appearing as keynote speaker at a recent conference for the far left, anti-Israel group J Street. Israeli government officials have gone on record as saying that J Street's agenda is harmful to Israeli interests. At least a dozen Members of Congress who were originally slated to speak at the J Street conference backed out once they learned of the group's anti-Zionist views. Yet the President's National Security Advisor - who knew full well that others were pulling out because of J Street's dangerous agenda - still delivered the keynote address at this conference. Jones himself has made controversial statements about Israel in the past, and another Obama advisor, Samantha Power, is rabidly anti-Israel. So, from Freeman to Mary Robinson to J Street to Hagel and beyond, there is a troubling pattern here. That is not even mentioning this administration's unprecedented pressure on the State of Israel or President Obama's previous friendships with anti-Israel zealots like Jeremiah Wright, Bill Ayers and Rashid Khalidi.

Gordon: The Obama administration has postponed enacting bipartisan Iran nuclear sanctions legislation passed by Congress. Why in your view did they do that? Further, what would the sanctions legislation actually do to deter Iran from completing workable nuclear weapons?

Stakelbeck: I'm going to answer the second part of the question first. The main focus of those sanctions would be to cut off the import of refined gasoline to Iran. The Iranians spend far too much time focusing on building nuclear weapons and not enough time figuring out how to refine gas. As a result, they have to import 40% of their refined gas from foreign companies. A number of those companies are based in the West, so if we could get these companies to stop supplying refined gas to Iran it would hurt the Iranians, without a doubt. There could be gas shortages; you could have some unrest in the streets that would result in a further weakening of the regime. At least, that is the hope. But Iran has a fallback option. Hugo Chavez, the oil-rich Venezuelan dictator, has already promised to supply Iran with refined gas if sanctions are enacted. The Chinese and Russians will step up to the plate and work with Iran to get around these sanctions. So could sanctions have an impact? Yes, and the administration should enact them immediately. But in the end, I think their impact would be dulled by the likes of Venezuela, China, Russia and others assisting Iran. Right now, the Iranian people are in a position where we could support some subversive activities among those who hate this regime and cause real problems for the mullahs. Sanctions, even if only moderately effective, would be another strong blow to the regime. Unfortunately, President Obama has completely dropped the ball in this regard. In June, he stood back and stayed mum as the Iranian people rose up against the dictatorship. President Obama said he did not want to "meddle" in Iranian affairs. I talked to several Iranian dissidents afterwards who were incredibly disappointed in Obama and despondent over his lack of action.

Back to sanctions. At the end of the day, it is real simple. Nothing - and I mean nothing - will stop Iran from her drive to acquire nuclear weapons. The Iranian regime views the acquisition of nuclear weapons as their divine right. This is a religious mission for the Iranians. Neither President Obama nor lawmakers here in the U.S. and the West can grasp that. This is not the Cold War, where you had a situation of Mutually Assured Destruction, where we wanted to live and the Soviets also wanted to stay alive. In the Iranian case, that regime has shown that it is willing to sacrifice thousands - if not millions - of their own people to further their jihad. Look at the Iran/Iraq war. The Iranians sent waves of young Iranians to clear mine fields. Tens of thousands of them were killed. So if the Iranian regime can take out Tel Aviv and the surrounding areas - where most of Israel's population lives - and effectively end the State of Israel as we know it, I believe the Iranian regime will find it irresistible: it will, at some point, take its chances and launch an attack. Or the regime will supply a nuclear weapon to a terror group to let it do the dirty work. Remember, Iran is a big country, 70 million people. Hashemi Rafsanjani, the former Iranian president, said a few years back, essentially: "One Islamic bomb would be the end of Israel. But we could survive an Israeli counterattack."

So if Iran goes nuclear, you are going to have people with their fingers on the nuclear trigger who are not rational, who are religious zealots, people like an Ahmadinejad who believes that he, personally, can help usher in the return of the Mahdi, or Islamic Messiah. These are not people with whom you can have a rational dialogue. The Iranians are steeped in taqiyya - deception - the Islamic concept that justifies lying to non-believers. They have done it to the West time and time again in these ongoing nuclear negotiations. In the end, the ultimate reason the Obama administration is delaying these sanctions is because President Obama has the utmost belief in his own magnificent charisma and powers of persuasion. He still thinks he can convince the Iranians to take a different path and knows that sanctions would sabotage his grand efforts at normalizing relations with Iran. I think his Nobel peace prize has emboldened this delusion. Unfortunately for him and for all of us, nothing will stop the Iranians from acquiring nuclear weapons other than military action. I wish it wasn't so and it's not going to be pretty. But it is a fact.

Gordon: Do you think Israel has any choice but to undertake a military assault on Iranian nuclear and missile development facilities? When might Israel launch such an operation and how complicated and effective would it be?

Stakelbeck: I don't think Israel has any choice. I think the Obama administration and the "international community," have really backed Israel into a corner. I would be shocked if the Obama administration took any kind of military steps against the Iranians. I think the administration has made a conscious decision that they can live with a nuclear Iran and seem to believe that Mutually Assured Destruction will work with the Iranians, that we can isolate and contain them. But that's just not possible with Iran: a radical Islamist, expansionist state that seeks to export its Jihad throughout the world.

The Obama administration, based on Secretary of State Hillary Clinton's comments a few months ago, may plan to offer a nuclear umbrella for Israel and the Arab Gulf states to help deter nuclear Iran. Yet a nuclear Iran would surely spark a Middle East arms race, U.S. umbrella or not. It is interesting that the French are now taking a much tougher stance against the Iranian nuclear program than the U.S. That tells you how misguided and ineffective our approach to Iran has become. You are never going to get Iran's allies, China and Russia, on board with any kind of sanctions. They have close business and economic ties with the mullahs and are helping to arm the Iranians. The Russians are helping to build Iran's nuclear plant in Bushehr. So it's pure folly to think that you are ever going to get Russia or China on board, not only for sanctions but any kind of real international pressure on Iran.

The Iranians, according to various intelligence estimates, could have a nuclear device by 2012. The Israelis can't wait much longer than they already have, and the recent revelation that Iran has a hidden nuclear facility outside Qom just raised the stakes even higher. I have spoken to Israeli officials at length both on and off the record about this. The Israelis feel they have no choice but to let the Obama administration's diplomatic game play out. If Israel were to attack Iran while negotiations were still ongoing, the full anti-Semitic fury of the UN and much of the EU would come down upon Israel in a vengeful manner. The Israelis realize this, and feel they need to exhaust every possible option before possibly taking that ultimate step of military action against this existential threat of a nuclear Iran. That way, they can tell the world, "hey, we tried it your way and we've waited long enough. We either act now or a second Holocaust awaits us." The Israelis do not want to take military action. It is the last thing they want and a true nightmare scenario. All the Israelis want is to live in peace with their neighbors, including Iran. If the Iran nuclear issue could work out diplomatically, the Israelis would be absolutely thrilled and relieved. Sadly, I do not see that happening.

I think the Israelis will give negotiations until January 1st, and then make their decision. My gut tells me that by spring of 2012, if we have seen no momentum or real progress in these talks between the West and Iran, Israel will take military action. If they wait beyond the spring of 2012, it may be too late. The U.S. and Europe don't want to do it. They are going to leave it up to Israel, once again, to take care of the West's dirty work. It's going to be interesting to see the public response by the Obama administration if and when Israel does take that action.

I thank God that Benjamin Netanyahu, a man of strength and character, is the Prime Minister of Israel right now. A man who will be willing to make unappealing but absolutely necessary decisions for Israel's survival. Israel has no other choice. You have a 1939 type situation here with Iran. And I can assure you that when Netanyahu says "never again," he means it with every fiber of his being.

Gordon: How important is the U.S. alliance with Israel in preserving our Middle East strategic interests?

Stakelbeck: The U.S. alliance with Israel is arguably our most important, given the stakes in the Middle East. You have a Westernized democracy in the heart of the Middle East. The most restless, volatile, dangerous region in the world, a region consumed with anti-American extremists who seek to erase the U.S. from the map and are working actively to do it. In the middle of all that, we have a staunch friend, a beacon of hope, in Israel. A democratic, Western nation that loves and supports the U.S., has strong ties to the U.S., with many American expatriates living there. The intelligence sharing and military cooperation that goes on between our nations has been constant and invaluable. This has been a special relationship for years, back to President Harry Truman's brave recognition of Israel's nationhood in 1948. Israel is the original bedrock of Judeo-Christian civilization, and we all know the religious, cultural and biblical reasons for supporting the Jewish State. But there are many other reasons. An excellent and thought-provoking new book by George Gilder, *The Israel Test*, describes how Israel is growing into a technological and economic powerhouse with top-flight scientists, entrepreneurs and technological innovators. Israel has become a Silicon Valley in the middle of the desert. So that's another obvious reason to maintain and promote the alliance.

At the end of the day, putting everything else aside, it all comes down to this: Israel's enemies are America's enemies. I spent time last year in Sderot, where they keep the rocket casings that are constantly fired into their city by Palestinian jihadists in the nearby Gaza Strip. They have hundreds of them on display at the police station in Sderot. Stamped on many of those rockets, in Farsi, are the words, "Made in Iran." So the same jihadist madmen who have been shouting death to America for 30 years also want to exterminate Israel. If that fact doesn't bring us together and strengthen our alliance, I don't know what will.

Gordon: Will the Obama administration adopt a winding-down strategy in Afghanistan as suggested by Vice President Biden or a surge in military forces as requested by General McCrystal?

Stakelbeck: I think Obama will find what a happy medium is, for him. You will see more troops in Afghanistan, but not the 40,000 that General McCrystal is asking for. Unfortunately, I think you are going to see a strategy closer to what Vice President Biden is pushing. Biden, by the way, is a guy who has been wrong on every major foreign policy issue over the past 35 years. So to have the President taking Biden's foreign policy advice is profoundly disturbing. But I think Biden's view could largely win out here. I think McCrystal will get some additional troops but not the 40,000 he needs for counterinsurgency and population protection. I'm not for nation-building or winning Islamic hearts and minds, because I don't think that is possible, particularly in Afghanistan. But McChrystal and General David Petreaus, two counter-insurgency experts for whom I have the utmost respect, believe that making the local population feel safe and secure is a big key to victory. You need more troops to do that with any kind of effectiveness, much as we did in Iraq with the surge.

Apparently, what the Obama administration is considering is fortifying Afghan cities - having a strong presence in cities like Kabul and Kandahar but pretty much ceding the countryside and rural areas to the Taliban. What you would have under this strategy is a situation similar to what we have with Hezbollah in Lebanon. The administration talks about this as if it would be a good thing. This is madness, as anyone familiar with the situation in Lebanon will tell you. You are not going to be able to fend off the Taliban for long. If you give the Taliban any kind of territory and any kind of "peace" via treaties, like Pakistan has done, they will only push for more. In Pakistan, the Taliban seized so much territory that in April they got within 60 miles of the Pakistani capital of Islamabad before they were turned back.

I think we potentially have a similar situation in Afghanistan. If you cede large areas of the country to the Taliban, you are going to have them fortify these areas and create al-Qaeda training camps. Eventually they will move on those Afghan cities. The Obama administration now seems to be thinking, "hey, you know, we can live with the Taliban. They are not an immediate threat to the U.S." Even though Taliban leaders, over the last two years, have repeatedly threatened to carry out attacks on U.S. soil and work hand in glove with al-Qaeda. So to say that the Taliban is not a direct threat to U.S. interests or the U.S. mainland is misleading at best. Biden seems to think that sporadic drone missile strikes against Taliban/Al Qaeda targets in the Afghan countryside will do the trick. I think you might have some success with that strategy in the short term, but in the long term it can't work. The goal in Afghanistan should be to ensure that the country never again gets to a point like it did before 9/11, when it was run by anti-American, jihadist barbarians who gave Al Qaeda safe haven to plan attacks on U.S. targets. We should take every step needed to prevent that - if that means more troops, which I think it does, so be it. Jeffersonian democracy is not going to happen in Afghanistan. It certainly shouldn't be a driving force in our strategy there. Protecting American lives, at home and aborad, should. If we leave too soon or do this with half measures, Afghanistan will descend into pre-9/11 chaos once again.

Gordon: How dangerous is the Pakistani nuclear arsenal and what assurances and controls can the U.S. exert to prevent weapons getting into the hands of terrorist groups in the Islamic world?

Stakelbeck: Pakistani government officials, and even Secretary of State Hillary Clinton, have said that they think Pakistan's nuclear arsenal is secure. When the Taliban moved within 60 miles of Islamabad last spring, they were apparently close to some of Pakistan's nuclear facilities. The Pakistani military obviously has a very strong presence and they ultimately hold the keys to Pakistan's nuclear arsenal. The problem is that the Pakistani military and Pakistani intelligence services are infiltrated by Taliban and Al Qaeda sympathizers. Pakistan never misses a chance to remind us that it is a sovereign country and we have been very mindful of that. But if you have the Taliban seize major metropolitan areas in Pakistan, everything is off the table. If it came to a point where it looked like the Taliban was going to overthrow the Pakistani government and a nuclear-armed, jihadist state was going to ensue, the U.S., along with NATO, may have to take drastic measures, perhaps even attempt to destroy Pakistan's nuclear arsenal (if India didn't first). It would be that dire of a situation. A nuclear-armed jihadist state run by the Taliban and al-Qaeda, with designs against the West, is an apocalyptic scenario.

Gordon: Finally, what thoughts do you have regarding improving U.S. counter-terrorism and Homeland Security?

Stakelbeck: I think the most important thing is to acknowledge who we are fighting. Yet again, know your enemy. Be straight with the American people. Tell the American people that we are fighting a global jihadist enemy who seeks our destruction. Terrorism expert Walid Phares has written in *Future Jihad* that we should be teaching what jihad is and what our enemies believe to American kids in high schools and universities, informing the American public about the threats we face. We did it during the Cold War. Most Americans knew what Communism was about and were aware of the severity of the Soviet threat. People today are very uneducated and misinformed about Islamism, thanks to a variety of factors, including the mainstream media. I would say that 90% of Americans couldn't even tell you what jihad is. Yet jihad, global Islamic expansionism through military force or stealth means, is what drives our enemies. There needs to be a sustained effort to educate the American public about the enemy we face. We are going to be fighting this radical jihadist enemy for years to come, and if the average American doesn't know who we are fighting, if they don't grasp the ideology and theology of our enemies, there is no way we can win this war in the long term.

6
RICHARD L. RUBENSTEIN
MARCH 2010

Dr. Richard L. Rubenstein is an ordained rabbi, noted theologian and author. He began his religious training at Cincinnati's Hebrew Union College, receiving a B.A. from the University of Cincinnati. He was ordained and received the Master of Hebrew Literature from the Jewish Theological Seminary. He earned the Master of Theology from Harvard Divinity School and a PhD in the History of Religion from Harvard. He was also a post-doctoral fellow at Yale. For a quarter of a century he taught religious studies at Florida State University where he was named a Robert O. Lawton Distinguished Professor, the University's highest academic honor. Following his retirement from FSU, Dr. Rubenstein served from 1994 to 1999 as President of the University of Bridgeport (UB), Connecticut, where he continues to serve as Distinguished Professor of Religion. Upon retirement as president, UB's trustees named him President Emeritus for his years of meritorious service.

Dr. Rubenstein was a founding member of the Editorial Advisory Board of *The Washington Times*, later serving as chairman. His views on the Shoah (Holocaust), Jewish and Christian theology, and the psychology of religion have been much sought after by Christian colleagues. His opinions on these and other subjects have been published in *The New York Times*, *Time Magazine*, *Newsweek* and even *Playboy*. He has published widely in scholarly journals and attended international theological and interreligious conferences where he encountered Muslim jurists and Imams and their views on Islam, the Shariah law of the Quranic canon and their attitude toward unbelievers.

He is the author of many books on religion, the Holocaust, and the impact of surplus populations on immigration, social destabilization, war and genocide. Among his works are: *The Religious Imagination: A Study in Psychoanalysis and Jewish Theology*, based on his Harvard PhD thesis, for which he received an Italian literary prize in Rome in 1977. His seminal book, *After Auschwitz: History, Radical Theology and Contemporary Judaism* and its companion volume, *Approaches to Auschwitz: the Holocaust and Its Legacy*, co-authored by John K. Roth, are highly regarded by Holocaust scholars. *The Cunning of History: Mass Death and the American Future*, with an introduction by the late Pulitzer Prize winning author, William Styron, and *The Age of Triage: Fear and Hope in an Overcrowded World*, are considered important readings in the study of surplus population and historical causes of conflict. His latest book, *Jihad and Genocide: Studies in Genocide, History, Religion and Human Rights* is the product of several years of research on the threat of annihilationist Islam to Western civilization and Jewish survival.

Gordon: What was it like growing up as a Jew among pro-Nazis in the Yorkville section of New York during the 1930's?

Rubenstein: In 1937, East 86th Street was the heart of Yorkville. It was then the German section of New York and was almost completely Nazi. Wherever you went, there were swastikas flying. I remember that at one end of the block, there was a tourist agency advertising trips to Germany on the Hamburg-America Line. This was when the German American Bund was strongest. One of my friend Bob's acquaintances was a German by the name of Henig. We barely talked to each other. I was aware of what was going on, both over in Europe and also in the United States, not that it directly affected me.

Then it did affect me. I think it was in 1938, when I was walking along the street at about 10:30 at night, after having been at a school affair and I heard, across the street, three drunken men – I think they were Irish – shouting, "Goddamn dirty Jews!" I said, "Shut up," and they came over and they beat the hell out of me. My parents complained to the police who came up and I noticed two things: One, the police were trying to find me guilty – "Why were you out that late? Why were you making trouble?" and my parents were being quite weak about it. They did not stand up for me. So, I had the feeling of Jewish powerlessness in a very graphic way.

I thought to myself, "Well, if this is what being Jewish means..." (I had had no Bar-Mitzvah. I had no emotional ties to anything Jewish at the time, except that I knew that my background was Jewish.) I asked myself, "Why should I be Jewish?" I thought it was a matter of choice in those days. So, I went to All Souls Church at 80th Street and Lexington Avenue in Manhattan, and talked to the Director of Religious Education. She invited me to join the Young People's Group. Shortly thereafter, I took the right hand of fellowship and became a Unitarian. I decided that I was going to become a minister. I had come to feel that religion was overwhelmingly important.

One day, I got a letter from somebody I had met whose father was the executive secretary of the American Unitarian Association. He said, "You are going to make a fine minister, but you need to change your name from Rubenstein to one that is less Jewish, more Anglo-Saxon." That sort of hit me like a lightning bolt. I went home and thought about it and said to myself, "I'm not going to do this, change my name." First of all, I would have spent the rest of my life worrying about being found out. Secondly, all of a sudden, I began to worry about ancestry and I thought, "I can't rat on my background."

Living on Manhattan's Upper East Side, I had friends who went to Temple Emanu-El on Fifth Avenue. They introduced me to Rabbi Nathan Perelman of Temple Emanu-El. I told him, with a lot of chutzpah (nerve), "I want to be a reform rabbi." I couldn't read Hebrew. I never had a Bar-Mitzvah. I knew very little about Jewish tradition, but he thought I was presentable and could do it. So, he decided to mentor me and invited me to become a member of the Junior Society of Temple Emanu-El, in preparing to become a student at the Hebrew Union College in Cincinnati, Ohio

Gordon: What was it like going through the Reform Jewish Hebrew Union College in Cincinnati during World War II?

Rubenstein: Early on, there was one crucial encounter when Julian Morgenstern, who was the president of the Hebrew Union College, came to New York. Rabbi Perelman said, "You ought to call on him and tell him that you're interested in becoming a student at the College," which I did. We got along especially well when I made a comment that I will never forget. "Dr. Morgenstern," I said, "if being a rabbi means being a Zionist, then I could never become a rabbi." He smiled broadly and said, "Richard that will not be a problem." It was obvious that he was looking for presentable, American-Jewish young men who did not have a Yiddish trace in their spoken English, and who could become presentable American Reform rabbis. In spite of my ignorance, I seemed to fit the bill.

As a student at the College, my opinions began to change drastically. I realized what was happening to Europe's Jews. I also realized that anti-Zionism was absolutely no answer, that basically, Jews were being slaughtered because they lacked the power to defend themselves and that Zionism was an attempt to provide empowerment and sovereignty for Jews. By 1944, I had completely abandoned my hostile views on Zionism and saw the logic of the Zionist position. Theodore Herzl (1860-1904), founder of political Zionism and an assimilated Jew, was one of the thinkers whom I most greatly admired. Like me, he understood the role that power plays in human and group relationships. I had come to realize that anti-Zionist groups simply didn't understand what was going on. I understood that it was a very desperate effort on the part of Europe's surviving Jews to get to Palestine, but there was no other place for them. My attitude changed completely. The problem with Martin Buber and many of the other people who talked about a bi-national state of Jews and Arabs was that they would have reproduced the same powerlessness in the refuge that had caused them to flee from Europe. This would have been a disaster.

At the same time, my theological opinions began to develop. By the fall of 1944, I was very troubled by the Reform Judaism of the time. In some respects, I've never ceased to be a Reform Jew, even though I'm an ordained conservative rabbi.

When I arrived in Tupelo, Mississippi as a student rabbi, the news came that the Russians had reached the Majdanek death camp near Lublin, Poland and found 600,000 pairs of ownerless shoes. I was preparing to deliver a sermon, reading the Reform Prayer Book. There was one sentence that I never forgot: "And now that we live in pleasanter times and pleasanter places," and it stuck in my craw. I said to myself, "This is wrong. We don't live in pleasanter times and pleasanter places. If anything, we live in the worst of times." So, I could not continue to think of God as I had thought of him, and my ideas of God began to change.

Gordon: After graduating from the Hebrew Union College you attended the Jewish Theological Seminary in New York. How did that lead to attending Harvard Divinity School and later earning a Doctorate from Harvard?

Rubenstein: By the time I was about to graduate from the Seminary, I was married with two children. I had one crucial meeting with my teacher, Abraham Joshua Heschel. I had written a paper on some aspects of theology and he said to me, "You must go on, and you mustn't be a congregational rabbi." I asked, "Why not?" He said, "You will not have the time to do the work you need to do intellectually." I decided to apply first to Harvard Divinity School.

Why did I want to go to Harvard Divinity School? Because I had come to believe that a lot of what had happened in the Shoah was the result of Christian animus towards Jews and Judaism. I wanted to know more about Christianity. Because I was a married man with two children, I had to take a small congregation in the Boston area so that I could go to Harvard Divinity School. I took a congregation in Brockton for two years and then one in Natick for two years, and in 1955, I received a Master of Theology in Christian Theology from the Divinity School. I then went on to get my doctorate in the history of religion at Harvard's Graduate School of Arts and Sciences.

At the time, I was also in psychoanalysis. Fortunately, the outcome was very good. Psychoanalysis gave me an appreciation of the importance of ritual, religious symbolism and how the non-intellectual, non-conceptual elements in religion are very powerful. I did a doctoral dissertation on the Aggadah – the legends and myths of the rabbis of the first three centuries of the Christian era on the issue of sin and deviance.

The thesis became *The Religious Imagination*. It was translated into French by France's leading publisher, Gallimard. It's called *l'Imagination Réligieuse*. The Italian translation also won a literary prize in 1977, the Portico d'Ottavia Prize.

My ideas had begun to develop with a strong social science and historical bent. I saw religion as an enormously potent force, both in individuals and groups. By this time, there was absolutely no doubt as to where my fundamental commitment lay within the Jewish community.

Gordon: What encounter with a German theologian in 1961 defined your post-Holocaust theological views?

Rubenstein: In 1961, I was the guest of the *Bundespresseamt*, the Press and Information Office of the West German Republic. I was scheduled to spend two weeks investigating conditions in Germany. There had been a series of what they called *Schweinerei* – antisemitic attacks on [a] synagogue in Cologne, etc. They wanted people to see that the Germans were clean. I was supposed to arrive on the 13th of August, 1961. I was living in the Netherlands that summer. That was the day that the Wall went up between East and West Berlin. I postponed going until the 15th of August, and instead of going to the Rhineland, at their urging, I went directly to Berlin. I was in Berlin two days after the Wall went up. Four days after the wall went up, I had an interview with Dean Heinrich Grüber, one of the most important interviews in my life. Dean Grüber's church was in East Berlin. He lived in West Berlin. He couldn't get from West Berlin to his church and he was very upset about what was going on.

The reason they wanted me to meet with Dean Grüber was because he was the only German who testified against Adolf Eichmann at the Eichmann trial in Jerusalem, that summer. Also, he had spent three years in Sachsenhausen, sent there by Eichmann for having tried to rescue Jews. I mean, there was nothing fake about the man.

When we met, Gruber was understandably very upset. He said, "Well, you know, Dr. Rubenstein. We Germans made people refugees. Now we are refugees. We destroyed churches and synagogues. Now our churches are being destroyed. God is punishing us." Then he got carried away and said, "Dr. Rubenstein, it was God's will to send Adolf Hitler to punish the Jews at Auschwitz." In that atmosphere of crisis, when nobody knew whether there would be war, I said, "Dean Grüber, I'd rather be an atheist than believe in such a God." He said, "How can you say that and be a Rabbi?" I said, "There's one thing I need more than God, to be a Rabbi, a few live Jews. By your logic, I would be praising God for his destruction of almost all the Jews of Europe."

Gordon: How did you become involved in the "Death of God" movement in the 1960's?

Rubenstein: In 1965, William Hamilton, who was one of the leading "Death of God" theologians, pointed to me as perhaps a Jewish "Death of God" theologian. There was a *Time Magazine* cover, "Is God Dead?" I was invited by Emory University to a conference called "America and the Future of Theology" and I was supposed to respond to Thomas Altizer, who was a leading "Death of God" theologian. The conference was covered by *The New York Times* and other media. Altizer's basic message was: "God is dead and this is a great liberation for us." I knew, as a Jew, instinctively, that the death of God is no problem for Christianity because of Good Friday which is always followed by Easter

Sunday. Because Good Friday is not the end of the story, Altizer could rejoice in the death of God. The crucial sentence in my response was, "If God is dead, I will not dance at the funeral." It is a tragic event, with tragic loss. Although we live in the time of the "Death of God," there is a God, and in fact, in the second edition of *After Auschwitz*, the final chapter is, "God after the death of God."

The Shoah was the most perfect example of what it meant to live without God. The Nazis felt they could do as they pleased. They understood that nobody would or could stop them. That's basically what I meant. I've never retracted a word, but there was shock in the Jewish community. At the time, there was also some anger that I had asked the question, "If you hold that God has chosen us, what do you make of the Shoah?" There were several possible responses: One can say that the Shoah was divine punishment for Israel's sins. This was what Dean Gruber was saying. Some very orthodox rabbis were saying the same thing, although the rabbis and the Dean would have different sins in mind. Alternatively, one might say that God is less than God, that He's not fully powerful, or one might say that the idea of a direct relationship between the existence of God and human actions is questionable. That's the position I took.

I had a lot of media attention. There was an interview in *Playboy*. *The New York Times* had a four column story, and I did an op-ed piece for *The Times*. My views were widely disseminated. I was trying to make sense out of the Jewish situation, both politically and theologically in our times.

Gordon: What do you consider the basic Jewish value at the core of your writings?

Rubenstein: I think the idea of Jewish values can be a trap because for 2,000 years Jews had no experience being the masters of their own destiny and had no experience with what that meant, what its responsibilities were. As Israeli Ambassador to the U.S., Michael Oren said in an *Azure* article, "They had no experience with sovereignty." If you have an army, if you have enemies you know are out to destroy you, then having abstract values that are unrelated to the actual context of danger in which you live does yourself a disservice and one which is potentially suicidal.

Now, I believe that Jews should practice justice, but what I mean by justice is to give each man and each group its proper due. This is fundamental. That means that if you have an enemy who is out to kill you, you don't necessarily have to kill him, but you have to do whatever is necessary to defang his power so that he cannot kill you.

Nevertheless, I do not believe, for example, in doing more than you have to against an enemy. I don't believe in gratuitous killing or torture.

In that same article, Oren describes how David Ben Gurion, Israel's first Prime Minister, sat by himself on Israel's first Independence Day, wondering whether the people understood what they were getting themselves into, whether they understood what sovereignty meant. He was afraid that they didn't. He knew that neither Martin Buber nor the German-Jewish professors at the Hebrew University understood sovereignty. Sovereignty means that you possess an army and, as the German sociologist Max Weber put it, "The sovereign state is that human community that successfully claims the monopoly of the legitimate use of physical force within a given territory." Ben Gurion understood that insight when he forcibly disarmed the Irgun militia at the start of the new State of Israel in 1948. Ultimately, the conflict between the Israelis and the Palestinians is over the question of who possesses a sovereign monopoly of the use of force. Such a monopoly cannot be shared.

To me, the most basic Jewish value is to survive with dignity as an individual and as part of a people. However, learning from tradition can be a trap. Rabbis, whose background was that of a powerless minority, neither understood sovereignty nor were they able to exercise it.

Make no mistake about it. I have enormous respect for Jews who exercised restraint under conditions of powerlessness. They had no other choice then. The way I used to put it to my students in class, was, "If a person comes along and says, 'You dirty Jew boy,' I'm going to go after him, but if five people come and surround me and say that, I'm going to have to learn to hold my temper." That was the situation of Jews for almost 2000 years.

Gordon: What is your political philosophy?

Rubenstein: In the world of politics, I'm a Hobbesian. Thomas Hobbes believed that originally men lived in a state of nature in which there were no rules. Inevitably, the very strongest prevailed and the weakest served them or fell by the wayside. Finally, in order to protect themselves, men agreed to delegate whatever powers they had to one sovereign who would protect them and who would prevent them from behaving towards each other as if they were in a state of nature. For example, if my neighbor and I have a dispute over where my property line ends and his begins, we don't take out guns and settle it that way. We believe that, through the sovereign state, there are impartial institutions which will decide whether my claim or his is right. However, Hobbes also says something else. He says, "Sovereigns always live in a state of nature with regard to each other." That is, between nations, there are no permanent, fixed rules. Nations may agree on rules, because it is within their interest to do so, but the same nation that makes a rule can break a rule. There is no such thing as an international community. There are only states with different interests which sometimes conflict, and I don't think that's always understood. I think this is especially true when it comes to Jews in Israel. They don't understand that when you are faced with a mortal foe who is out to destroy you, you owe that foe absolutely nothing. That foe has announced in advance that he owes you nothing and he will use your conscience, which restrains your action, as part of his weapon against you.

Gordon: How do you view the historical relationship between Jews and Islam?

Rubenstein: In some sense Muslim Spain was a golden age; that is, it was a great center of culture. Both Averroes, the Muslim jurist, and Maimonides, the Jewish doctor and sage, were born there. However, as a young adolescent, Maimonides had to flee Cordoba because of its conquest by another Muslim group, the Almohads. They were rigid in their Islamic extremism and in their insistence on conversion or death. Under the Sharia Islamic law of the so-called Golden Age of Spain, Jews and Christians were dhimmis, second class subjects. They were allowed to exist within Muslim civilization, but only in certain professions and under humiliating circumstances. I don't know anywhere Islam was dominant that wasn't the case. The reason why Jews left Spain in 1492 and went to Turkey was that their conditions at the time were less harsh in Turkey than they were in Spain. It wasn't because they received religious freedom in the Ottoman Empire, they didn't. They were given the choice in Spain of death or conversion. In Turkey, they were given a third choice, dhimmitude, and they accepted dhimmitude, the status of second class citizens. There was never a time when the Muslim world was dominant that Jews or Christians were anything but subordinate second-class citizens. That they were used for their talents is true; as financiers, as doctors, but never as the decision-makers. This was always done by the Sultan or the Emir.

Since dhimmis were Jews or Christians under Muslim domination who accepted their subordinate, humiliating status, they had to employ the strategies of the powerless in their dealings with those who had power over them. They tried to argue or to use words of persuasion to do what they could not do by force of arms. They thought, "Well, we will try to persuade the Muslims to see our point of view." That didn't work, because the Muslims said, "We are in power."

With regard to interreligious dialogue with them, I do not see the point. I've been involved in a number of Jewish/Muslim/Christian dialogues with noted British and American Imams and Sheiks. One of the Arabic words for dialogue with infidels, unbelievers, is takyyah. Takyyah in Arabic means religiously sanctioned dissimulation. There is no real engagement with non-Muslim thought.

There is another element to this, the Muslim claim that the original will of God for all eternity is expressed in the Qur'an. The Qur'an wasn't simply what came into existence with Muhammad. It was revealed to Muhammad in the 7th Century, but it was already there from the very beginning of creation. They believe that the Qur'an was revealed to Abraham, the first great Muslim prophet. So, how do they explain the Bible and the New Testament? They claim the Jews and Christians misrepresented and distorted the original message of God and that is why the texts appear so different. No Jew or Christian can accept that.

If you start with the idea that the Qur'an existed from all eternity and that the Bible and the New Testament are distortions of this original version, how do you get to historical study of the Bible? Jewish and Christian scholars can usually at least agree on the history of the Bible, not completely, but mostly, because they understand that there was an historical process. However, to admit that there was a historical process and that Islam came after the other two is to deny an absolutely fundamental belief of Islam. They won't do it, so there's no such agreement on the one thing that could allow for dialogue; historical examination and criticism. All they will do is tell you their truth.

Gordon: Recent polls of Israeli and American Jews reveal a vast difference of opinion regarding the current Obama Administration in Washington. To what do you attribute that?

Rubenstein: Most Israelis understand that the Obama Administration is the most pro-Muslim, anti-Israel American government since the founding of the State in 1948. They further understand that their own lives as individuals and the existence of their nation can disappear in an instant if a nuclear Iran, governed by messianic, apocalyptic theocrats, uses the weapons it is acquiring to fulfill its oft-repeated promise to annihilate Israel. Yet, in spite of Iran's threats, the Obama administration has repeatedly announced sanctions then delayed their imposition.

Moreover, most Israelis understand that the Obama administration has used its very considerable leverage to encourage Israel to surrender territory to the Palestinians in East Jerusalem and the West Bank with no credible guarantees of an ensuing genuine peace. Since their lives are on the line, Israelis are far less likely to delude themselves than liberal American Jews, large numbers of whom are not unlike "Yellow Dog Democrats," those Southerners who used to say they would rather vote for a Yellow dog on the Democratic ticket than vote Republican.

When 78 per cent of American Jews voted for Obama, they were continuing without reflection a tradition of Jewish loyalty to the Democratic Party that goes back at least to Franklin Delano Roosevelt. I have always thought that both the historic experience of persecution and the injunction repeatedly pronounced by Moses to the Hebrews, "Remember that you were slaves in Egypt..." (Deut. 5:15; 15:15; 16:12; 24: 18, 22) has instilled in Jews identification with the victim or underdog. Such identification is impossible for Israel. In ancient times, the slave was either an enemy defeated in war or the descendent of such an enemy. Israel exists because it was militarily victorious and will continue to exist only as long as it can keep its enemies at bay. For 2,000 years, Diaspora Jews lacked sovereignty. Put differently, for 2,000 years Jews never had the weapons with which to defend themselves. The result was the Holocaust. If Israel means anything after the Holocaust, it is that Israelis would not lack such weapons. That is why Israel built its nuclear arsenal and it's military. Moreover, every young Israeli must serve in the military. Israel would perish as a nation if its youth refused. Military service is a matter of choice for American youth, Jewish and non-Jewish. Lacking military experience, American young people find it difficult to understand that force remains the foundation on which civilizations are built. The Israelis understand this, because they must.

Gordon: How dangerous is the deepening rapprochement with the Muslim world that began in the Bush Administration and is now flourishing in the current Obama Administration?

Rubenstein: There is every reason why Barack Obama's Administration should seek good political relations with Muslim nations, insofar as it is consistent with our national interest. It is something very different when the President seeks a rapprochement with Islam as a religion. Unfortunately, that is what he set out to do as indicated by his Inaugural Address in which he stated: "The United States is a nation of Christians and Muslims, Jews and Hindus and non-believers." The President is a lawyer trained at Harvard Law School and had the distinction of serving as editor of the *Harvard Law Review*. He knows the importance of every word, indeed of every comma, in public documents such as the Inaugural Address. His words were no accident. Not only did he reject the traditional formulation, "a nation of Christians and Jews," but as Hugh Fitzgerald has pointed out, he allowed Muslims to claim "some kind of historic or cultural or other connection to this land, when everything that makes America, America … is in direct opposition to, and is permanently threatened by the texts, the tenets, the attitudes, of Islam."

The President either will not or cannot understand that a religious war - for that is what jihad is - is being waged against the United States by people who are unshakably convinced that they are doing God's will by seeking to destroy us. It is extremely dangerous when our enemies understand the nature of the war and our leaders do not.

Gordon: What do you wish to be noted for as a legacy?

Rubenstein: I have not given much thought to my legacy. I may be deceiving myself, but at age 86 I believe there is still much work for me to do. Above all, I want to do all that I can to make people understand that radical Islam is the most dangerous adversary the United States has ever confronted. It means what it says when it threatens a second Holocaust against Israel. It expresses confidence that jihad can subvert and then bring down the United States. I have little hope for Europe which is in the process of being subverted into submission. I would be more confident if the leaders of both Israel and the United States understood that they are in a long-term religious war with an ancient enemy. Further, that the strategies necessary to overcome that enemy, involve a transformation of consciousness and a knowledge of the religion and history of Islam. I hope that I will be granted some years to use the knowledge and insights I have acquired to help in the transformation if both Israel and the United States are to prevail. Of one thing I am certain, if Israel were destroyed, radical Islam would not be satisfied. Such an outcome would only whet its appetite to complete global Islamic domination.

7
SAM SOLOMON
AUGUST 2010

Sam Solomon was raised as a Muslim, trained in Shariah law for fifteen years, and then, after reading the New Testament and undergoing an intense transformational experience, he became a Christian. Solomon was imprisoned in his home country and fully expected to be put to death when the decision came to exile him instead. He is one of the leading experts on Islam and Shariah law in the Western world. He has testified before The US Congress and is a consultant to the British parliament on matters regarding Islam.

Gordon: Let us start with the simple question, what is a mosque and what is its basic function in the Muslim community?

Solomon: A mosque, totally unlike a church or a synagogue, serves the function of orchestrating and mandating every aspect of "life" in a Muslim community from the religious, to the political, to the economic, to the social, to the military. In Islam, religion and life are not separate. They are indivisible. In Islam religion is not just a part of life, but "life" is absorbed and regulated to the tiniest detail by religion (See Figure 1). In other words every aspect of a man or woman's life must be defined and governed by religion. So there is no concept of personal choice whatsoever, or in theological terms, there is no "free will," but only limited preferences between prescribed courses of action. In addition, there is no concept of a personal relationship between the person and the entity being worshiped, so "worship" itself, is of a different nature than that performed in a church or synagogue.

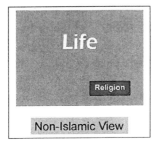

Figure 1: Comparison of Non-Islamic vs Islamic views of one's freedom of choice and options in life.

So we see that a mosque is a seat of government. A mosque is a school. A mosque is a court. A mosque is a training center. A mosque is a gathering place, or social center. It is not a place of "worship" per se as understood and as practiced in Western societies.

Gordon: Specifically, how is a mosque a threat to the community within which it is built?

Solomon: Every single mosque in the world, by definition, is modeled on the mosque of Mohammed in Medina in accordance with the Sunnah. The Sunnah interprets the Qur'an by reporting exhaustively on everything that Mohammed said, did, or consented to. Therefore, his Medina mosque, the first mosque, was a place where he gave judgments, where he decided who would be executed, where he instituted policy—domestic and military—where jihad war strategies were designed. Consequently, it was a storage place for arms, a military training base, and was where troops were blessed and dispatched. Literally they were sent to conquer - first the whole of Arabia, and then the rest of the known world. Therefore if the present-day mosque is modeled as per the Sunnah of Mohammed then there should be very serious concern. As is well-known, Muslims are required to follow the example (Sunnah) of Mohammed—and according to Sura 33:36 it is not an option or a matter of opinion: "It is not for a believer, man or woman, when Allâh and His Messenger have decreed a matter that they should have any option in their decision. And whoever disobeys Allâh and His Messenger, he has indeed strayed in a plain error." This explains and establishes beyond doubt why arms have been found in mosques in various countries, and in different capital cities in the West.

In addition to the undisputed significance of the Medina mosque as the role model for all mosques, there is also the Islamic policy of establishing strategic mosques as beachheads with interconnected networks. Taken together, these two policies do constitute a clear and present danger—and a need for concern.

For example, when Abu Hamza[1] was the Imam of the Finsbury Park mosque in the United Kingdom, he trained people, he sent out terrorists and British authorities found arms stored there. He was well within his Islamic mandate as these activities were sanctioned by Islam. He didn't find it wrong because it is in the Islamic manuals. Another prime example of a mosque being found to have engaged in high-level political, military and intelligence activities is the Munich mosque, which is now considered by Islamists to be on a par with some of highest-ranked mosques in Muslim countries.[2]

Gordon: What comment do you have on the significance of the "Ground Zero mosque" set to open on 9/11, 2011?

Solomon: First of all, the sponsors and supporters of the Ground Zero mosque insist that the significance of the building of this mosque is that it constitutes a refutation of the radical "fringe" within Islam, and as such, is a gesture of peace and reconciliation toward America and the victims of 9/11.

But, it is ludicrous for anybody to accept that this is a gesture of peace in the Western sense—rather it is a different definition of "peace." It is the Islamic definition of "peace" as a suspension of "struggle" which is ultimately said to emerge once opposition ceases, and Islam reigns supreme as Mohammed has stated, "Islam rises and nothing rises above

---

[1] Imprisoned as a terrorist, wanted by the U.S.A. as a terrorist, but at the moment entangled in legal maneuvers. He has taken his case to the European court to fight extradition to the United States. His son was caught in Yemen engaged in terrorist activities. See http://www.timesonline.co.uk/tol/tools_and_services/specials/article433669.ece and http://www.jewishvirtuallibrary.org/jsource/biography/Masri.html

[2] See: Johnson, Ian *A Mosque in Munich: Nazis, the CIA, and the Rise of the Muslim Brotherhood in the West* (Houghton Mifflin Harcourt Trade, 2010)

it."

The rationale of the sponsors is that acts of terrorism are being carried out by misguided "radicals" rather than true Muslims and that as a consequence, Islam itself has been victimized and defamed and needs to be defended. Their solution is to appear to decry all "radicalism", and to take the bold symbolic act of erecting a 13 to 15-story mosque—ostensibly representing true Islam—on the site itself, in their words, to "bridge and heal this divide."[3]

So, if allowed to be built, this mosque would consolidate, solidify, and embody a fallacious and pernicious interpretation of what really happened at the World Trade Center on September 11, 2001.[4]

In one fell swoop, it will be a re-writing of American history with American cooperation, and will achieve another major Islamic goal of setting a high profile beachhead at a strategic location in the seat of American economic power.

Gordon: When you speak of setting a "beachhead," is building this mosque tactically similar to Muslims building the Al Aqsa Mosque adjacent to the Western Wall in Jerusalem?

Solomon: Most Westerners do not realize that there are two Mosques on the Temple Mount. One is called Masjid Al-Aqsa, the Mosque of Ascension, and the other is called "Qubbat Al-Sakhra," the Dome of the Rock.

To provide the groundwork for answering your question more specifically, the basic principle is, that a mosque, totally unlike a church or synagogue, is a "sign" and a "symbol" of the establishment of "authority"—both religious and political—not just a place of worship for its adherents.

A mosque is the symbol of the establishment of an Islamic authority, and an announcement of the beginning of the "rightful restoration" of the land according to Islamic claims that the "whole world is a mosque," and is echoed in Mohammed's words, "the whole earth has been declared unto me a mosque." Therefore it is a matter of "restor-

---

3 See comment by the imam in charge of the Ground Zero mosque proposal, "The imam behind the center says it's designed to 'bridge and heal a divide' and says 'fighting radicalism is his personal mission.'" (http://www.newser.com/story/90422/right-goes-nuts-over-ground-zero-mosque.html)

4 See "The Mosque and Its Role in the Society," (www.Pilcrowpress.com)

ing" rather than "claiming" the land to Islam, as any land not in current submission is at virtual war with Islam, and must be brought "back" according to the Qur'anic version of history.

This process of "bringing back" has a name, it is called "Islamisation," and is implemented progressively though immigrating, segregating, gaining rights, and slowly asserting the supremacy of Islam politically, socially and even culturally. So, yes, the Ground Zero mosque would be a beachhead—and an important one, but it is not exactly the same as in the case of the Al Aqsa Mosque.

The building of the Al Aqsa Mosque adjacent to the Western Wall was a necessary consolidation of prior Qur'anic claims to the Holy Land and the spiritual base of Judeo-Christian Monotheism,[5] whereas the building of the Ground Zero mosque would be more in line with the tactical aspect of spreading the base. (See footnote 3)

Having said that, some "beachhead" mosques are more strategic than others. As we have seen earlier, the Munich Mosque became the most influential of those built outside Muslim lands prior to the proposed Ground Zero mosque.

If built, the Ground Zero mosque will be the most influential sign and symbol of Islamic authority in the Western World.

Gordon: Can you explain the significance of the 'Hijra' or migration?

Solomon: You need to understand an important distinction: In Islam, migration is a mental concept as well as a physical action.

To answer your question about the significance of the Hijra itself, it was the physical migration of Mohammed and his followers from Mecca to Yathrib [Medina] in 622 AD, making it the most important event in Islamic history and the reason for starting the Islamic calendar—while at the same time instituting it as the model for future expansion by immigration.[6]

However, the concept of migration in its broader sense is highly significant.

Conceptually, mental migration can be from one mode of opera-

---

5 See *Al-Yahud: Eternal Islamic Enmity and the Jews*, by Al-Maqdisi and Sam Solomon for the status and purpose of the Al-Aqsa Mosque (http://www.adnamis.org/)

6 See *Modern Day Trojan Horse: The Islamic Doctrine of Immigration, Accepting Freedom or Imposing Islam* by Sam Solomon (http://www.adnamis.org/)

tion to another, in other words from a non-Islamic mode to an Islamic mode.

The non-Islamic mode is known as Al-Jahiliyyah meaning "the age of ignorance," which has nothing to do with the Western concept of ignorance. So Al-Jahiliyyah, is a broad title given to all sorts of practices which might be regarded as un-Islamic. For example a woman who used to dress in Western-style, (considered as Jahiliyyah practice), her "migration" toward Islamic practice would be that she now adorns herself with the Hijab (head scarf) or total Nikab (full face and body cover). This movement from Western dress to Islamic veil would constitute a migration in dress code and behaviour.

Examples of other conceptual migrations would be imposing Islamic values and systems within host countries, such as Shariahh-complaint finance. It is all to achieve one purpose, the Islamisation first of the Muslim community by bringing it more and more in line with Islamic principles and, second to condition and transform the host society.

The foregoing was an explanation of a conceptual, spiritual, or mental transformation.

The physical migration of Muslim communities, from one country to another or from one area to another is just as important. It is to extend the rule of Islam. For instance, there would be no need for Islamic schools if there were no Muslim children. There would be no need for Halal meat if there were no Muslim consumers. There would be no debate about the Hijab if there were no Muslim women to wear it.

Therefore, any such demand by the Muslim community within a host country is an expression of their desire to be governed by Islam. Demanding Islamic banking is a direct imposition of the Shariahh Law on non-Muslims, even if there may not be any Muslims in the community.

Gordon: Why does Islam celebrate Mohammad's journey from Mecca to Yathrib (Medina) annually rather than his birthday?

Solomon: The celebration of Mohammed's birthday is controversial within the community of Islamic scholars, as it is considered as an innovation (a "Bid'a")—though practically, it is recognized as a holiday in most Muslim countries. However, your point is well taken.

All Muslims do celebrate the Islamic New Year, based on the Islamic Calendar—which after deliberations regarding other dates in Mohammed's life, was dated from the Hijra, his journey from Mecca to

Medina, rather than from his birthday.

The Islamic calendar was established by Umar bin Al-Khattab, the second Khalifah in response to letters of concern from the various judges and governors in the new Islamic empire saying to him, "your letters are undated." Thus he was confronted with a dilemma, as any dating system at that time was un-Islamic. So he called a committee to look into it and they initially decided not to start the Islamic calendar with the birth of Mohammed, and then considered various other important events that occurred in Mohammed's life as the starting point of the new calendar.

However, Umar concluded that it would be appropriate to start the calendar from the day of Mohammed's flight or Hijra, because from that day forward he was transformed from a haunted man to a victorious ruler.

Thus the Islamic calendar, called the "Anno Hijrah Calendar," or "Immigration Calendar," abbreviated as "A.H." replaced all existing calendars and was established as a declaration of the victory of Islam over the rest of the world.

Gordon: What is the most important thing for us to know about Islam?

Solomon: The most important thing for a non-Muslim to understand about Islam is that Islam is not simply a religion. Islam is a social and political system, an indivisible melding of religion and state.

It is a socio-political, socio-religious, socio-economical, socio-educational, socio-judiciary, legislative militaristic system cloaked and garbed in religious terminology.

We must never forget that Islam is an all-encompassing ideological system, and as such wherever there is a Muslim community there will be Shariah and wherever there is a Shariah there is an Islamisation of the territory and ultimately of the nation.

8
LARS VILKS
NOVEMBER 2010

Lars Vilks, Swedish artist and controversial art theoretician, created sketches of Mohammed as a roundabout dog for a "Dog as Art" exhibit in 2007. Swedish news reports about withdrawal of his sketches at sponsored exhibits led to an eruption of controversy and threats against his life from Muslims in Sweden and around the World. That roiling controversy has made him an iconic figure in the conflict between Freedom of Expression versus Islamic totalitarian doctrine. Vilks was in America in the autumn of 2010 for a series of talks sponsored by the International Free Press Society (IFPS) with scheduled events in Philadelphia, Boston, Toronto and Ottawa. Two of those events, Philadelphia and Ottawa, were cancelled because of alleged security reasons. Even the event in Boston had to be moved to a secure private setting from a local synagogue. Rabbi Jonathan Hausman contributed to the following interview.

Vilks' Theory of Art

Lars Vilks is one of Sweden's most distinctive contemporary artists. He holds a Doctorate in Art History and has received academic appointments throughout Sweden. He taught art history and art theory at a number of universities. His artistry focuses on process. As Vilks explained, his task as an artist and as a proponent of absolute freedom of expression is to test the limits of artistic expression in each piece, thereby creating several slightly different versions of each drawing. In so doing, he presses against the conventional wisdom that a design has inherent boundaries.

Vilks considers art similar to a bow and arrow. You pull the bow back and shoot the arrow. However, you don't want to hit the bulls-eye. You want to strike slightly off-center. In so doing, you have all kinds of creative possibilities within the initial construct that you envision. A true artist never knows where he or she will end up in the creative process. A cartoonist knows the exact, defined message he or she wants to convey from the start. Not so with the artist. Vilks' artwork is very conceptual. His other work which prompted much controversy were the wooden sculptures of Ladonia at the Kullaberg Nature Reserve in Sweden.

In addition to drawings and sculptures, Vilks has also assembled video art projects. One video that he created criticizes those he feels should have defended his stance on the absolute right to freedom of expression. They have either criticized him for the Mohammed drawings or condemned him for not exercising self-censorship. Vilks sees his objective in art to provoke. Vilks can be seen as an equal opportunity offender to what constitutes convention and authority.

R'aison d' Être for the Mohammed Sketch

Mohammed as a Roundabout Dog by Lars Vilks

Vilks created the Mohammed sketch for an exhibition in Sweden entitled "Dog in the Roundabout." He explained that Sweden's road/highway system is dotted with roundabouts (rotaries). Often, parks are created in such rotaries or there is simply open area in which people take their dogs for walks. In 2006, there was a national competition to create dogs in roundabouts. With his artist's eye, Vilks drew dogs in the roundabout. He then began to play with different forms of dogs...solid form, blurry form, different sizes, dogs in different settings, interchanging the body of a dog with the head of a man, Mohammed. Vilks has stated that this series of drawings stirred the ire of the Muslim world. The catalyst for his sketches was the growing violence and changes in Swedish cities caused by Muslim immigrants who displayed unbridled anti-Semitism and anti-Western animus.

Islamic Taboos against Figurative Depiction of Mohammed

Vilks' controversial sketches of Mohammed as a roundabout dog require delving into Islamic doctrine and history.

The Qur'an does not explicitly forbid images of Mohammed, but there are a few Hadith which have explicitly prohibited Muslims from creating the visual depictions of figures under any circumstances. Most contemporary Sunni Muslims are particularly averse to visual representations of Mohammed. The key concern is that the use of images can encourage idolatry, where the image becomes more important than what it represents.

Many Muslims take a stricter view of the supplemental traditions. Such adherents will sometimes challenge any depiction of Mohammed, including those created and published by non-Muslims.

Verbal descriptions of Mohammed in the Hadith abound. Ibn Sa'ad's Kitab al-Tabaqat al-Kabir, contain numerous verbal descriptions of Mohammed. Athar Husain gives a non-pictorial description of his appearance, dress, etc. in *The Message of al Quran*.

Great controversy surrounds visual depictions. The Qur'an forbids idolatry, but does not specifically forbid representative art.

"Behold!" He said to his father and his people, "What are these images, to which ye are (so assiduously) devoted?" They said, "We found our fathers worshipping them." He said, "Indeed ye have been in manifest error - ye and your fathers." - Sura 21:52-54

The figure of Mohammed seldom occurs in a picture painted by a Muslim artist, and when it is found the face is generally veiled or the prophet is symbolically represented by a flame of golden light. To do otherwise is to court blasphemy, according to Muslim religious leaders.

The past decade has witnessed controversies over any depiction of Mohammed, whether caricatures, cartoons, artwork, television shows, or film. Lars Vilks' drawings of The Dog in a Roundabout series, one of which featured the head of Mohammed on the body of a dog (an unclean animal in Islam) were perhaps one of the most controversial.

We had the opportunity to interview Vilks upon his return to Sweden following the IFPS American "tour" and prior to his second Uppsala University lecture.

Jerry Gordon: Professor Vilks, you are considered a prominent member of the post-modern conceptual art movement in Sweden. Could you tell us about your views on conceptual art and the importance of free speech?

Lars Vilks: Conceptual art means working with ideas, projects and processes. Contemporary art is conceptual in opposition to modernism which is concerned with formal matters. In general art is about transgression which also means provocation; the history of art is a story about provocations. Thus freedom of speech is utterly important for art.

Gordon: Could you describe for us the background and public reactions to your conceptual art projects, most notably Nimis and Arx?

Vilks: Nimis and Arx are big constructions made of wood and concrete. I started in 1980 on a remote place in a nature reserve. After two years the authorities reacted and started a twenty years long trial. During the first years this project was very controversial but it became a well known and popular tourist attraction.

Gordon: What prompted your Mohammed as a Roundabout Dog sketch for the Tellerud Exhibit in July 2007?

Vilks: I was interested in the fact that it is often declared that "today everything can be made in art there are no longer any boundaries." As the art world has a political agenda which is leftist the standard criticism is against capitalism, US and Israel. The Muslim world and Islam are excluded. I found that there were good reasons to bring about this subject.

Gordon: Did you intend the Mohammed sketch as a public statement against Islamic intimidation and in favor of free speech?

Vilks: That was a part of the content when bringing up a discussion about the borders in art.

Gordon: Why in your view did the sponsors of the Tellerud exhibit withdraw the sketch? Where else did you offer it and what was their reaction?

Vilks: The curator said that security was the reason. Later they said that one should not offend a weak group. I also offered the drawing to an art school, Gerlesborg, where I was invited to exhibit. They said no for security reasons.

Gordon: What happened when the Swedish newspaper *Neirkes Allehanda* published the sketch in mid-August 2007?

Vilks: There were demonstrations and the news spread to the Middle East. A Swedish flag was burnt in Pakistan and President Ahmidinejad of Iran made a statement where he declared that Zionists were behind the drawing.

Gordon: Following the publication of your sketch you were subjected to condemnation and death threats by domestic Swedish and Foreign Muslim groups, countries and even an affiliate of al Qaeda. Who made the threats? What were your and the Swedish government's reactions?

Vilks: I got many death threats through e-mail, telephone calls and SMS. In September, 2007, I received a fatwa from Al-Qaida in Iraq. The Swedish government arranged meetings with the ambassadors of the Arab League and met with the Organisation of Swedish Muslims. For me it was not easy to understand what to do.

Gordon: When were you placed under 24/7 Swedish police protection? Does that protection continue?

Vilks: I had some protection when I undertook official lecturing. In 2007 the Swedish police was not of much help. I found a hideaway place by myself, but I was there only for a couple of days. Today it is different though I have no direct protection. The Swedish security service is very active and covers all my arrangements. I also have a warning system installed in my house.

Gordon: Could you describe the extent of Islamization in Sweden? Have there been demands by Muslims in Sweden for creation of so-called no-go areas? What cities are most at risk currently?

Vilks: The problem in Sweden is that many Muslims are gathered in ghettos where they do not have any contact with the Swedish society. I haven't heard anything about no-go areas. More problematic is that the society accepts all sorts of strange requests from Muslims. For example, the Swedish left party leader Lars Ohly wants Ramadan to have the same position as Christmas.

Gordon: Is there any general public reaction to these developments in Sweden akin to what has occurred in Holland with the rise of Geert Wilders?

Vilks: I guess the fact that the Swedish Democrats entered the Parliament is such a reaction. But in a less extreme way there is a general discontent among many people.

Gordon: Have you met or conferred with Danish Cartoonist Kurt Westergaard about your common predicaments? Do you both share the same concerns about protection of free speech in the face of Islamic threats?

Vilks: I speak with Westergaard now and then. We are both firmly behind the protection of free speech against Islamic demands.

Gordon: US charges against Colleen Renee La Rosa AKA "Jihad Jane" were unsealed on March 9, 2010 in a US Federal Court in Philadelphia indicting her in a plot to assassinate you. On the same day seven alleged plotters were arrested in Ireland. What happened and what were your reactions?

Vilks: When I learned about this it was all over. It is difficult to say what ability "Jihad Jane" had in being the killer. I found it rather amusing. You should remember that everything that happens is included in my artwork. This was a nice piece of soap opera even if I was playing at high risk.

Gordon: On May 11th, 2010 you were attacked while lecturing on Free Speech at Uppsala University. What in your view prompted this attack? Were the perpetrators detained and charged under Swedish law?

Vilks: No doubt that showing a video work by an Iranian artist on homosexuality and religion (especially on Islam) prompted the attack. I was showing where the borders are in art. This video though had a very good point but could not be shown in an exhibition. However an Islamic mob attacked me. The security guard was fast enough to run interference between me and a Muslim attacker. He was charged and had to pay fines.

Gordon: A few days later on May 15th your home was firebombed by two Kosovar-Swedish Muslims. Were the perpetrators apprehended and have they been charged and convicted?

Vilks: These guys were amateurish enough to set fire to themselves during their planned arson attempt. One of them was severely burnt and was taken by the police the next day. Obviously the two men panicked and threw things away: drivers license, keys etc. They were convicted to two and three years in prison.

Gordon: In early October you came to North America on a tour sponsored by the International Free Press Society in Philadelphia, Boston, Toronto and Ottawa. Why were your talks in Philadelphia and Ottawa cancelled?

Vilks: The security arrangement needed became so expensive that it was not possible to cover the costs.

Gordon: You also spoke near Boston, Massachusetts. Who arranged that talk? What were the security arrangements that enabled you to speak? What were the audience's reactions to your talk?

Vilks: Rabbi Jon Hausman made the arrangements. It was cancelled at the original space but the Rabbi found a private home where it could take place. Rabbi Hausman also made security arrangements through the local police. The audience was very positive.

Gordon: Where did you speak in Toronto? What were the reactions of Canadian audience to your presentation?

Vilks: I spoke before a Jewish sponsoring group with a lot of security. The audience response was quite positive.

Gordon: Mollie Norris, cartoonist for Seattle Weekly, creator of "Everybody Draw Mohammed Day" has been the victim of death threats. At the urging of the FBI, she has gone into hiding. Do you believe that Mollie Norris, Kurt Westergaard and you are victims of Muslim demands for blasphemy laws?

Vilks: There are many groups around the world who are Islamists and totally ruthless. More moderate Muslims negotiate for blasphemy laws but they do not come with death threats.

Gordon: Do you believe that the Ayaan Hirsi Ali - Daniel Huff proposed US legislation that would empower our federal government to provide protection and enable victims of Islamic death threat intimidation to seek civil damages if adopted in the EU would help stop the kind of threats that you, Kurt Westergaard and others have experienced?

Vilks: No, I don't think it would stop the death threats but it would provide important support in fighting for free speech.

* * *

Lars Vilks' security is still a matter of concern. Several attempts on his life have been made since the publication of his "Mohammed as a roundabout dog" sketches in 2005 outraging the Muslim ummah. In February 2011, Colleen La Rose, a Muslim convert known as "Jihad Jane," plead guilty in a Philadelphia Federal courtroom after being indicted on four counts, including conspiring to support terrorists and conspiring to kill Vilks in 2009. La Rose faces life in prison and a $1 million fine. In March of 2011, an accomplice of La Rose, Jamie Paulin-Ramirez, plead quilty to aiding terrorism and to conspiring in the plot against Vilks by traveling to Ireland to live and train with jihadists. For that Ms. Ramirez received 15 years and a fine of $250,000.

In late December of 2011, a matter was dismissed in a court hearing brought against three men accused of planning to murder Vilks at the Röda Stengallery in Göteborg, Sweden on September 11th. The Swedish court found for the defendants whose counsel said, "the evidence presented by authorities was weak."

9
DAVID YERUSHALMI
DECEMBER 2010

Shariah, Islamic law, has become increasingly visible in the debates concerning possible Islamization in the West. It is at the core of opposition to and debate about expansion of mosques in this country. Shariah is a total system that governs every aspect of the life of a Muslim including fulfillment of jihad against non-believers, whether through da'wa, persuasion, or ultimately, violence. Shariah is a political, legal, social and military system that threatens basic constitutional liberties and freedoms that we take for granted in America. The lure of multi-billion dollar transactions has created Shariah-compliant international corporate finance markets with active participation by major commercial and investment banks and financial rating organizations. Shariah advisers to these eager financial institutions are proponents of violent jihad and Islamic antisemitism. One egregious example is Pakistani Federal Sharia Court Judge and Hanafi Scholar, Mufti Muhammad Taqi Usmani, who advised Dow Jones on creation of its Islamic Market Index. Egyptian-born Islamic scholar, Yusuf al-Qaradawi used the term "financial jihad" to describe Shariah-compliant finance (SCF), as Andrew McCarthy noted in a *National Review* article, "American Taxpayer, Financial Jihadist."

> Because Shariah bars interest (although it permits "profits" that Islamic authorities, in their infinite wisdom, deem reasonable), SCF requires that investments be constantly monitored and that

any interest payments be purged. This is done by skimming off a percentage that is then channeled - at the direction of the advisory board - to an Islamic "charity." Of course, as no one knows better than the Treasury Department, many such charities are merely fronts for the financing of terrorist organizations. This is not an accident. When Sheikh Qaradawi speaks of "financial jihad" as an Islamic obligation, he's not kidding. In Islamist ideology, funding those who "fight in Allah's cause" - e.g., Hamas - is one of the eight categories of permissible *zakat*, the Muslim obligation of almsgiving.

Shariah has entered our legal system through the backdoor of arbitration and mediation panels and even directly though our court system.
One of the prominent opponents of Shariah in our legal system is David Yerushalmi, Esq., a New York and D.C.-based lawyer, litigator and developer of uniform laws aimed at curtailing and outlawing its spread. Yerushalmi designed and sponsored the Mapping Sharia Project whose findings revealed the extent of extremist Shariah compliance in a study of American mosques that was published in the *Middle East Quarterly* in June of 2011. He has initiated ground breaking legal actions involving Shariah issues, advancing important federal cases, and has won cases in matters of free speech under the First Amendment. Among these are:

> Murray v Paulson brought in the Federal District Court of the Eastern District of Michigan against the Treasury for using TARP monies in the bail-out of insurance giant AIG which markets and sells Shariah compliant insurance products. The case has advanced given the denial by the court of the federal government's motion to dismiss. The court rejected the plaintiff's motion for summary judgment in 2011. The matter is now on appeal.

> A federal case brought by five former Muslim clients of the Council of American Islamic Relations (CAIR) in the DC Federal District for fraud and racketeering in misrepresenting legal representation. The RICO charges were dismissed by the Court. However, the fraud charges have been upheld in a recent decision.

> Several cases brought on behalf of the American Freedom

Defense Initiative against the Rapid Transit Systems in New York City, Miami, Florida, and Dearborn, Michigan for violation of First Amendment rights in connection with bus ads advising Muslims of assistance in leaving Islam. The threat of the lawsuit forced Miami to acquiesce and filing of the lawsuit in New York resulted in a victory in two days. The lawsuit in Michigan required an evidentiary hearing.

Working with The Public Policy Alliance, Yerushalmi has drafted uniform laws for addressing Shariah at both the State and Federal levels. More recently, as General Counsel to the Center for Security Policy (CSP) he co-authored the CSP Team B II Report, *Shariah: The Threat to America, An Exercise in Competitive Analysis*.

Given the recent passage by popular referendum of an Oklahoma anti-Shariah State Constitutional Amendment, SQ 755, seeking to ban Shariah, and immediate legal actions brought by CAIR in federal court to stop the law from being implemented, we invited David Yerushalmi to discuss that controversy and others against the backdrop of his courtroom battles, research investigations and legislative proposals.

Gordon: David, you have been prominently involved in anti-Shariah litigation and legislative development in the United States. What is Shariah?

Yerushalmi: Shariah is Islamic law. Normally, when we speak about Shariah we include both the rules of jurisprudence termed *usul 'ul-fiqh* or the science of the jurisprudence of the law. *Al-fiqh* are the positive law rulings that are usually generated by way of a question and answer process or fatwa. Together they make up the Shariah.

Gordon: Do you consider Shariah a clear and present threat to our constitution?

Yerushalmi: Well, I don't consider anything a clear and present threat to the Constitution. That is to say, the Constitution is a legal document forming the basis of our legal and political system in this country. I do consider Shariah to be a threat to both our physical existence and our way of life in that we require our political and legal systems to abide by the supreme law of the land grounded in the Constitution. Shariah's purpose is to destroy our legal and political systems.

Shariah is law based upon the word of Allah as represented in the Qur'an and the rulings of the Hadith on various subjects together with the interpretations of the recognized Shariah authorities over a millennia bounded by consensus, what is termed *ijma*.

The fundamental principle of Shariah is that no law can coexist much less reign supreme over Shariah. So, to the estent that Shariah's purpose is that no law anywhere in the world where Muslims live should coexist or rule over Shariah that would suggest to any rational person that Shariah poses a threat, at least in principal. It is rendered a threat because the methods that are required by Shariah to achieve this end include violent jihad.

Thus we have a principled or theoretical threat in that Shariah must reign supreme and exclusively over every place Muslims live. We have a method, at least in speech, to achieve that end or purpose which includes violent jihad.

The question then becomes whether that threat in theory is a threat in fact. To answer this question, you must ask if there are sufficient numbers of Muslim who adhere to Shariah and if they are prepared to achieve Shariah's purposes through Shariah's methods of violent jihad? In other words, do Shariah-adherent Muslims represent an existential threat?

The answer to this question is available to us by simply reading the newspaper or just opening one's eyes. The answer is of course they are. They are engaged in a full scale global war against the United States outside our borders and they successfully recruit and infiltrate our borders with home grown terrorists all the time. So the answer to your question is yes, I consider Shariah a threat to our way of life.

This of course is underscored by surveys in the Muslim world like the World Opinion Survey which find that 50-70% of the 1+ billion Muslims in Muslim countries desire a global Caliphate and the forced imposition of an al-Qaeda like strict Shariah.

Gordon: Given your involvement in the Mapping Shariah Project, what are the principal findings and in particular, degree of Shariah compliance in American mosques included in the survey?

Yerushalmi: The Mapping Shariah project was a study that we began in 2008 to determine if there was a correlation in U.S. mosques between Shariah-adherence and violent literature promoting jihad. We sent researchers into a random representative selection of 100 mosques throughout the United States. We then measured Shariah adherence along several behavioral axes as independent variables, such as gender separation in prayer, strictness in Shariah-required prayer ritual and dress. Then we measured the existence or the presence of Shariah-promoting, violent literature as the dependent variable, including the imam's recommendation to study the violent material.

What we wanted to test was the thesis that as mosque worshippers becomes more and more Shariah adherent, one would expect a greater likelihood of violent jihad literature and its promotion by the imam.

While we confirmed the thesis, we also discovered something eye-opening. As mosque worshippers became more Shariah adherent, the presence of violent jihad literature increases commensurately. The correlation between Shariah-adherent mosques and imams promoting this violent literature also held. What was eye-opening, however, was that we found that 80% of mosques in the U.S. are Shariah-adherent and promote this violent literature.

Of that 80% a majority were actually Salafi mosques, which are the more orthodox or puritanical sects of Shariah-adherents. Now this overwhelming presence of Shariah-adherence and promotion of violent jihad doesn't necessarily reflect the demographics of American Muslims. That is to say, we were measuring mosque attendees, not necessarily American Muslims in the population. Indeed, most anecdotal data suggests that the demographics of American Muslims are that they are fairly assimilated and that the general population would more accurately be represented by the 20% of the mosques that were not deemed to be Shariah adherent and which did not include the violent literature. So what this tells us is that most American Muslims stay home and they would only attend mosques for example during the season of Ramadan. They typically don't attend mosques during the week or even on their Sabbath on Friday.

We measured mosque attendance randomly throughout the week; however, we specifically did not measure it during Ramadan so as not to skew the results. So one thing we find is that the so called moderate Muslims tend not to be consistent mosque-goers. The ones who do go are very Shariah adherent and they are permeated with literature which calls for violent jihad.

The study did not address what the sources and amounts of funding for these mosques were.

Gordon: What evidence is there of the growth of de facto Shariah in the U.S.?

Yerushalmi: There is plenty of evidence of Shariah in US courts. We have recorded many different cases that have appeared at the appellate level where, under three different circumstances, courts in fact entertain Shariah and actually end up applying it as the law of the case. The first example arises when the U.S. court grants comity, or formal recognition of the foreign judgment rendered by a foreign court which applies Shariah, as in Saudi Arabia, Iran, Pakistan or Gaza. If the court were to grant comity or legal reciprocity to that decision then it would be essentially enforcing Shariah law.

Typically when you come to the United States and ask a domestic court to recognize a foreign judgment per the rule of comity, you are asking the court to enforce the foreign judgment as its own. The same would hold true of a private arbitration decision rendered here in the United States or abroad where a Shariah-based religious court issued a ruling based upon Shariah. The winning party typically walks into a court and asks that the court enforce that arbitration decision by granting it comity and to enforce the judgment, which may include sending the marshal out to collect and sell the losing party's assets. In other words, the police power of the state is being exploited to enforce Shariah.

The second example of Shariah being applied in our courts is where two parties enter into an agreement and they include a "choice of law" provision in their contract that requires a court to apply Saudi law, for example, which is Shariah, to adjudicate their dispute. The same result would occur if the contract included a "choice of law" provision requiring Iranian law, or Pakistani or Indonesian family law.

In a domestic matter like child custody disputes, you have cases where U.S. courts are applying a national law based upon Shariah.

Choice of law issues also arise when a tort or injurious event occurs in a Shariah jurisdiction but the litigation takes place in the U.S. If all of the evidence and witnesses are in the Shariah jurisdiction, given that the tort occurred there, the U.S. court would typically apply the law of the foreign jurisdiction.

The third avenue for Shariah to find its way into our courts is when courts must decide which forum or venue should host the litigation. This occurs in one of two ways. As in "choice of law" cases, this can occur because the parties agree to litigate in a Shariah jurisdiction. If the U.S. citizen learns of the oppressiveness of Shariah after the fact and asks the U.S. court to void that contract provision so the litigation may occur in the U.S. with our constitutional protections, most courts would deny that request and force the litigation to take place in the Shariah jurisdiction.

Choice of venue also occurs when the tort occurs in the Shariah jurisdiction. If the U.S. party does not want to litigate in the Shariah jurisdiction because it discriminates against non-Muslims and women, most courts would likely ignore these offensive aspects of Shariah and force the litigation to take place abroad.

We find cases of each of these examples applying Shariah de facto in our courts. For these reasons, states are well advised to pass a law like the one we developed at my law firm called the uniform draft American Laws for American Courts Act.

Gordon: Since 2008, you have been involved in a lawsuit in the Federal Eastern District Court in Michigan the Federal Court of Appeals for the Sixth Circuit. Matters that are concerning Federal TARP funds used for the bailout of insurance giant AIG with regard to the latter's marketing and sale of Shariah compliant insurance products. What is the background of the AIG suit against the Federal government and its present status?

Yerushalmi: AIG, before its fall from grace, was the largest insurance company in the world. It might still be for that matter. It was a multinational corporation with the parent company domiciled in Delaware with its main headquarters in New York. Its subsidiaries, and there are hundreds, are located all over the world. In that capacity it was also the world's largest aggressive promoter of Shariah compliant insurance products in the world. These are insurance products that abide by Shariah, with Shariah authorities supervising them; deciding how and where the premiums will be invested; and where charitable contributions by the company, which are required under Shariah, would be directed.

AIG, not only sold these Shariah insurance products, but actually promoted them and Shariah simply.

As we all know, AIG then ran into the financial mess driven by its underwriting of financial insurance products such as credit default swaps for the real estate subprime mortgage market. On the verge of its collapse the U.S. Government stepped in and took ownership and control of AIG. The federal government acquired 80% of AIG through both Federal Reserve and taxpayer TARP funds. Once it acquired 80% of the common stock ownership of AIG, the U.S. Government was effectively in the business of promoting Shariah.

So we filed suit on behalf of Kevin Murray, a former US Marine who served in Iraq, on the grounds that this was an Establishment Clause violation under the First Amendment. The status today is that we survived a motion to dismiss by the U.S. Government. We then engaged in a year's worth of very hard core discovery both of the government and of AIG. What we discovered was that the U.S. Government had transferred up to a billion of our taxpayer dollars to Shariah compliant insurance subsidiaries. We also found that the U.S. Treasury had actually promoted Shariah and the idea of a global unification of Shariah rules and regulations. Literally, the US government was intimately involved in the very concept of Shariah and Islamic legal jurisprudence.

We filed a motion for summary judgment in the Summer of 2010 essentially stating that based upon these undisputed facts there is no question that we win as a matter of law. The government filed a cross-motion for summary judgment and the court against plaintiff's motions. We believe that given the court's ruling on the motion to dismiss we have made our case and expect a ruling in our client's favor and against the government upon appeal.

This case is important because it is the first time a federal court has considered Shariah-compliant finance and the danger posed by Shariah.

Gordon: The Center for Security Policy in mid-September issued a report, Team B II: *Shariah - Threat to America*. What were the principal findings?

Yerushalmi: The Team B II report was modeled after the "Team B" report during the Cold War era when the Administration put together a team of outside national security experts to prepare a "competitive" assessment of the national security threat posed by the Soviet nuclear program and gave the Team B access to classified information. The report "competed," as it were, with the government's establishment national security professionals

The Center for Security Policy Team B II Shariah Threat report is not based on classified information. Further, it was not set up by the Administration but rather operated as a kind of shadow assessment of the threat from Shariah. The principal findings are as follows.

First, the threat from Islamic terrorism, radical or extremist Islam, or "man-made disaster," whatever nomenclature the Administration places on it, is in fact all driven by the same doctrine, Shariah and its law of jihad.

Second, the Team B II report assesses Shariah as followed by the various global jihadist groups and finds that it is neither some perverted or extreme version of Shariah. It is extant authoritative Shariah with a pedigree derived from classical Shariah.

Third, and most important, the Team B II Report finds that there is a concerted conspiracy by the Muslim Brotherhood and by other groups similar to the Muslim Brotherhood to infiltrate and insinuate Shariah into our legal and financial systems through a variety of methods. These methods include "lawfare." immigration, political lobbying and other forms of what we deem pre-violent jihad. By "pre-violent" we mean that it is based upon the Shariah doctrine that mandates violent jihad, but permits da'wa or social, political, economic and legal jihad based upon persuasion or stealth methods if violent jihad is not viable. However, the moment that violent or kinetic jihad is possible, Shariah obligates the full subjugation of the enemy, the infidel, through violence or the threat of violence. In effect, then, this stealth or pre-violent jihad is in accordance and very much a part of the violent jihad required by Shariah. That third finding is the most important of the Team B II Report.

Gordon: What has been the reaction of Members of Congress and the media to this report?

Yerushalmi: Neither positive nor negative. Remember, the Team B II report came out in the run-up to the last mid-term election. I just don't believe anyone has paid much attention to it.

Gordon: Do you anticipate attention might be paid to the Team B II report in the 112th Congress?

Yerushalmi: Yes. The Center for Security Policy is definitely going to engage the new Members of Congress once they have settled in. I believe that it will be the subject of serious Congressional inquiry, possibly including sub-committee hearings.

Gordon: Oklahoma voters recently passed an amendment to the State Constitution, Question 755 that would ban judges from recognizing Shariah rulings. The Federal Court in Oklahoma has accepted a motion for temporary restraining order by the Oklahoma Chapter of CAIR. The restraining order was temporarily granted and a hearing held recently. What in your opinion are the problems associated with the Oklahoma law and what are the prospects for it being changed or remediated?

Yerushalmi: I don't think that there is much opportunity for change if it's held to be unconstitutional. They will just have to redo it. The problem with the amendment as it stands is that it imposes a blanket prohibition against courts using international law, which is not feasible or logical because some disputes might require the application of international or foreign laws as we discussed earlier. The problem is not foreign or international law per se, but the use of those laws when they are patently offensive to state and federal constitutional liberties and privileges. Further, the Oklahoma amendment does not define what Shariah is. It was left open to court interpretation, which is always dangerous. In fact, this "undefined Shariah" has opened the door to the CAIR lawsuit which effectively argues that Shariah is really nothing more than Islamic religious practice which of course it is not. While Shariah includes Islamic religious practices under its legal mandates, it is far closer to a legal, political and military system than it is a religious one.

What we would suggest is something that my law firm developed for our client, The Public Policy Alliance. As noted earlier, we drafted a uniform law called, "American Laws for American Courts" in which we define as void as against public policy and not recognizable by a state court any foreign law or religious law for that matter that would violate fundamental constitutional liberties and privileges. This facially neutral law would apply to Shariah because Shariah violates all sorts of constitutional liberties and privileges, not the least of which would be the free exercise of religion, equal protection and the due process clauses.

Thus a state may accomplish the same end without identifying Shariah per se and avoiding the stickly problems of our First Amendment jurisprudence. In the Oklahoma case, I still believe the state could have created a Constitutional amendment which targeted Shariah directly, but it would have to make it very clear that the provision was attacking a political, legal, military doctrine and system and not referring in any way, shape or form to some purely religious worship called Islam. So those are the problems that I see in terms of the Oklahoma Federal case that is now pending.

Having said that, I do think the Federal Court was wrong to accept standing. I don't believe the Court has standing and there are some Amicus briefs that have been filed on that question that properly address those issues. I think the court needs to take another look at the briefs filed by CAIR in support of a temporary restraining order. The court will find that it does not have standing because an individual cannot claim that he has been hurt just because an Amendment to the Constitution is passed if it doesn't apply to him. In this case it certainly doesn't apply to the plaintiff unless he is claiming that somehow he has some Shariah question pending in a court.

In truth, what the plaintiff has done is exploit the vagueness of the amendment by arguing that his personal religious worship is the same as Shariah.

Moreover, the plaintiff's specific claim is entirely bogus. He claims that the court would not probate his will since his will follows Islamic family law dictates. But this most certainly cannot grant standing to the court because if the plaintiff has a will that follows Shariah, the court will simply follow the specific instructions without even considering Shariah. But if the will instructs the court to probate his will by devising his estate according to Shariah, the court would not be able to do that anyway because no secular court may do so now under the Establishment Clause of the First Amendment. Courts cannot be in the business of trying to divine what Shariah is and what it says about inheritance because that would require an "entanglement" between the secular state and religion which is currently not permitted. Thus, irrespective of the problems inherent in the Oklahoma amendment, the case now pending before the court is bogus and should be thrown out.

Gordon: What states have successfully enacted anti-Shariah legislation and are they models for adoption elsewhere?

Yerushalmi: Only two states, Tennessee and Louisiana that I am aware of. They have adopted a version of our "American Laws for American Courts" model legislation. Tennessee's law was a valiant first effort but there were some amendments that reduced the scope of the model law in ways that I believe need to be corrected. For example, Louisiana endeavored to push through our uniform draft law but the final bill added a provision that excludes from its application any kind of corporate entity. That effectively limits the Louisiana version applicable almost entirely to domestic law cases or contract or tort cases only between two natural persons. That provision in the Louisiana law doesn't address legitimate kinds of cases that the law should preclude from entering into domestic courts. Both of those states in my view should go back and try to correct those versions. However, they at least made an effort and effectively passed a version of the model law. It was an important start and I applaud them and the legislative sponsors.

There are many states currently considering the uniform model law. There are probably a half a dozen other states currently considering the legislation.

Gordon: There is a booming Shariah-compliant international corporate finance market that grew dramatically during the last several years. We have also seen evidence of Shariah-compliant finance and banking in several states in the U.S. How widespread is that development and is it in violation of existing state and federal anti-discriminatory banking legislation?

Yerushalmi: Well it wouldn't be a violation of anti-discrimination laws because anybody could obtain a Shariah-compliant mortgage or invest in a Shariah-compliant fund. That is not the problem. The problem is when a security is sold in the public markets with a prospectus issued by a corporate structure of a public company and the sponsors of the public offering don't properly disclose what Shariah is. How does a company sell a security without disclosing to the post 9-11 investor that this law seeks our destruction? I believe the failure to disclose this material fact would violate securities market disclosure laws that are on the books today. Unfortunately, the SEC and the Department of Justice are in bed with the Islamists.

Now in terms of its pervasiveness, almost every major international bank engages in Shariah-compliant finance in some markets. That is to say, they sell Shariah-compliant products. Dow Jones and Standard & Poor's have developed Shariah-compliant investment indexes. In terms of state level banking, there are a few regional and state banks that offer Shariah-compliant mortgage products. That is probably less of an issue than the international banks like HSBC, Citibank, JP Morgan, or Chase, all of which promote their Shariah-compliant financial products worldwide.

Gordon: Do you see any basis for developing state level legislation that would contend with Shariah-compliant finance issues?

Yerushalmi: Yes. Our client, The Public Policy Alliance has retained us to address this problem and we have completed a model amendment to the 2002 Uniform Securities Act, the model "blue sky laws" are applicable at the state level. Almost every state has already passed some version of the Uniform Securities Act which parallels the federal regulatory structure for securities. Our amendment makes very clear that any bank or financial institution that offers a security in a particular state bound by a foreign legal system, which would include Shariah, whose laws violate state and federal constitutions is under a requirement to disclose all of the relevant facts about those offending provisions of that foreign law. You could still buy that security with the knowledge that it is governed by a foreign law, but you would be doing so fully apprised of its offending provisions. I would dare say that this kind of disclosure would effectively kill a Shariah-compliant security offering in this country.

Gordon: There have been a number of controversial mega mosque projects that have erupted throughout these United States. What is your view as to how local opposition can block development of Shariah-compliant mosques in this country?

Yerushalmi: I don't think you can oppose the mosques, other than on the basis of zoning issues. I don't think you will effectively block mosques and I don't think that is necessarily the right way to deal with the problem - at least in the courts. I don't think that you will ever engender real support legally for the idea that you can block a mosque even if some of its founders or its directors were Shariah-compliant. I think what you have to do is get at the underlying problem which is effectively outlawing Shariah in the United States.

We also have developed a legislative proposal for the Public Policy Alliance for doing just that at the State and Federal levels. That is a harder nut to crack because of First Amendment jurisprudence but I do believe it can be done. The Ground Zero mosque in Lower Manhattan, the mosque in Murfreesboro, Tennessee and the mosque in Temecula, California, have engendered a lot of opposition by local grass roots activists for very good reasons. I just don't think that this is a courtroom battle that can be won on those terms.

* * *

As the creator of the US anti-Shariah litigation and legislative initiatives, David Yerushalmi has become a highly visible and controversial figure in the mainstream press. Yerushalmi has been labeled an extremist by Abe Foxman of the Anti-Defamation League. A front page *New York Times* article on July 31, 2011 by Pulitzer Prize winning reporter, Andrea Elliot, who covers Muslim affairs boosted Yerushalmi's role as "The Man Behind the Anti-Shariah Movement." Yerushalmi commented in a Letter to *The New York Times* re-published in the American Thinker:

> Unfortunately, Ms. Elliot exposed herself as biased and in denial, and has since given an interview to NPR in which she more openly evidences journalistic condescension, in addition to the bias one normally expects from the mainstream media. The story was quite explicitly intended to link a national movement to a single individual, me, and then to suggest that this individual -- again, me -- was manipulative, hidden, and controversial.

The AIG case involving use of more than $153 million in Federal TARP funds to promote the insurance giant's world-wide Shariah compliant financial products is now pending before the Sixth Federal Circuit Court of Appeals. His "American Law for American Courts" (ALAC) uniform legislation is in its second legislative season in more than 20 states. In 2011, one additional State, Arizona, enacted a version of ALAC bringing the total to three; Arizona, Louisiana and Tennessee. Several of these neutral state statutes have prospects for passage in 2012 legislature sessions.

In January 2012, Yerushalmi and Robert Muise, co-counsel from the Thomas More Law Center in the AIG and other anti-Shariah litigation, announced the formation of a new pro bono law firm, the American Freedom Law Center (AFLC). Yerushalmi commented in the AFLC announcement:

> "AFLC will fight for faith and freedom by advancing and defending America's Judeo-Christian heritage and moral foundation through litigation, education, and public policy programs. Fighting for our Judeo-Christian values is more than simply defending religious liberty; it is fighting for the very survival of our Nation." He added, "Throughout history, great nations have fallen from within. Make no mistake, America is a blessed Nation, but only so long as it remains faithful to the Judeo-Christian values upon which it was founded."

10
CHARLES JACOBS
FEBRUARY 2011

Dr. Charles Jacobs is an entrepreneur activist based in Boston. We have written about his exploits in "Chelm on the Charles River" (*New English Review* August, 2009) as he endeavored to arouse the Boston community against the rise of jihadism in his battle over the Islamic Society of Boston Cultural Center which is controlled by Muslim Brotherhood front group, the Muslim American Society (along with terror financier enablers and antisemitic trustees). We have also witnessed his valued attempts to warn the Boston Jewish Community of the dangers and delusions of interfaith Muslim dialogue.

Jacobs co-founded several enduring pro-Zionist and international human rights organizations. Among them are the Boston branch of CAMERA, the Middle East media monitoring group which became that organization's national office; the David Project, which endeavors to train young Jews in advocacy for Israel on college campuses; Americans for Peace and Tolerance, a diverse group formed to combat extremist Islam and the American Anti-Slavery Group (AASG). Jacobs was listed by *The Forward* newspaper among the 50 most influential American Jewish leaders.

Jacobs recently returned from South Sudan where he witnessed the freeing of several hundred slaves and the internationally supervised referendum to partition the Sudan into the Arab-Muslim North and the Christian and animist South. Sudan has been racked by Muslim-on-infidel civil war since the country's founding in 1956. This ongoing jihad has taken the lives of more than two million Southern Sudanese and several hundred thousand nominal Muslims in the Western Darfur region. The current President of Sudan, Omar al Bashir, publicly declared the conflict a jihad. The Arab dominated regimes in Khartoum have perpetrated an active barbaric and brutal slavery that Jacobs, a Jew and co-founder of AASG and John Eibner of Christian Solidarity International (CSI) based in Zurich have combated. Eibner is also a board member of AASG. CSI's slave liberation program has freed hundreds of thousands of jihad slaves and in the process, working with Jacobs' American group, convinced the US to free the Christian/Animist South by brokering the Comprehensive Peace Act of 2005 that laid the basis for the country's partition.

Gordon: You've had a career as an activist entrepreneur in Zionist and International Humanitarian causes for more than three decades in Boston. When did you first arrive in Boston and what drew you there from your origins in New Jersey?

Jacobs: I got a full scholarship at Brandeis University for a doctoral program in Psychology. I had graduated from Rutgers University in Newark with a dual major in Psychology, and History. I received this wonderful scholarship to attend Brandeis about 30 years ago and I came up here.

Gordon: One of your important activities in international humanitarian causes has been the freeing of slaves in the Southern Sudan before many people in the United States understood what jihad was about. What caused you to establish the AASG?

Jacobs: We didn't know what jihad was either at the time. I think perhaps few experts except for Bat Ye'or and maybe Walid Phares really understood in those days what jihad was. I was just angry that the human rights community was ignoring black African women and children being bought and sold for $15 (or $50) dollars. This anger and perplexity led to my obsession – for over a decade and a half – to crack an intellectual puzzle: how to understand "human rights selectivity?" If these groups would not be moved to act by the enslavement of blacks in North Africa, we needed a general theory to explain their priorities. What will the people who run Amnesty International and Human Rights Watch do with their resources? On what basis do they decide their priorities?

I read in the *Economist* magazine, a short entry that you could buy and sell people in North Africa for a few dollars. It prompted me to do some research. I went to Amnesty International and Human Rights Watch and all the people who were supposed to know about this. I found that the subject of slavery was in their back files. My first compilation of data concerning slavery came from the very human rights groups who knew but hadn't acted. I was very lucky. I met someone at the Harvard Hillel services on Shabbat who was a black convert to Judaism. I told her about this and she had a friend at the *New York Times* Editorial Board and arranged for me to hold a conversation with her. She solicited an op-ed that I wrote called "Bought and Sold" with a Muslim from Mauritania whose people were also enslaved. His name is Mohamed Athie. That was the first exposure, the first widely read report that broke the story about a slave trade of blacks in our own time. The response from that was enormous. I went and met Southern Sudanese and Mauritanians in New York City, refugees both from their respective countries. I put them together as people who were victims of slavery. The three of us, a Christian, a Jew and a Muslim, Mohamed Athie, David Chan from Sudan and I met and formed the AASG. If we were younger we would have cut our fingers and made ourselves blood brothers. We decided that we had to do something about this. That meeting was dramatic. It took place at the home of Mohammed Athie and in the presence of his 9 year old daughter, who happened to look exactly like the photo of a slave girl that I saw in *Newsweek* magazine. We looked at her and felt inspired.

It took a long time to convince the Southern Sudanese community here in America that they needed to talk about slavery. They complained that no one was helping them. They went to churches and they went to NGO's and they went to government officials and nobody paid attention about this war that had taken 2 to 3 million people. I told them, of course not - it is just another war in Africa. Take a number and get in line. But if you tell Americans that people are raiding your villages and taking the women and children and making them slaves, and if you bring proof of that – Americans will help you. This is an abolitionist nation. We argue over everything: abortion, gun control, foreign policy… but the definition of every American is that he and she belongs to a nation that tore itself apart over the issue of one man owning another. America will fight against slavery.

But slavery is a humiliation. They were reluctant to talk about it. They took me to their most important intellectuals in Washington. Frances Deng said not to raise the issue. They explained: it's like a woman being raped. Do you want us to talk about our people being raped? I said "yes." You have to. Because it will wake up America.

That is what happened. I got on The Tony Brown Show on PBS. He was one of the first Black TV hosts. I was interviewed with Muhamed Athie and we discussed slavery and that caused a storm of controversy in the black community. (You can see this show at www.iabolish.org.)

We then worked hard to put together an unlikely left-right coalition. We had Pat Robertson and Barney Frank. Of course, we didn't put them in the same room. The Christians knew that this was an anti-Christian issue, although they hadn't known about Islamic jihad at the time. Still, they knew about anti-Christian slaughter, enslavement and blacks. Barney Frank knew that slavery was a bad thing. We had Nat Hentoff from *The Village Voice*, some support from the NAACP and many members of the Congressional Black Caucus. We had white Republican Senators like Sam Brownback of Kansas who took a leading role in this. So it became a rainbow left right coalition. We testified before Congress three times. We had former slaves – especially Francis Bok, whose tale of being enslaved as a boy still brings tears to my eyes. I've watched him give his talk dozens of times. Francis and other liberated or escaped slaves spoke at churches, synagogues and campuses around the country and on radio and television. President George Bush finally picked up the black slavery issue because he was persuaded this was the right thing to get involved in as an international issue. Bush enlisted the assistance of former US Senator John Danforth as Special Envoy to negotiate the Comprehensive Peace Agreement (CPA) between the Islamic North and the Christian/animist South in the Sudan that was concluded six years ago in January, 2005. A key provision of the CPA was the right of South Sudan to separate. That dream came true a few weeks ago with the referendum that will likely partition the county and create self rule in South Sudan.

I have just returned from Sudan having gone there to witness the referendum and to redeem more slaves. It should be understood that this is miraculous. Africa has rid itself of Western colonialism. But what you have here is an African roll-back of Arab colonialism – which preceded European dominance and still persists today. I believe that this never would have happened without the abolitionist movement.

We are posting on our website - www.iabolish.org - video interviews of redeemed slaves. This is the saddest heart crushing experience I have ever had. These people are stolen from their villages. The Arab militias would storm African villages, shoot the men; capture the women and children as slaves. The little girls are domestics until they reach puberty at which time they would become sex slaves. The boys are goat herders. If you lose a goat they would chop off your finger or your hand. I just interviewed a man whose eye they gouged out because he lost some goats or cows. On our AASG videos you'll see him. It's just horrific. We are very proud about saving these slaves.

Gordon: When did you meet John Eibner of CSI and how has that partnership developed in the black Jihad slavery abolition movement?

Jacobs: John Eibner is the unsung hero. He is the man who almost single handedly brought peace to the South and brought them independence. I am in awe of John. He is too humble to ever speak about his exploits. But that is the reality. I met John Eibner at the first abolitionist conference in this country since the Civil War at Columbia University in 1995. He presented a slide show of people from Sudan. He had pictures of men who had lost wives and children to slave raiders in Sudan. John – and his partner Gunnar Wielbalk – have gone to Sudan over 100 times for CSI. They miraculously have redeemed about 100,000 people from Northern Sudan. They did this through a very brilliant and courageous program. They discovered that there had already been a peace treaty between local Arabs and Dinka tribesmen who live close to the blacks in the Northern part of South Sudan. These Arabs needed Dinka wetlands to graze their cattle and they want to sell their goods in Dinka markets. So in return for those rights the Arabs would send retrievers up North and get slaves and return them to the Dinka community. They would buy them or "appropriate" them, find them wandering around and help bring them back South. CSI figured out that it could amplify and increase the number of slaves brought back if they would incentivize more Arab retrievers to do it. At first they used cash, now they use cattle vaccine. They came under tremendous attack from the United Nations, from UNICEF, which was thoroughly humiliated. UNICEF is the presumed primary protector of women and children in the world. UNICEF would not even tell the world that there were child and women slaves in Sudan. So when CBS News had a featured documentary showing CSI's slave liberation program, UNICEF was humiliated. They were forced to admit there were slaves, but they came out against CSI's method of redemption. I debated them on NPR. They said that by paying cash for flesh, we were acting like slavers. I tried to be calm, and I explained that we in America already had this debate: abolitionists debated whether or not to pay for Frederick Douglas' freedom. He escaped his master who had a claim upon him. Rather than lose the most effective abolitionist voice, the abolitionists decided to pay his master for his freedom. They insisted that we should not buy slaves back. I pointed out that they were giving mothers in India money to buy back their daughters who had been sold into slavery. They had no answer. I asked what we should do then, to free the slaves. They said we must wait till the end of the conflict for the slaves to be set free. I said, "That's what the West told the Jews in Auschwitz! Wait there until we defeat Hitler."

So UNICEF did for a period admit there was slavery in Sudan until Khartoum threatened to block UNICEF from operating in the country. Then they pulled back from saying that there were slaves. They went along with Khartoum's threat and started to call the slaves "abducted people." Absolutely unbelievable. So Eibner was the key player in the struggle against slavery and for freedom for Southern Sudan. It was his ability to provide actual cases of real people in slavery that forced attention and political pressure. He is the hero, still pretty much unsung.

Gordon: Let us talk about your most recent trip. You were there with John and Gunnar of CSI to redeem several hundred former slaves and you witnessed the referendum to free South Sudan from the North. What was that experience like?

Jacobs: Well, I have to say if you would have asked us even six months ago if it was possible that South Sudan could be a self-ruled Christian break-away nation, freed from the Arab realm, none of us would have said there was much hope of that happening, even though we had fought for it. The fact that it is going to happen is – and I must use this word again - "miraculous." This is the second time in history in the region that a former dhimmi non-Muslim people have achieved self-rule by pushing back at Arab colonialism. The first is, of course, Israel. This is not lost on South Sudanese who, when they heard I was Jewish, responded with great wide open grins, hugs and said, "You were the first to defeat Arab armies." And, "you are from the Chosen people… welcome." I can't tell you how heartwarming that was. None of us in the coalition would have told you that we expected anything like this to happen. We went there and I never saw such happy, smiling, gleeful, excited, expectant people. We went to two polling places in Wanyjok, which is in Bahr el Ghazal in the Northwestern part of Southern Sudan. At these polling places we video interviewed with the aid of translators several people waiting in line to vote. The voting took a week. There were huge lines on January 9th. All of the people we interviewed pretty much said the same thing. What are you voting for? "Separation," they replied. Most of these people couldn't read or write. So there were two signs you could have chosen from in the voting booth: one sign that had hands clasped together which symbolized a vote for "Unity" and another sign with thumbs up which meant "Separation." So we would ask them via translators what are you voting for and virtually all gave us the separation hand sign. When we asked them why, almost to a man and woman, they would say, "They stole our women. They stole our children. They enslaved us. They killed our cattle. They murdered us. They hate us. We need to separate." When we interviewed bus loads of returnees, people who were not slaves but who had fled to the North because of famine or war, they cited two reasons for coming back south: there is hope for them that they can live in a free place and that they would not be treated in a racist manner by the Arabs. The Arabs call them Jange which is equivalent to the "N" word or they called them simply "Abeed" which is Arabic for black slave. Anybody with black skin can be called Abeed or they call them Kafirs, infidels. While they are in pretty harsh circumstances upon arrival in the South they wanted to come home. They were also fearful of possible Arab retaliation when a partition is officially declared. So we saw the people coming back to virtually nothing. They are coming back for political and social freedom. The Government is poor. I think the South Sudanese earns an average of 41 cents a day. We saw the busses delivering people to empty countryside. CSI tries to supply them with plastic sheeting for cover and some food. I didn't see any United Nations people there helping them at all. I think that the partition looks like it will happen. Sudan's President, Gen. Omar Bashir was likely bribed by the Obama administration to go along with the referendum outcome. It has been said that the Obama Administration offered to take Sudan off the State Department terrorist list if they abide by the election results. Keep your fingers crossed but it looks like there is going to be a second non-Muslim state emerging from Arab colonialism.

Gordon: John Eibner of CSI has done important work defending minority Christian groups elsewhere in the world. Could you tell us about those activities?

Jacobs: John is working very hard on the desperate problem of Christians in Iraq. He went to Iraq. It is horrible for the Christians there and he's trying his best to lobby and organize efforts on their behalf. The same is true in Alexandria, Egypt when the Coptic Christian church there was bombed on New Year's Eve. CSI is doing enormously important work for the Coptic Christians. I know something about his work during the Nagorno Karabakh conflict where Christian Armenians were surrounded and besieged. CSI broke the siege with helicopters full of food. I'm told that emergency air lift helped save that Christian population. CSI, a non-denominational evangelical Christian group, is doing important work defending minority Christians besieged in the Islamic world, and elsewhere. They opened up an office in Washington DC. They are blessed people, and enormously talented.

* * *

Charles Jacobs returned in July of 2011 for the celebration of the founding of the independent Republic of South Sudan, the 193rd member of the UN. Notwithstanding that jubilant moment, turmoil and violence continues in the north south border regions fomented by the jihadist Arab government in Khartoum.

11
KENNETH TIMMERMAN
MARCH 2011

Kenneth Timmerman is an author, columnist and foreign correspondent. He has authored important non-fiction works on domestic and international foreign policy issues and thriller novels about contemporary national security and human rights issues. Starting in 1977, Timmerman spent nearly two decades abroad reporting on developments in Europe and the Middle East from his base in Paris. From that vantage point he had an early view of the Iranian Islamic Revolution that overthrew the late Shah and gave rise to the theocratic Islamic Republic of Iran. He fashioned important relations with the Iranian opposition and dissident community, both in Europe and inside Iran. This led to his co-founding the Foundation for Freedom in Iran upon his return to America in the mid-1990's. Beginning in the late 1980's, Timmerman spent over 20 years tracking the development of Iran's nuclear weapons program, presciently predicting the current threat to the world. For that investigative effort he was nominated along with US Ambassador to the UN, John Bolton, for the Nobel Peace Prize. While reporting from Beirut during the First Lebanon War in 1982, he was briefly a prisoner of the Fatah faction of the PLO. That experience of several weeks' confinement in a PLO dudgeon in Lebanon influenced his views about the Palestinian cause and Israel, transforming him into a Christian Zionist. While reporting on the signing of the Jordanian-Israeli Peace treaty, he interviewed many leaders of the Muslim Brotherhood affiliates, the Islamic Action Front and Hamas for the Simon Wiesenthal Center which exposed him to the core of Jew hatred in political Islam.

Timmerman has been critical of both the Bush and Obama Administrations' lassitude in supporting pro-freedom movements in Iran and their reluctance to employ stronger sanctions against the Islamic regime in Tehran for its brutal suppression of dissidents. He has also exposed pro-Islamic regime lobby groups in Washington, DC that have influenced White House policies. His most recent human rights activities and reporting have endeavored to spotlight the precarious predicament of the indigenous Assyrian-Chaldean-Syriac Christian community in Iraq which is teetering on the brink of possible extinction. We were fortunate to have interviewed him following a recent return from assignments in Northern Iraq.

Gordon: How did you become a foreign correspondent?

Timmerman: I began while I was in Paris as a young man with a trip to Prague behind the Iron Curtain in 1977 to cover the Charter 77 Movement. I guess I have always had a thing for dissidents and people who are resisting an oppressive authoritarian or totalitarian regime and have been covering similar types of conflicts ever since. I started working as a reporter full time in Lebanon covering the 1982 war. Ever since, it's been a long, passionate, fascinating story.

Gordon: What happened to you when you were in Beirut during the first Lebanese war with Israel?

Timmerman: I went into Lebanon having lived in Europe for many years, so I bought the Euro-leftie mind-set that Israel was an Imperialist aggressive state which was massacring the "poor Palestinians." I was accredited to the PLO to cover the war. I arrived in Beirut and not long afterwards was kidnapped by guerillas on the street and turned over to Fatah in West Beirut. Over the next three and a half weeks I was held in an underground cell with about 20 other people, most of them Lebanese, some from neighboring Arab countries, and I learned a lot about the way the PLO operated. Most of the people with me were being punished for trying to leave Beirut during the siege. The PLO wanted to make an example of them, so they would keep people for a week or two weeks, beat them up, some of them they would take out and shoot, and the others they would release onto the streets as a warning to anybody who wanted to leave Beirut. Their intention was to hold the civilian population of West Beirut hostage and then claim any civilian casualties were the result of Israeli barbarity. I gradually woke up to this during those 3-1/2 weeks, and by the end was tracking the advance of the Israeli tanks, whose shells were exploding all around us, waiting with great anticipation for one of them to bust down the walls of my prison and set me free.

Gordon: Did that experience transform you in terms of your views about Islam, your Palestinian captors and Israel?

Timmerman: Oh, absolutely. But not in the way you might think. I never hated my captors, the Palestinians. I was born again in the rubble of my prison, both in the literal sense and as a Christian believer. I understood that the only reason I survived was because God had a plan for me – to be a witness, not a martyr - and had sent guardian angels to protect me and deliver me from evil. I went back to Lebanon soon afterwards. I also went to the West Bank, Egypt, and to Israel and realized early on that it was hard to view the Middle East struggle at an individual level at least in black and white terms. I spent a lot of time with ordinary people in the Palestinian areas and could certainly identify with their suffering. I also spent a lot of time with ordinary Israelis over the years and I certainly identified with their suffering, with their history and with their struggle. Today, I consider myself a Christian Zionist. That belief has come to me over a number of years as I look at the bigger picture and the larger politics involved. But it's hard not to feel sympathy for individuals on both sides of the conflict on a very personal level, and I think it's very important to remember that.

Gordon: What prompted your book, *Preachers of Hate – Islam and the War on America*?

Timmerman: Well it's kind of a funny story. I'd been doing some reports for the Simon Wiesenthal Center on weapons of mass destruction in the early 1990's, so when I had the opportunity to cover the signing of the Jordanian-Israeli peace treaty in 1994, I made a phone call to Rabbi Abe Cooper, who was the Associate Dean of the Center. He said, "Ken, why don't you take that opportunity to interview some of the leaders of Hamas and the Muslim Brotherhood and ask them just one question." I said "O.k., what is it?" He said, "Ask them what they think about the Protocols of the Elders of Zion." I laughed and I said, "Come on, Abe, you've got to be kidding. These guys are sophisticated. Some of them have been to medical school. They have Masters degrees, business degrees. They are not going to fall for that kind of nonsense." He said, "Ken, just ask the question and let me know what happens."

So I asked the question and I was absolutely floored by the responses I got. It was my introduction to Muslim antisemitism 101. To a man every single Muslim leader I spoke with - and I spoke to people at the top of the Islamic Action Front, the Muslim Brotherhood front organization in Jordan, I spoke to leaders in Hamas, some of whom have since been dispatched to their maker by the Israelis, some of whom are still in power, and to a man they all believed that the Protocols were factual and true. Some of them got out their own copy of the Protocols and flipped to certain pages and said, "you see, it is written right here: the Jews have a plan." And they would go on and on as if this stuff was actually real. I was floored, and so I taped all of these interviews and eventually put out a monograph with the Simon Wiesenthal Center in 1994 called, "In their Own Words" which was exactly that. It was the transcription of these interviews.

It changed my view forever to realize that if you scratched the surface of political Islam, almost immediately you hit these core antisemitic beliefs. Political Islam simply couldn't exist without this deep hatred of the Jews. The Jews had victimized them, the Jews were the cause of all evil, the cause of their under-development, their scientific and social backwardness, you name it. I must say that understanding this basic underlying truth made it easier in the ensuing years to see more clearly what was going on here in this country with the Muslim Brotherhood penetration of American political institutions and even conservative institutions such as CPAC.

Gordon: When did you become involved with the Iranian Democratic Opposition and when did you assist in establishing the Foundation for Democracy in Iran?

Timmerman: I started following Iran during the Revolution of 1978 while in Paris. The uncle of my then girlfriend owned a bicycle factory in Tehran and was traveling back and forth between Paris and Tehran during the revolution trying to keep his factory open and his workers paid before it eventually was nationalized and taken over by the revolution and everyone was laid off. He brought back a little green book of sayings of the Ayatollah Khomeini. Two thirds of them were about sex. How do you keep the fast of Ramadan if you have sex with a goat? How do you keep the Ramadan fast if you have sex with a woman who is not your wife or a 12-year old girl? I won't get into too many of those details, but it was graphic. Now, needless to say this should have made Khomeini a laughing stock, but the media never read it. There is a story that Richard Perle likes to tell about Bernard Lewis who had a copy of one of Khomeini's books and he gave it to the CIA in 1979 and they said, "We've never heard of this." Then they came back and said the book didn't exist because they couldn't find it for sale in Iran. It was typical of the kind of intellectual shallowness and a lack of inquisitiveness that has led the CIA to make such monumental errors again and again.

I began tracking the first dissidents that came out of Iran once the Islamic Republic was established in 1980. First came Bakhriar, the Shah's last prime minister. Then came the first president of the Islamic Republic, Banisadr, was forced to flee in 1981. Then came Qassemlou, the leader of the Kurdish Democratic Party. And many more. I developed personal relationships with them as a reporter based in Paris. When I came back to the U.S. after living abroad for 18 years, I set up the Foundation For Democracy in Iran in 1995 with Peter Rodman, now sadly deceased, who served in six Republican White Houses and was a top aide to Donald Rumsfeld at the Pentagon and Ayatollah Mehdi Rouhani, a dissident Iranian Shiite Cleric who taught me everything I know about Shia Islam. We spent days drinking tea in his Paris apartment when he would teach me what *Itjihad* was all about. Also, there was Joshua Muravchik, a human rights activist here in the United States, and Nader Afshar, who had worked with the Iranian opposition in Pakistan when it was actively infiltrating Iran in the 1980s and early 1990s. We initially applied for and received a grant from the National Endowment for Democracy (NED) to monitor human rights abuses in Iran. We quickly realized that the internet was starting to become a powerful tool for promoting civil society and democratic expression and by the time the student rebellion took place in 1999 in Tehran University, we had good enough contacts inside Iran that we got the first photographs of students being tossed out of their dormitory windows by the Basij - within ten or fifteen minutes of the actual events. We posted them on our website, iran.org. We were funded by NED through about 1999, but since then no one seemed to care.

Gordon: You were among the first to publish about the Iranian nuclear development program with your non-fiction work, *Countdown* to Crisis, *The Coming Nuclear Showdown with Iran*. Where did most of that information come from? What positions did you espouse in the book to counter the threat and in your opinion, what has prevented the Bush and Obama Administrations from pursuing them?

Timmerman: *Countdown to Crisis* was actually the culmination of nearly 20 years of investigation into Iran's nuclear programs. I first wrote about them in the mid-1980's when I was in Paris working for *Newsweek* and earlier, the *Atlanta Journal-Constitution*. In 1987, I launched a confidential newsletter called, *Middle East Defense News* (MED News) and wrote about a relatively obscure Pakistani nuclear engineer named A.Q. Khan who had just signed a nuclear cooperation agreement with the Iranian regime. I thought that relationship was quite noteworthy, but no one seemed to pick up on it. My sources? You know I'm a veracious reader of what used to be called Foreign Broadcast Information Service which translated the Pakistani, Iranian and Arab media. I also had many sources among the dissidents, former intelligence officers and even family members of top leaders of the Islamic regime itself. I thought it was most important to roll out the long chronology of Iran's nuclear weapons development, something not very well known here in this country. Then I predicted in 2005 that this would lead to a nuclear showdown between Iran and the West. It has taken a little bit longer than I initially thought. There have been many ups and downs in the Iranian Nuclear Weapons Program. The most dramatic admission of which is the computer malware Stuxnet, which appears to have done serious physical damage to Iran's centrifuge program and to the Busheir nuclear power plant.

I argue in the book that it's absolutely, number one, for Western governments to recognize the threat from a nuclear armed Iran; number two, to take steps to prevent that from happening - economic sanctions that could include an oil blockade and even a total trade embargo. And, number three, if the West really cares about preventing a nuclear-armed Iran, it should do the most effective thing, the moral and the right thing, and that is to help the pro-freedom movement in Iran. I have always believed that the problem with nuclear weapons in Iran is not the weapons themselves. We don't really fear a nuclear armed France. But a nuclear armed radical Islamic regime in Iran is a threat to the entire world. So it's the combination of a radical regime and nuclear weapons that make it a clear and present danger.

Gordon: Why in your opinion has neither the Bush nor Obama

Administrations provided support for the democratic opposition in Iran?

Timmerman: That's a good question. The Bush administration did earmark 75 million dollars to help the pro-freedom movement, but the money was misspent. Most of it went to the Farsi Service of the Voice of America, which has been heavily infiltrated by pro Iranian regime elements. I think part of the reason that the money got misspent was ignorance. Part of the reason was deliberate efforts by State Department bureaucrats who detested George W. Bush and his agenda of bringing freedom to the Middle East and to Muslim countries. They actively tried to sabotage his efforts. I remember we applied for a State Department grant for the Foundation For Democracy in Iran to assist the opposition movement inside Iran. They told us as we were preparing the application to make sure that our programs targeted groups and individuals inside Iran, because they didn't want to fund think tanks and studies on the outside. I said great, we can do that. They green lighted us for about a million dollars and then the grant was reviewed, and it went to a woman named Suzanne Maloney who was not even a permanent State Department employee. She was the State Department fellow from Exxon Mobil. She argued that our proposal was "way too provocative." She said, we can't possibly approve this kind of thing. And so they funded think tanks and studies. That happened in the Bush administration. It was sabotage. The President's agenda was sabotaged by bureaucrats and political activists masquerading as bureaucrats he didn't even know existed.

With the Obama administration I think there is simply no desire to even pretend to help the pro-freedom movement. When given the chance in June 2009 of giving moral support, not even financial material support to the millions of protestors who were asking simply to have their votes counted in the election in Iran, President Obama chose to stay silent for three weeks. His silence as protesters were beaten and murdered in the streets by regime thugs sent a devastating message to the pro-freedom movement. It also sent an empowering message to the Iranian regime. They understood what he meant. Afterwards they would refer to Obama with a play on words, "Oo ba m'ast." In Persian, that means "he's with us."

Gordon: Are there in your opinion lobbying groups in Washington who are in fact foreign agents of the Islamic regime in Tehran?

Timmerman: That is a legal determination that I'm not capable of making. What I can say is that there are lobbying groups that support an agenda of changes in U.S. policy that directly coincide with the interests of the Islamic Republic of Iran. Most notably there is the American Iranian Council (AIC), run by Hoosang Amirahmadi, and the National Iranian American Council (NIAC) run by Trita Parsi – who actually is not Iranian-American but Swedish-Iranian. Both groups have been lobbying for a number of years to remove U.S. sanctions on Iran, to open negotiations with Iran and to strike a so-called grand bargain with the Iranian regime. Trita Parsi in particular has been an avid purveyor of fake documents purporting to demonstrate that the Iranian regime had made an offer of a grand bargain to the United States in 2003 shortly after the liberation of Iraq. In fact the State Department examined the document and their Iranian specialists told Secretary of State Colin Powell that the offer was not authentic. It came from the Swiss Ambassador to Tehran, not from the Iranian regime. Yet to this day, Trita Parsi and people like Flynt Leverett – another pro-regime shill, who worked for the National Security Council under Clinton and was held over by President Bush - still claim it was an authentic offer. In fact, it was a fake, a fraud. In my opinion, Mr. Parsi, whose positions seem strangely to coincide with the positions of the Iranian regime in Tehran, is also a fake and a fraud.

Gordon: How did both you and former U.S. Ambassador John Bolton get nominated for a Nobel Peace Prize?

Timmerman: I received a call one day in late 2005 from Per Ahlmark, Former Deputy Prime Minister of Sweden, saying that he wanted to nominate us. I was obviously thrilled and honored. I couldn't believe it at first and so I asked him how the process worked. He explained to me that the only people who have the authority to make official nominations for Nobel Peace Prize are current or former members of the governments of Sweden, Norway or Denmark. So I said "Wow," that is quite an honor. He wrote a six page letter to the Nobel nominating committee where he detailed my work in exposing Iran's nuclear weapons work years before the International Atomic Energy Agency became aware of it, and detailing John Bolton's work to set up the Proliferation Security Initiative. He argued that our efforts were worthy of a Nobel Peace Prize because they helped to prevent the spread of technologies that enabled regimes like Iran to build nuclear weapons or ballistic missiles.

Gordon: Your first thriller, *Honor Killing* was the fictional treatment of a nuclear nightmare from Iran. Is that a case of art following life?

Timmerman: I have always believed that art precedes life, that the imagination precedes reality. The novel has two plots. One involves an Iranian effort to bring a nuclear weapon into the United States on a cargo ship, so we follow the cargo ship around the world and watch as the hero, who is a Spec-Ops officer now working for DIA, warns about it and nobody listens. The second plot involves the honor killing of a young Muslim girl of Pakistani origin whose bloated corpse was discovered by a dog walker on a riverbank beneath a dam in Montgomery County, Maryland, with her hands bound behind her back with cable ties. She was 17 years old, and the state medical examiner soon discovers that she was three or four months pregnant. Quickly the investigation by the FBI and the local police determines that it could be an honor killing. So as the threads are pulled together by the FBI investigation, the ship carrying the Iranian nuclear weapon sails closer and closer to the United States, and gradually the two plots intertwine. We find that some of the same characters are involved in both plots. One of the subplots that I found very important, and it was one of the reasons I wrote the book, was the infiltration of the U.S. political leadership by Americans who are agents of radical Islam. People at very high levels with influence and extremely senior officials in the administration of the United States Government are agents of radical Islam. There is a scene in the book where one of the fictional characters, a conservative activist with ties to the White House, barges into the office of the FBI Director, outraged, literally jumping up and down and calling him a racist and a bigot because FBI agents had dared to interrogate the brother of the girl who was murdered in the honor killing. He argued that instead they should be going after her white boyfriend, who he claims probably impregnated her. Well it turns out that the FBI had DNA that proved it wasn't the white boyfriend who impregnated her but one of the Muslim friends of the brother. This was done in fact so she would die not as a virgin and go to heaven but die as a woman and go to hell. So I thought it was important to tell the story of the infiltration of the U.S. Government with real characters and dramatic scenes, and also to dramatize what I perceive to be the ineptitude of the U.S. intelligence community to deal with that infiltration and to deal with the sophistication and the determination of an Iranian regime that is absolutely convinced that it can and will destroy the United States of America.

Gordon: In a parallel scenario, your non-fiction book, *Shadow Warriors, the Untold Story of Traders, Saboteurs and the Party of Surrender*, you identified several members of the U.S. intelligence establishment working against our national security interests. Are there among these so called shadow warriors you've identified people who have surfaced in the Obama administration and in your view how dangerous is that to our national security interests both here and in the Middle East?

Timmerman: Look for example at the President's top advisor for counter-terrorism, John Brennan, who is a former top CIA official. I believe it is extremely troubling when you examine Brennan's role as a private contractor after he left the CIA in a scheme to "sanitize" the passport files of the three main candidates in the 2008 Presidential election, including his soon to be boss, Barack Obama. The State Department investigation into what happened in the spring of 2008 remains so highly classified that all you and I can read of it are page after page of redacted text.

Gordon: Do you believe that current Obama administration diplomatic initiatives have given rise to the downfall of the sectarian government in Beirut posing a direct threat to Israel?

Timmerman: I don't think it was the intention of the State Department to cause the collapse of the government of Saad Hariri. However, I think the diplomatic initiative that was Obama's signature foreign policy issue during the 2008 Presidential campaign to open negotiations with the Islamic Republic of Iran had the effect of empowering the Iranian regime, and made them believe that they could get away with things that they didn't think that they could get away with doing under the Bush administration. I think they believed they had a good opportunity to get rid of a government they did not like and the United States would do nothing to oppose them. Let's remember what this was all about. Saad Hariri is the Prime Minister because his father Rafiq Hariri was murdered on February 14th, 2005. Now we are learning from the International Tribunal in the Hague, run by the United Nations, that Hariri was probably murdered by Hizbullah on the direct orders of the Iranian regime. So there is no love lost between Iran and the Hariri family. The Iranians believe that the Hariris, who were Sunni Muslims, were also in the pocket of the United States, the Saudis and more generally the West. So it was just a matter of time before they acted. I do think that Obama's initiative towards Iran, emboldened and enabled Hizbullah to sabotage the government of Saad Hariri.

Gordon: Were the recent events in Egypt and across the Arab Muslim world in your opinion abetted by President Obama's June 2009 Cairo speech about outreach to the Muslim Ummah.

Timmerman: It's very curious to see the way Obama has dealt with Islam and the Middle East in general. You mentioned his Cairo speech. I would say more important than that was his response to the millions of protestors in the streets of Iran in June of 2009. There you had a radical Islamist regime in Tehran fighting against millions of pro-freedom protestors who were begging the United States to show them some support. Obama made his choice. He chose the radical Islamist regime. Fast forward to what happened in Egypt. You had an Egyptian leader Hosni Mubarak who was an autocrat, but not a dictator. People have exaggerated vastly the oppressiveness of the Mubarak regime. I have gone to Egypt many times under Mubarak's reign and Egypt is an authoritarian country but people are a lot freer there than you might think. Remember, the Egyptians also love to talk and they have a reasonably free press, compared to many other countries in the Arab world. In Egypt you had a staunch U.S. ally, and opposing him you had the Muslim Brotherhood. Two months before his Cairo speech, President Obama met in the White House with several senior leaders of the Muslim Brotherhood from Egypt. He told them that he favored them coming to power in Egypt. Moreover, if they came to power his Administration would do nothing to oppose them. Fast forward to the first protests in Cairo against Mubarak. Within two days President Obama is pounding his fist on the table saying that Mubarak has to take into account the demands of the protesters. Then within a week he sent a special envoy to Cairo, Frank Wisner, to tell Mubarak that he has to step down. Within 18 days it was all over. Now, so far we've been lucky and the Egyptian army has stepped into the void. The Egyptian army is not pro Muslim Brotherhood although they have Muslim Brotherhood officers. However, lurking beneath the surface is the Muslim Brotherhood and we will not know the end of this story for many months. We didn't know how the 1979 Revolution against the Shah of Iran was going to finish until almost a year later. It could easily take that long to see how Egypt's revolution finishes, whether the Muslim Brotherhood seizes power or whether there is some kind of soft landing. However, I believe the common thread between Obama's response to the cries for freedom of the Iranian people and his enabling of the Muslim Brotherhood in Egypt is this: Obama likes radical Islamic rule.

Gordon: Do you believe that the rise of the Muslim Brotherhood affiliates across the Arab Muslim Ummah will pose a serious threat to both Israel and U.S. interests in the region?

Timmerman: Without a doubt. This is as dangerous and its impact would be as far reaching as the collapse of the Shah in Iran in 1979.

Gordon: Given your recent trip to Iraq, what if anything is the U.S. doing to alleviate the plight of Christian minorities in the Middle East threatened by annihilationist Muslim majorities and in particular with the Assyrian Chaldean community in Iraq and the Copts in Egypt?

Timmerman: Under President Obama the U.S. is doing nothing. They are putting no pressure on Al-Maliki in Iraq. In Egypt when we had on Christmas Eve a horrific bombing of a Coptic church in Alexandria, you know there was some huffing and puffing from the Obama Administration but nothing serious. I just returned from Northern Iraq to celebrate the Rogation of the Ninevites, which is a three day ceremony of prayers to commemorate the Prophet Jonah as he calls the Ninevites to repent. I was in many different places on the Nineveh Plain in the North. I went to churches in Erbil and in Mosul. I can tell you that this is a community that is on the verge of extinction. The Assyrian Chaldean community in Iraq constitutes the indigenous people of Iraq. They have been there for millennia. They are being driven out by jihadi Muslims on the one hand and by Kurdish Nationalists on the other.

I think that the Kurds are divided. Many members of the Kurdish Regional Government such as Prime Minister Barham Saleh and many others in his government, are striving to do the right thing and see themselves as protectors of the Christians. President Massoud Barzani and the former Prime Minister Nechirvan Barzani see themselves as protectors of the Christians. The President of Iraq, Jalal Talabani, and the Foreign Minister Hoshyar Zebari have publicly stated that they want to protect and maintain the Christians in Iraq, so this is not a religious persecution on the part of the current Iraq government. What you do have is an ethnic conflict between the Assyrian Chaldean Syriac community and the Kurds that dates back hundreds of years. You have land encroachment, you have the Kurdish Democratic Party Intelligence Service harassing Assyrian leaders throughout the Nineveh plain. This is part of a larger goal on the part of the Kurds to bring the Nineveh plain within the Kurdish regional government and annex it. The Arabs, on the other hand, and Da'wa party of Prime Minister Al-Maliki simply want to drive the Christians out of Iraq entirely. In fact I have just finished a story for Newsmax.com with new information about the October 31st attack on Our Lady Salvation Church in Baghdad where 58 worshippers were murdered in cold blood and nearly 100 others wounded. The information that I received in Northern Iraq from credible sources suggests very strongly that Al-Maliki's Da'wa party was directly involved in the attack on the church. This was not just jihadi Muslims trying to drive Christians out. It was an organized political act to drive the Christians out. I believe that Congress and the President should become engaged and push Prime Minister Al-Maliki to purge his security forces and allow the Christians their rights under the Iraqi Constitution to form an autonomist province in the Nineveh plains. This is the only thing that will keep Christians in Iraq.

Gordon: Your latest thriller, *St. Peter's Bones*, talks about this background. Do you think this is an example of triumphalist Qur'anic Islam endeavoring to rid the region of all Christians and non-Muslim minorities in the Middle East?

Timmerman: Absolutely. That is what the Muslims themselves say. Now I'm not saying Iraq's Muslim leaders say this, but the jihadi leaders say that they would like to rid the Middle East of the infidels and they say this openly and repeatedly. They say this in letters that they put on the windshields of Iraqi Christians. They say this when they burst into houses and murder Christians, and when they machine gun liquor stores owned by Christians in Baghdad. When I was recently in Northern Iraq I had the opportunity to meet a young man, an Iraqi Christian who worked as an interpreter for U.S. Coalition forces. He told me of a number of operations that he had been on when they were taking down terrorist cells and interrogating terrorists. While sitting there with him, I was thinking he could have been the original model of the fictional narrator in my book, *St. Peter's Bones*. Yet another case of art preceding life!

He told many of the same stories that my narrator tells in the book. There is no real coincidence because the narrator in *St. Peters Bones*, was based on a number of real characters who I have met during my previous trips. Nevertheless, it was really extraordinary to come across somebody in the flesh who thoroughly embodied this composite character who narrates *St. Peter's Bones*.

The tragedy of the Iraqi Christians is just heartbreaking. I wrote *St. Peter's Bones* as a novel to try to get this emotional impact across to ordinary American readers, so when they read news stories about churches getting bombed, liquor stores getting machine gunned and Christians being threatened because of their faith, they will realize that these things are happening to real people. When you create characters in a novel, you hope that they will jump off the page, and that your reader will identify with them, and care about them. In *St. Peter's Bones*, bad things happen – really tragic things happen - to good people. I wrote this novel to wake up Americans, wake up Christians in this country, and wake up Jews in this country, to the threat of extermination of the Christian minorities in Iraq, by hopefully getting them to care about these characters as real people.

Gordon: Whom do you see as the strongest political candidates in the upcoming 2012 Presidential race capable of making make a major mid-course correction in the devolution of American moral presence, both at home and abroad?

Timmerman: Now it probably won't surprise you Jerry that I like John Bolton. People will say John Bolton has no experience. He is not a politician. All that is true. However, he certainly has plenty of experience in executive positions and in policy positions in government. He has a track record of running things and confronting crises that people can very easily examine and evaluate. Between Barak Obama and John Bolton, it's easy to see which one has got more executive experience, even today. John Bolton is the only thoughtful person in the GOP camp who has the timbre and intellectual fortitude coupled with experience to deal with this rising threat from Iran and the Muslim Brotherhood against the West and the U.S. But can he raise the money he needs to run? I don't know.

Kenneth Timmerman

* * *

Kenneth Timmerman tossed his hat in the ring as a Republican candidate for Maryland's 8th Congressional District (CD) in January of 2012. Should he win the GOP primary, Timmerman will be facing veteran Democrat Chris Van Hollen, former Congressional member of the Joint Select Committee on Deficit Reduction. Van Holen is an assistant to US. House of Representatives Minority Leader, Nancy Pelosi.

This is not the first foray by Timmerman into politics, he ran in the 2000 GOP primary for the US Senate in Maryland. Timmerman received an endorsement from Maryland's lone GOP conservative, Congressional Representative Roscoe Bartlett in the adjacent Maryland 6th CD. Roscoe said:

"Like me Ken Timmerman is not a career politician and I would welcome a chance to serve in Congress with Ken. He will bring to Congress a lifetime of experience in foreign affairs and investigative reporting which would serve Congress well in its oversight role over the executive branch of government."

12
ROBERT WISTRICH
APRIL 2011

Antisemitism has coursed through Middle Eastern and Western history for nearly two millennia. It was the hatred of Jews nascent in Christian theology in the 4th Century that reached heights of racism during the long period from the Inquisition through the 20th Century until finally extinguished from the official Catholic Catechism during Nostre Aetate, Vatican II in the mid-1960's. Religious writer James Carroll has chronicled this long history of official Church antisemitism in his work, *Constantine's Sword: the Church and the Jews, A History*. Scholar Bat Ye'or has demonstrated the long history of Islamic hatred and subjugation of all unbelievers (Jews, Christians and "polytheists") in her several studies of Islamic jihad, beginning with *The Dhimmi: Jews and Christians Under Islam* in the 1980's and in more recent works. Dr. Andrew Bostom in his seminal work, *The Legacy of Islamic Antisemitism: From Sacred Texts to Solemn History* has presented the historical evidence of Jew hatred that is at the core of doctrinal and historical Islam. Both Bat Ye'or and Bostom have documented evidence of Jew hatred from Islam's inception with Mohammed's brutal depopulation of Jewish centers in Arabia. The great waves of jihadist conquest of former Christian, Persian and Indian realms left pockets of Jews subject to dhimmi status and periodic pogroms including those that erupted in the 20th Century in Casablanca, Tripoli, Alexandria, and Baghdad.

Jew hatred of a more sinister nature in the West erupted in the 19th and 20th Centuries with the rise of European antisemitism as evident during the Dreyfuss Affair in France at the turn of the last century and the creation of the "blood libel" in the notorious Czarist secret police forgery, *The Protocols of the Learned Elders of Zion*. Even Henry Ford published more than half a million copies of the *Protocols* in America under the title of *The Eternal Jew*, some of which persist to this day in Arabic translations, despite Ford's later disavowal of the forgery. The *Protocols* heavily influenced the rise of Nazism in Germany under Hitler culminating in the genocidal murder of six million European men, women and children in the gas chambers and crematoria of the death camps of the "final solution" adopted at the Berlin SS Wannsee Conference in early 1942. Hitler welcomed notorious antisemitic Muslim leader, the Grand Mufti of Jerusalem, the Haj Amin al Husseini, as his house guest during WWII in Berlin. Al Husseini sponsored recruitment of Bosnian, Kosovar and Caucasian Muslim Waffen SS units and urged destruction of Jews in Nazi death camps to ensure that they didn't reach Jewish Palestine. Nazi era *Der Sturmer's* lurid cartoons of Jews still flourish in Arab Muslim publications, despite the Jewish state of Israel being defamed as the "new Nazis" by Arab Muslims referring to alleged mistreatment of the Palestinians.

Notwithstanding the heinous history of the WWII Holocaust, antisemitism in the West and especially Muslim realms persists. In many areas it thrives, despite the absence of Jews because of primordial hatred of the Jew as the "Other." That is evident in recent studies conducted in the EU and polls of Muslims. Recently, the Friedrich Ebert Foundation in Germany reported persistent high levels of antisemitism among Germans, Hungarians and Poles. The Pew Global Attitude Survey found increasing negative attitudes towards Jews in European countries like Spain, Poland, Russia and Germany. Pew Global Attitude Surveys of seven Muslim countries show a consistent level of antisemitism, a reflection of both cultural and Islamic doctrinal Jew hatred. In a recent Pew Global Attitude survey over 90% of respondents in the Arab Middle East viewed Jews as "unfavorable."

With this background in mind, we had the opportunity to interview, Professor Robert Wistrich, a renowned international expert and author of several major works on antisemitism. Professor Wistrich is Neuburger Professor of European and Jewish history at the Hebrew University of Jerusalem, the head of the University's Vidal Sassoon International Center for the Study of Antisemitism and editor of its annual research journal, *Antisemitism International*. We reviewed the 2010 edition of *Antisemitism International* in preparation for this interview with

Prof. Wistrich.

Gordon: Professor Wistrich, could you tell us about your family background and escape to the West from Soviet Russia following WWII.

Wistrich: My parents were born just before World War I in the Galician province of Austria-Hungary. They lived in Cracow until 1939. On the first day of Hitler's invasion of Poland, they moved east and for the next 7 years they lived in the U.S.S.R. In 1946 they returned to Cracow as part of the Soviet-Polish repatriation agreement.

Gordon: What do you consider the most significant benchmarks in your distinguished academic and professional career - a career that culminated in your Neuberger Professorship of European and Jewish history and your assumption of the directorship in 2002 of the Vidal Sassoon International Center for the Study of Antisemitism at Hebrew University?

Wistrich: There were several major landmarks. In 1980, I was invited to be a scholar-in-residence at the Hebrew University of Jerusalem's Institute of Advanced Studies and a year later I already had tenure; receiving the Austrian State Prize for History in 1991; writing the script and editing the three hour film *The Longest Hatred* on antisemitism for Thames Television; and, being given a lifetime achievement award in 2010 for my research on antisemitism.

Gordon: What prompted your interest in the study of antisemitism?

Wistrich: I think that from an early age I was aware of the seemingly ineradicable nature of antisemitism. Even in its relatively milder British variety it was always present – at school, university, in social life. As a student of history at Cambridge, I became more aware of its longevity and enigmatic character.

Gordon: Which of your published works do you consider of seminal importance?

Wistrich: *The Jews of Vienna in the Age of Franz Joseph* (O.U.P.)/1989); *A Lethal Obsession: Antisemitism from Antiquity to the*

Global Jihad (Random House, 2010) and my forthcoming, *From Ambivalence to Betrayal: The Left, the Jews and Israel* (University of Nebraska, 2012) are the three I would pick out as truly seminal.

Gordon: Your books, *Demonizing the Other: Antisemitism, Racism and Xenophobia* and the recent *A Lethal Obsession: Antisemitism from Antiquity to the Global Jihad* establish a framework for historical analysis of the phenomenon of antisemitism. Why in your view has this phenomenon persisted through two millennia?

Wistrich: Ultimately, antisemitism exists because the Jews are considered a "chosen people," an anomaly, and an exception that defies all the known "laws of history." They should have disappeared but they did not; they are influential beyond their numbers; and they are God's "special treasure." That arouses envy, perplexity, anger, hatred and sometimes even exaggerated love. Whether we like it or not, we're stuck with the label.

Gordon: Do you believe from your experience with the International Catholic Jewish Historical Commission, that the door has been closed on the Vatican's role during WWII on the question of rescue of European Jews during the Holocaust?

Wistrich: The real question about the Vatican and World War II can only be resolved when all of the Holy See's archives on Pius XII are open to independent researchers.

Gordon: In your essay, "Jewish Otherness in European History, Past and Present," you cite evidence of persistent antisemitism in the EU. Why does this meta-myth continue? How much of this is a reflection of fundamental antisemitism among rising émigré and native born Muslim populations?

Wistrich: Antisemitism in Europe today is different from what it was 60-70 years ago. There is some continuity on the populist Right with the old-style racist/ultranationalist desire to exclude foreigners and Jews; but the hysteria about Israel has helped turn more liberals and leftists towards anti-Jewish ways of thinking; and Muslim resentments about the West as well as their own social alienation reinforce the long-standing anti-Jewishness in their religion and culture.

Gordon: You noted in an essay "Antisemitism: the European and Islamic Legacies" examples of European and Muslim Jew hatred. Could you provide us with your insights as to the persistent historical doctrinal hatred at the core of Qur'anic Islam?

Wistrich: I think the core problem is the way that the Islamists have succeeded in hijacking the Qur'an for anti-Jewish purposes. There are many hostile passages in the Qur'an, especially towards Jews, but also towards Christians and "polytheists." But today we have an entire Muslim "culture of hatred" towards Jews and non-believers which is increasingly totalitarian.

Gordon: Jeffrey Herf in *Antisemitism International* discusses Nazi Broadcasts to the Arab World during the Holocaust from the "Kirk transcripts" of the US National Archives recorded by the US Ambassador in Cairo during WWII. Could you discuss the importance of Herf's analysis of these wartime Nazi broadcasts to the Arab and Muslim world?

Wistrich: Herf has helped us to better understand how in the wartime period, the Nazi antisemitic poison was transmitted to the Arab and Muslim world, sinking roots which affect the region to this day.

Gordon: Matthias Schuetz interviewed you for the German webzine *Prodomo*. A recurring theme in the interview was the alleged export of 19th and 20th century European antisemitism to the Arab Muslim Middle East. Doesn't Jew hatred in the core of Islamic doctrine antedate the alleged importation of European antisemitism into the Muslim ummah?

Wistrich: Undoubtedly Jew-hatred pre-existed the import of European-style antisemitism into the Arab world in the 19th and 20th centuries. Jews experienced pogroms; they suffered an inferior status, many disabilities and were an object of contempt. Nevertheless, only through fusion with modern European antisemitic theories, did a fully-fledged demonization of Jews (and Israel) emerge.

Gordon: Menahem Milson in his essay, "A European Plot on the Arab Stage" chronicles the adoption of the Czarist forgery, *The Protocols of the Elders of Zion* in the Arab Muslim world, which he considers a reflection of "deeply-ingrained stereotypes of Jews . . . rooted in Arab culture." Isn't that a reflection of the Jew hatred conveyed in doctrinal Islam?

Wistrich: I agree with Milson on this point and expanded on the theme in *A Lethal Obsession*.

Gordon: Liberal Jews in the EU, and the US have aligned themselves with leftist advocates of anti-Zionism supporting the so-called Boycott, Divestment and Sanctions (BDS) movement directed at demonizing and delegitimizing the Jewish State of Israel. Doesn't this amount to Jewish support of antisemitism?

Wistrich: The BDS movement is in my view exclusionary, discriminatory and antisemitic in its consequences – whatever the motivations of its advocates. So "liberal Jews" who support it are betraying their principles as well as aiding and abetting an insidious form of racism and double standards!

Gordon: Is Islamization in the EU and possibly in America a threat to fundamental Judeo-Christian values at the core of Western democratic traditions?

Wistrich: Islamization (as opposed to Islam) stands in flat contradiction to Western Civilization today. If it expands, it would be a death-warrant for individual liberties, free speech, and freedom of criticism, democracy and the rule of law – all of which owe much to the Judeo-Christian tradition.

Gordon: From your long association with American Jewish groups, do you believe the leadership has an adequate understanding of Islamic antisemitism?

Wistrich: The short answer is NO! But reality is a hard taskmaster. The question is how long it will take for their eyes to be opened.

Gordon: What do you view as the cause of the emergence of virulent antisemitism in international bodies like the UN Human Rights Council and the General Assembly of the United Nations?

Wistrich: The causes are mainly political. There are 22 Arab States and nearly 60 Islamic States, but only one Jewish State. Ganging up on Israel in the UN is an easy way of avoiding the real issues of Human Rights. Anti-Jewish bigotry at the UN carries no price and is a function of Israel's isolation, the tyranny of the automatic majority and Third World resentments against the West.

Gordon: Do you consider the body of work of non-academic scholars such as Bat Ye'or, David Littman, and Dr. Andrew Bostom among others helpful in elucidating Islamic antisemitism?

Wistrich: The scholars you mention have made a contribution by pointing to the darker corners in Islamic attitudes to the Jews which others sought to avoid. There is too much conformism in Academia when it comes to treating the record of Muslim antisemitism.

Gordon: What do you see as the future of research into antisemitism and what advice can you provide for policy makers in the West and elsewhere?

Wistrich: I am sure that we will be seeing in the next few years a long-overdue resurgence of interest in antisemitism. I believe that my own work and that of SICSA (our Centre in Jerusalem) has been a major catalyst. Policy-makers need to take very seriously the saying: "What begins with the Jews never ends with the Jews." Above all, they should stop talking in euphemisms and call a spade a spade.

13
LARS HEDEGAARD
MAY 2011

In George Orwell's *1984* the totalitarian credo of the Party is: "Who controls the past, controls the future: who controls the present controls the past." If one looks at what passes for speech control in the European Union (EU), we see continued assault on basic freedoms. Freedoms that we take for granted in America under our Constitution's First Amendment - the masthead of the Bill of Rights. Notwithstanding this American bulwark in defense of free speech, we are witnessing lawfare waged by Muslim Brotherhood front groups abetted by the US Department of Justice that seek to derogate and even supplant basic Constitutional protections via intimidation and the gradual insinuation of Shariah into our judicial system. That would explain the efforts led by David Yerushalmi, Esq. and the Public Policy Alliance who are endeavoring to introduce bills in a number of state legislatures seeking to bar Shariah from being used in our legal system based on the model "American Laws for American Courts."

The EU unfortunately views criticism of Islam as tantamount to racism and official hate speech. It is a stalking horse for de facto adoption of Islamic blasphemy laws as sought by members of The Organization of Islamic Cooperation. Their most recent effort was overturned by the UN Council on Human Rights in late March. Criticism of any religion is protected under the US Constitution. Not so in many EU member countries. This is evident in several legal actions brought by public prosecutors in Holland against Freedom Party leader Geert Wilders, in Austria against Elisabeth Sabaditsch-Wolff and in Denmark against Lars Hedegaard, President of the Danish Free Press Society, who is also leader of the International Free Press Society. They all have dared to criticize Islam, a protected religion in many EU countries. Hedegaard's case is particularly troubling, because he was ensnared in an interview, disseminated without his permission, during which he told the truth about Shariah – Islamic doctrine - that permits rape within a Muslim family and honor killings of women - daughters and wives. He was tried on a Kafkaesque hate speech complaint under an arcane Danish law and was acquitted on a technicality in late January of 2010, only to have the matter appealed by the public prosecutors. The case was heard again on April 26th by the Superior Court in Copenhagen. It was a show trial in liberal, tolerant Denmark. Hedegaard is seeking to advance the view that Islam is a totalitarian doctrine seeking world domination with what we have called, "the thin veneer of religious practices."

Hedegaard has clearly rankled the politically correct ruling Danish elite by taking on the cause of criticizing Islam. They are trying to muzzle him for telling the truth. He was informed by public prosecutors that the matter of truth about Islam has nothing to do with the adjudication of the hate speech charges brought against him. Hedegaard will not be silenced. In this regard, he joins courageous Scandinavian champions of free speech and free expression. Fellow Dane and political cartoonist Kurt Westergaard and Swedish artist Lars Vilks have also dared to criticize, at great personal risk, the exemplar of jihadist Islam - Mohammed. The Danish prosecutors' arguments are akin to the exchange between Humpty Dumpty and Alice in the topsy turvy world of *Though the Looking Glass*:

> "When I use a word, it means just what I choose it to mean — neither more nor less."
>
> "The question is," said Alice, "whether you can make words mean so many different things."
>
> "The question is," said Humpty Dumpty, "which is to be master — that's all."

Prior to Mr. Hedegaard's Copenhagen Superior Court hearing, we were afforded the opportunity to interview him.

Gordon: Could you provide us with your background as a journalist, historian, free speech advocate in Denmark and the EU?

Hedegaard: I hold degrees in history (my major subject) and English from the Universities of Aarhus and Copenhagen. This prepared me for a teaching career, but after five years at a junior college, I decided that teaching was not for me. My wife and I moved to California, where I somehow landed a job as a book editor in Beverly Hills. After five years in the US, I moved back to Denmark and took up a career as an author, journalist and editor and for three years I was chief editor of the Copenhagen intellectual daily *Information*. For ten years I was an almost daily columnist with the leading Conservative daily *Berlingske Tidende* until I was fired for writing too much and too un-pc on Islam and immigration. In my spare time I have written books on historical and political subjects – in the beginning from a clearly Marxist perspective. I no longer believe in utopia, but my analytical approach to history and power politics hasn't changed. Recently most of my writing has been on Islam and Islamic history. In 2004, I was asked to become the head figure of a new free speech organisation, Trykkefrihedsselskabet (The Free Press Society) and later of The International Free Press Society. I am still President of both organisations.

Gordon: You are one of several prominent Shariah opponents in the EU who have been put on trial for alleged hate speech and criticism of Islamic doctrine. Why in your opinion has this occurred with Geert Wilders in Holland, Elisabeth Sabaditsch-Wolff in Austria and you in Denmark?

Hedegaard: There is a simple explanation for these and many other such cases: For decades, Europeans have been told – by their governments, by the European Union, by the press and by so-called "experts" – that Islam is the religion of peace and tolerance and that mass immigration is an enrichment. Anyone who has voiced doubts about these supposedly self-evident truths has been labelled a racist if not a Nazi. Courageous opponents of the official fiction have had their careers ruined and have been expelled from polite company. The current lawfare tsunami is simply a logical extension of previous efforts to silence all critics.

By now it is becoming uncomfortably evident that European policies on Islam and integration have failed utterly. Most European countries are falling apart and governments have no idea how to reverse the trends they have set in motion.

So instead of facing a reality, they can do nothing about unless they were to admit that they have lied and deceived, they have chosen to prosecute those who talk about it.

Of course that strategy will also fail. Reality is a hard taskmaster, as our governments and elites will soon learn to their detriment.

Gordon: Do you find it ironic that hate speech laws in many EU countries were adopted in the 1930's and Post WWII environment to combat antisemitism and now are being manipulated by fundamentalist Muslims to further criminalize any criticism of Islamic doctrine, especially Shariah?

Hedegaard: Absolutely. Speech regulation and thought control haven't worked in the past and won't in the future. All you can accomplish is to create a bifurcated climate of debate. In the public sphere people will only say and hear what the government will allow – this will be very bad for the newspapers because few will want to pay for government propaganda or tracts by religious madmen. The real debate, what people really have on their minds, will unfold behind closed doors or man to man when agents of the rulers are not listening.

Speech regulation creates a pressure cooker of dissatisfaction and resentment that is bound to explode at some point.

Gordon: Could you describe the events that led up to your January trial in Copenhagen and the legal basis under Danish law for public prosecution of alleged "racist" remarks regarding Islam?

Hedegaard: There is no legal basis for the lawsuit against me. Article 266b of our penal code – despicable as it is – at least provides the protection that to be criminal, statements have to be made with the intent of public dissemination. I did not get a chance to authorise my comments for publication.

The public prosecutor is well aware of this fact, as was the judge in the lower court who acquitted me. The public prosecutor nonetheless went ahead and appealed to superior court.

I have no idea what has been going on between the government, the Justice Department and the prosecutor. All I know is that somebody is trying to get me, as they would have tried to get any president of The

Free Press Society. The keepers of the public faith consider our organisation a stone in their shoes that has to be got rid of.

Gordon: In your view, how radical are the Danish Imams and what are their connections to Salafist centers in the Muslim ummah?

Hedegaard: That is no secret. The leaders of Islamisk Trossamfund (The Islamic Faith Community) have made no bones about the fact that they are salafists with close connections to Saudi Arabia and other radical states. If there is one "moderate" imam in the country, I haven't heard of him.

Gordon: Have you been afforded personal protection by the Danish Police Intelligence service in view of threats made against you?

Hedegaard: I haven't received many threats. A couple of Muslims have written on the internet that they hope I'll be dead soon, but that is all. I have no police protection. My circumstances may change if I am convicted in superior court. With an official label as a "racist" and menace to society, men of violence may determine that I am fair and easy game.

Gordon: What facilitated the entry and growth in the numbers of Muslim immigrants to Denmark?

Hedegaard: To begin with – when it started in the late 1960s – immigration from Muslim countries was driven by the captains of industry who were in need of cheap, unskilled labour. The first immigrants were called "guest workers" and the assumption was that they would return to their native countries once they had outlasted their usefulness. Many of these immigrants were illiterate and had no idea of how to behave in a developed country.

As it happened, they never returned but were allowed to settle and bring their extended families – entire clans – to Denmark. This new policy soon facilitated an avalanche of Muslim immigration as it became known back in Anatolia, Pakistan and Somalia that one could simply get on a plane to Copenhagen, claim to be persecuted and then live a life of leisure at the expense of the Danish taxpayers.

This development was greatly facilitated by a Law on Foreigners passed by Parliament in 1983, which practically provided free access to anyone who could pay for forged documents or engage a people smuggler.

The real question is the *cui bono*. Here one has to remember that socialism was on its hind legs. The Soviet empire was crumbling at the same time as the traditional working class was becoming "bourgeois." Consequently, the Left was in need of a new "revolutionary subject" whose supposed plight might justify the Left's continued ideological hegemony.

This strategy succeeded famously. The Muslim immigrants had the immeasurable advantage over the traditional proletariat that they would never integrate and would thus constitute a permanent focus of resentment for which the Left elite could claim to be the genuine champion.

The Left substituted its traditional socialism with "antiracism," and as private property rights were no longer challenged, the parties on the right were only too happy to accept antiracism, blind toleration, multiculturalism and finally cultural relativism as the ideology of the land.

As it happened, that was precisely what the European Union advocated. The great historian and Islamic scholar Bat Ye'or has documented the entire story in her book *Eurabia: The Euro-Arab Axis*.

The implicit deal that came out of this unprecedented rapprochement can be summed up as follows: You – the Left – leave capitalism alone; we – the capitalists – won't challenge your ideological hegemony so long as you stick to "antiracism," "human rights" and such; the bill is sent to the taxpayers and good riddance to the country.

Gordon: How demographically assimilated is the Danish Muslim population?

Hedegaard: There is no question of assimilation. Quite the contrary. Islam does not penetrate the Dar al-Harb in order to assimilate or integrate but in order to dominate. That has not changed for 1400 years and won't change so long as Muslims believe that assimilation to the values of the infidels will lead straight to hell.

Gordon: How did they benefit from tolerant Danish cultural values, social welfare and legal system?

Hedegaard: They have been given the opportunity of settling in the country without changing an iota of their culture and ideology. So why would they accept our values or our legal system? It must be said, however, that many of the immigrants have assimilated wonderfully to our social welfare system as it affords them the opportunity to have all their expenses paid for by Danish taxpayers.

Gordon: Has the national parliament in Denmark debated any legislation to curtail Muslim immigration? If not, what has prevented it from being considered given l'affaires Westergaard, your own legal matter and other incidents?

Hedegaard: Never. Parliament has had many debates on immigration in general and has passed a number of laws aimed at limiting immigration. These laws have been systematically undermined by the EU and especially by the verdicts of the EU Court, which is a unique institution in Western culture. It does not operate under a fixed and transparent legal system. It is like God: it creates what it says. So Europeans have no idea what the law says until the EU Court has spoken. This is the same as saying that we have no law.

So far our governments have been happy to submit to this Star Chamber system of jurisprudence.

The number of Muslims in Denmark is kept as a state secret because the official ideology is that all religions are equally good. Unofficially it is believed that Muslims constitute approximately 5 percent of the population – not counting those who live here illegally. Muslims are expected to form a majority well before the end of the century.

Gordon: You facilitated the publication of Nicolai Sennels' book in Denmark, *Among Criminal Muslims: A Psychologist's Experiences from the Copenhagen Municipality*. His work is based on the failure of therapeutic programs involving young Muslim offenders in Copenhagen. Do you agree with his conclusions based on his clinical research that Muslims reject Western values and are not assimiliable?

Hedegaard: I edited his book for publication. I am not a psychologist and therefore not qualified to offer a scientific opinion. But as far as I can tell, Sennels' method is solid as are his conclusions. Otherwise The Free Speech Library would not have lent its good name to this publication. What Sennels documents is very much in line with what I would expect on the basis of my own extensive research on Islam and Islamic history.

Gordon: In your capacity as President of the Danish Free Press Society, what are you views regarding demands for criminalization of Islamic blasphemy as proposed by the Organization of the Islamic Co-operation at the UN Human Rights Council in Geneva?

Hedegaard: All along, we and the International Free Press Society have been campaigning against blasphemy laws. The very concept of blasphemy has no place in a civilised society. Although I am of little faith, I think it an abomination to consider God to be so impotent that he is in need of legal protection.

Gordon: Geert Wilders has been an advocate for the adoption of an EU parliamentary version of the First Amendment of the US Constitution. Do you believe that the EU Parliament would take up such a measure? If not, why not?

Hedegaard: The European Parliament would never do that as it aims to undermine the national cohesion of the EU member states. It could be done nationally. All it takes is the will to stand up, and I am all in favour of it.

Gordon: Do you view as significant the statements of German Chancellor Merkel, President Sarkozy of France and PM David Cameron of the U.K. on the failure of multiculturalism?

Hedegaard: Talk is cheap. It is significant that they should feel a need to make such statements. But are they going to do something about it? As far as I can tell, they have no such intention. They seem to think that they can fool all of the people all of the time.

Gordon: Do you consider the Swiss ban on minarets and the French National Assembly Ban on burkas indicative of a groundswell of public concerns about Islamic culture in their respective countries?

Hedegaard: Undoubtedly. These pinpricks are indications that something is going on among the aboriginal peoples of Europe.

Gordon: America currently has a legal doctrine that protects so-called hate speech under the 1969 Brandenburg v. Ohio US Supreme Court decision. Yet, there is a current effort to pass anti-Shariah legislation in a number of States and anti-Shariah Finance litigation in our federal courts. As an international observer concerned about free speech, how you view these developments?

Hedegaard: I'm familiar with the Brandenburg decision, which – by and large – I consider a fair compromise between free speech and the obligation to maintain security and free institutions.

I very much support current attempts to legislate against Shariah-based institutions and practices. A free and democratic state cannot have dual jurisprudence. I think that you have a great legal precedent in the US Supreme Court's decision on Reynolds v. United States in 1878, which stated that polygamy is incompatible with democracy. So are Shariah law and Shariah practice.

Gordon: Geert Wilders in his recent speech at the Magna Carta Foundation in Rome cited the dangers of politically correct multiculturalism supplanting sovereign cultures in the EU nations. Do you agree with his positions?

Hedegaard: Wilders' speech stands out as one of the great speeches of our time. I wish that every concerned citizen would read it. The speech is mercifully free from the usual fare of pc gobbledygook that European politicians serve up these days. Here is a man who speaks the truth as he sees it. No wonder that he is hated and feared by the European elites whose own project is coming down like a ton of bricks. In addition, Wilders' Rome speech stands out for its grasp of history. Our leaders haven't spoken this way since the days of Churchill and Enoch Powell.

* * *

Immediately following our interview with Lars Hedegaard, on May 3, 2011, he was convicted in the Eastern Superior Court in Copenhagen of "hate speech." Hedegaard noted the rough justice meted out to him by what passes for law in Denmark. To wit:

> It is with great sadness I have to report that Denmark's reputation as a haven of free speech and a bastion of resistance to Shariah encroachment is irreparably tarnished. Denmark is my country and I used to be proud of it.

On May 3 the Eastern Superior Court in Copenhagen convicted me of hate speech under Denmark's infamous Article 266 b of the penal code – a rubber provision that may be stretched to serve any political purpose dear to the hearts of the ruling elites. My crime is to have called attention to the horrific conditions of Muslim women and for my audacity the court has now enabled my detractors to label me a racist.

[. . .]

We cannot permit this outcome to stand. I have therefore decided to appeal my conviction to the Supreme Court and – if that is denied – to the European Court of Human Rights.

This is a fight for liberty against tyranny. It will be long and hard but losing is no option.

14
DAVID BEAMER
SEPTEMBER 2011

In honor of the tenth anniversary of the terror attacks in September of 2001, we spoke with David Beamer, father of Todd Beamer, one of the heroes of Flight 93. The younger Beamer along with many of the 40 passengers and crew attacked their jihadi skyjackers, thereby dooming the plane, but sparing countless lives and unknown trauma in our nation's Capitol, the ultimate target of these Islamic radicals. To the cry of "Let's Roll!" Todd Beamer and his fellow Flight 93 passengers initiated what his father David calls the first counter-attack on 9/11; all within an elapsed time of less than 30 minutes after seizure of the aircraft. The 9/11 episode aboard Flight 93 was memorialized in a Universal Studios production, one that David Beamer considers a faithful re-telling of the realities aboard the hijacked plane and the actions of his son Todd and other valiant passengers and crew.

The elder Beamer was in a business meeting in Palo Alto, California that fateful day, when the events aboard Flight 93 concluded in a struggle forcing the plane with its passengers, crew and Islamic jihadi attackers to crash in a field in Shanksville, Pennsylvania. The crash site is now the last of three memorials to the fallen on 9/11. The Pentagon memorial was completed and dedicated in 2008, while the memorial in Lower Manhattan, at the former site of the World Trade Center, was dedicated on the tenth anniversary. David Beamer did not get definitive word of the fate of his son and the other passengers and crew on Flight 93 until later that week. Because virtually no air traffic was allowed in the days following 9/11, the elder Beamer and a business partner drove across the US to Todd's home in New Jersey to prepare for a memorial service that weekend. The irony was that Todd Beamer and his wife Lisa were not expected back from a trip to Italy until the following week.

In the decade following the events of 9/11 that struck down his son and thousands of others, David Beamer has become an articulate opponent of the Islamic jihad doctrine, its proponents here in America and the politically correct attitude toward fundamentalist Islam espoused by both the Bush and Obama Administrations in Washington. He has appeared in frequent media interviews, hearings before Congress and public presentations across the US. I chanced to hear and meet him at two such occasions in Florida paired with an American Israeli father, a former IDF special operations officer, Tuly Wultz, who lost his son, Daniel, to a Palestinian suicide bomber in 2006 while on a visit to Israel.

We were fortunate to interview David Beamer in partial commemoration of 9/11.

Gordon: Where were you when you first got word of the 9/11 attacks?

Beamer: I was in Palo Alto, California and I frankly thought that Todd and Lisa were still in Italy. I didn't think they were coming back to the U.S. until later that week.

Gordon: When did you first get word of your son Todd's predicament aboard Flight 93?

Beamer: We first learned some of the details about what Todd and the other 39 passengers did on that plane either Thursday or Friday. I can't quite remember because I was in an automobile with a business colleague driving from San Francisco to New Jersey. There was a memorial service planned for Todd on that Sunday and as we all might remember there were no airplanes flying that week so the way to go from Palo Alto to New Jersey was by car. I frankly can't remember whether it was Thursday or Friday that I got the call that confirmed what in our heart and mind's eye we knew. Those passengers had done something and we knew that Todd would not be sitting quietly in the back. It was very reassuring frankly and a blessing to know, for the country to know, what the passengers and crew on that plane did. They had the opportunity to fight back and they did so.

Gordon: How did you and the family react to Todd's valor and that of the courageous passengers aboard Flight 93 who attacked their Islamic terrorist highjackers?

Beamer: We were proud of what they did. Those people on the plane had the opportunity to fight back. They launched a successful counter-attack. It was a victory for our country. No other lives on the ground were lost and we were proud and pleased about what they did. We were not surprised.

Gordon: Did you consider the *Flight 93* film as faithful to what happened to Todd and the other passengers?

Beamer: If we're discussing the *Flight 93* major movie that was done by Universal Studios with Paul Greengrass as the producer, we felt it was good. Mr. Greengrass assured the families as the film was being developed that he was going to make every attempt to faithfully recreate the realities of the day I believe that his research and his efforts to do so produced that kind of a result. The fact was that both he and his co-producers reached out to family members for additional background information and insight about our loved ones. He did that in a greater manner than the other productions or documentaries. I think it was either 10 or 12 people in that movie were not actors. They were playing themselves which also adds to its authenticity. Those good souls were not going to do anything other than present the realities of the day. We thought it was a good job.

Gordon: You have been active in the 9/11 families and friends group with regard to the memorial both in Shanksville and lower Manhattan. What in your opinion has stymied the completion of both memorials during the past decade?

Beamer: You know there are three national memorials to recall the events of 9/11: the Pentagon, New York City Ground Zero and the Flight 93 memorial in Shanksville. Two out of those three, Ground Zero New York and the Pentagon are fundamentally complete and happily will open on this the tenth anniversary. Great progress has been made on the Flight 93 memorial in Shanksville but the fact remains it is far from complete. I was there four days ago and I believe the Phase I effort is excellent. I believe the overall design is appropriate to honor, remember and educate subsequent generations about the realities of that morning. However Shanksville is largely out of sight, out of mind and, it's not pleasant to dwell on 9/11 every day. We do need to remember what happened and even though the economy is tough, I really call upon every American just to make a little sacrifice. If every working American gave just one hour's income then the Flight 93 memorial would be well on its way to completion. You know the fact is that 40 free people executed a successful counter-attack in a total elapsed time of about 30 minutes. I am a bit, more than a bit, disappointed that 10 years later all of the memorials aren't complete.

Gordon: You met with former President Bush during his re-election campaign in 2004. What was his reaction to meeting you and the other 9/11 families?

Beamer: It was a very warm, caring and concerned interaction. He was our President. He is also a gentleman and First Lady Laura Bush could not have been more gracious so it was a special meeting. First Lady Laura has, specifically helped, along with thousands of other people, to progress the Flight 93 memorial to the state that it is in. Her efforts and those of many people over these 10 years I deeply appreciate.

Gordon: Why do you believe this Administration has not aggressively pursued military tribunals for those involved in planning 9/11 like Khalid Sheikh Mohammed whom you call the chief operating officer of 9/11 and other Guantanamo detainees?

Beamer: That brings to mind what could be the possible agenda or motive. I don't know what motivates our Justice Department under the leadership of Attorney General Eric Holder. Is it a turf issue? Clearly, these would be high profile proceedings generating great publicity and great opportunity for limelight so is it a turf issue or is it just a general feeling about the military? Attorney General Holder came from a law firm where they felt compelled to provide pro bono legal support to enemy combatants at GITMO; so what is their motivation, what is their attitude, what are their beliefs? These enemy combatants, those stateless jihadis who plotted the attack, and frankly their comrades continue to do so; they do not deserve the rights of American citizens. They do not belong in our courts; they are not criminals. They are guilty of war crimes and military tribunals are exactly the right place and it's been way too long in coming.

Gordon: What was your reaction to the killing of Osama Bin Laden by the U.S. Navy Seal Team Six and also your view of Pakistan's response?

Beamer: May 1st, 2011 was a great day. Osama Bin Laden was the mastermind who perpetrated this evil. He directed the killing of thousands of innocent people, those that didn't agree with his particular philosophy, religion, political system and law. He was introduced to his maker by the Navy Seals, exactly the right outcome for Osama Bin Laden. I know that Osama Bin Laden had a really bad day and it was about time that he should have. It was a bit ironic to me that there were 40 Navy Seals carrying out that mission. There just happened to be 40 passengers and crew on Flight 93. I thought that was good. I especially thought it was great that 40 Navy Seals went in and 40 Navy Seals came out. None of their families got that terrible message where they would have said one of your loved ones was lost, so that was great. Pakistan, who we have supported and sent billions in aid, had obviously been complicit in protecting, harboring, allowing Osama Bin Laden to, have his compound near the walls of their equivalent of our West Point. Not trustworthy, hah!? I would say not trustworthy.

Gordon: Why have you opposed the construction of the 51 Park Place the Ground Zero mosque in lower Manhattan?

Beamer: The notion that we should somehow welcome with open cooperative arms our enemy and allow them to construct a victory symbol, which they see as an absolute victory, namely the destruction of thousands of Americans in the middle of one of our great cities, is to me unconscionable. The notion that it's a center for interfaith outreach and communication is just another Islamic lie. It clearly is indicative of our Islamic enemy to foster deceit, to lie and to play to our general feelings of liberty and tolerance. Interfaith outreach is an oxymoron when it comes to the goals and objective of Islam. There is no such thing. The bumper stickers that I see some naive Americans sporting on their cars, "coexist" written with every religious symbol known to man, do not understand something. Coexistence is an anathema to the ultimate goals of Islam which is to dominate planet earth.

Gordon: Why do you believe Mayor Bloomberg of New York supports the Ground Zero mosque?

Beamer: Intelligence and a lot of money don't necessarily in every circumstance overcome ignorance. One needs to read, learn and understand about the ultimate goal of Islam. That goal is absolutely inconsistent with the values we hold dear in America; of liberty, freedom of speech, and freedom of religion. We need to understand that the enemy really is serious about their objective to change our way of life into theirs with their system of Islamic law and lack of rights for women and religious liberty. I think many Americans, be they rich or in powerful positions of high responsibility, are operating from the stance of denial. We in America have enjoyed so much liberty for so long we just have a hard time believing that the goal of fundamental Islam is to change all that, but we better start believing it because I can assure you that is the enemy's goal.

Gordon: Following 9/11, has our country made sufficient commitments to combat homegrown Islamic terror threats?

Beamer: In my view our enemy uses tactics of not only terror but infiltration. Getting us to change our language making sure that we are so politically correct that threats and their ideas won't even see the light of day. I believe that our strategy of apology, capitulation and compromise makes sure that we don't do anything that might possibly offend them. We don't call out Islamic radicals for what they are. We just give them more time to indoctrinate, to preach their hate and to really target the disenfranchised members of our society with promises of a glorious better life and virgins in the hereafter. Our stance and our strategies to combat this threat in many ways just demonstrate weakness to the enemy.

Gordon: Do you regard as a major threat to the security of this country the so called "secret plan" of the Muslim Brotherhood to replace our Constitution with an Islamic Shariah regime as revealed in the Holy Land Foundation trial and convictions of 2008?

Beamer: We must understand the Islamic fundamentalist objectives of the front organizations of the Muslim Brotherhood in this country; groups like the Council of American Islamic Relations (CAIR) and others. Their goal is to overthrow our form of government and replace it with Shariah Islamic law. These groups use their tactics of stealth jihad, intimidation and infiltration which are dangerous to our country. Political correctness and unwillingness to speak openly and directly about the threat gives momentum to their strategies and approach to change our way of life.

Gordon: Are you concerned about our national law enforcement agencies like the FBI, the Justice Department and the Department of Homeland Security inviting Muslim Brotherhood front group representatives onto their staffs and advisory bodies?

Beamer: When groups like the ones you just mentioned invite, appoint, allow and encourage representation from Muslim Brotherhood front groups as a part of our administration, our agencies, and our law enforcement, it only reaffirms that ignorance abounds. People are unwilling to read, study, learn and believe what the enemy really says. Not their lies but what they really say, who they are and what their objectives are. Yes, the Muslim Brotherhood and their front groups, serving in places like our Department of Homeland Security, it really defies one's imagination. It's way beyond the fox and the chicken coop analogy, way beyond that.

Gordon: You've made joint presentations with Tuly Wultz, an American Israeli former IDF Special Ops Officer who lost his son Daniel to a suicide bomber in Tel Aviv in 2006. Do you believe that the U.S. and Israel are both engaged in a war against Islamic jihadism? Further, what more in your opinion could be done by our government to cooperate with Israel in defeating this common enemy and preventing other 9/11's?

Beamer: Tuly Wultz is one fine man and his loss of his son was terrible. Tuly is a warrior, a great man. Israel understands the Islamic threat. When leaders like President Ahmadinejad of The Islamic Republic of Iran proclaim their goal is to wipe "Israel off the map of the world," they understand that those comments are not made lightly. It's not just rhetoric. That's the intent. That's what they believe. Israel understands it. I do not believe that in the United States, our current Administration understands that we are at war with Islamic jihadism. In fact, our President I believe says explicitly, "we're not at war with Islam." Well, I guess not Islam in the sense of the moderate Muslims who are not a part of the jihad. We had better recognize, though, that there are elements of Islam that are at war with us and instead of backtracking and showing a deteriorating support for our long time ally Israel, we ought to be shoring them up, not telling them to give back their territory. It is absolutely the wrong policy and the wrong direction. It is another example that saddens me about what has happened in the last decade since 9/11. I sadly believe that America is weaker today than we were then both at home and in the eyes of our allies abroad.

Gordon: How important is it for you and other 9/11 families that the memories of loved ones be preserved and this country maintain vigilance against the threat of Islamic jihadism?

Beamer: Islamic fundamentalists with their jihad objectives are striving to have the entire world submit to Islam. This same enemy has been attacking us for decades; our Marines in Beirut in 1983, our embassies in Africa in 1998, the World Trade Center, the first time in 1993, the U.S.S. Cole in 2000 and the big bang on 9/11/2001 in our own homeland. How many times must the same enemy kill our loved ones and wreak havoc around the world to carry out their jihad war? How long must it be? How can we forget who the enemy is? How could we diminish our vigilance or attempt to fight back with strategies of political correctness? Denial is not a strategy. Capitulation and apologies are not strategies.

Gordon: In conclusion, what are your thoughts on whether the U.S. has learned the lessons of what your son Todd and others fought and died for on 9/11?

Beamer: A lot of what we've been discussing here is frankly some frustration on my part in that it's not apparent to me that we as a country have really understood the threat from this enemy. If we don't understand, if we don't act, if we don't employ strategies and tactics other than let's just pretend everything is going to be o.k., then we are going to be looking at more battles in this war. The enemy, the Islamic fundamentalists who have launched this jihad are not waiving any white flags.

15
BAT YE'OR
OCTOBER 2011

I met Gisèle Littman, better known as "Bat Ye'or," through her book, *The Dhimmi: Jews and Christians under Islam* while browsing through a Judaica section of a Barnes & Noble book store in Westport, Connecticut in 1985. Reading it opened my mind to the historical evidence of the subjugated treatment of Jews, Christians and other non-Muslims under Shariah in the wake of Islamic jihad over conquered lands. Her book threw into considerable doubt the then fashionable medievalist commentary that Jews and Christians had been well treated in Muslim Spain (Al Andaluz) and in the far reaches of the Caliphate of the Ottoman Empire. Bat Ye'or's penetrating historical analysis in *The Dhimmi* was followed by further investigations into the plight of Christians under the system of Islamic shariah "dhimmitude." Dhimmitude as an historical concept, was coined by Bat Ye'or in 1983 to describe the legal and social conditions of Jews and Christians subjected to Islamic rule. The word dhimmitude comes from *dhimmi*, an Arabic word meaning "protected." Through her latter writings, Bat Ye'or plumbed the depths of Islamization of Europe with her major work, *Eurabia: The Euro Arab Axis* and the recently published, *Europe Globalization and the Coming Universal Caliphate*.

I later met Bat Ye'or and her husband David Littman in person at a lecture at Brown University arranged by Andrew Bostom, then in the midst of research for his books, *The Legacy of Jihad: Islamic Holy War and the Treatment of Non-Muslims* and *The Legacy of Islamic Antisemi-*

tism: From Sacred Texts to Solemn History. In 2003, Bat Ye'or spoke at my synagogue in Fairfield, Connecticut. The matter came up about what topic to discuss. Her *National Review* article, a precursor to *Eurabia*, had recently been published. Colleagues, Fred Leder, Judith Greenberg, Dr. Richard L. Rubenstein and I agreed it should be about the threat of Islamization to Europe and the isolation of Israel and the Jewish people. When *Eurabia* was published in 2005, Dr. Rubenstein and I attended Bat Ye'or's lecture at Columbia University. We next met when she returned to New York in 2007 to give several lectures on her views about Islamization in Europe. She had been invited by a faculty member to lecture on these topics to a class of future staff officers at the US Army Command and General Staff College in Fort Leavenworth, Kansas.

Less well known is the saga of Bat Ye'or's family's ejection from Egypt as stateless persons following the first Sinai War in 1956. Deprived of resources, they made their way to exile in England. This interview focuses on her experience and that of her family as Jews in Egypt during this tumultuous period following the founding of the State of Israel and the Free Officers Movement coup in Egypt. It touches on her family heritage; her meeting with her future husband while both were students at London University's Institute of Archeology, their marriage and their little known exploits in clandestinely saving Moroccan Jewish children and enabling their emigration to Israel. Both Bat Ye'or and her husband David Littman were honored in 2009 for this rescue known by Littman's code name, Operation Mural.

Gordon: You were born and raised in Egypt. Could you tell us about your family's heritage?

Bat Ye'or: I was born in a family of mixed heritage. My mother was French and grew up in Paris. Her mother, who was British, had married a Frenchman. They were emancipated and non-observant Jews, well integrated into French culture, counting among their family painters and writers. Members of my mother's family were also living in Egypt and were prominent leaders of the Alexandrine Jewish community.

The picture was very different on my father's side. The Orebi were observant Italian Jews, who spoke Arabic, several other languages and were less Westernized. My grand-father received the title of *Bey* under the last Ottoman Sultan. He died when my father was thirteen years old.

Both families were related and belonged to the same educated and wealthy Westernized Jewish bourgeoisie, sharing the same social milieu.

My mother loved reading and followed the cultural events in France. She gave us her taste for literature. We always had plenty of books at home. As far as I can remember, I was always reading.

After the Italian racial laws were decreed by Mussolini in 1938, my father requested Egyptian nationality that had been established only in 1924. Usually it was denied to Jews, but he did obtain it. He could hardly guess then, that less then 20 years later he would leave Egypt stripped of everything, including his nationality.

Gordon: What was it like growing up as a Jew in Egypt prior to the establishment of the State of Israel in 1948?

Bat Ye'or: In my childhood we were more worried by the Nazi advance toward Alexandria and the war in Europe. In Egypt we knew about the extermination of European Jewry, my mother worried about her parents living in occupied Paris, wearing the yellow star. Her two brothers and uncles were hiding in the so-called free zone. When the Germans approached Alexandria, the populace around us grew menacing and we left Cairo and hid in the countryside.

Later, after the war, the Muslim Brotherhood and the nationalists triggered a wave of assassinations and violent demonstrations against the British and mainly against Jews. I only knew of the ordeals suffered by the Jews living in the poor quarters from my parents. We lived in a residential area, with many Europeans. We were protected children, going out only with our nannies and chauffeur.

My parents recommended that we never speak of Israel or of any policy even with friends. We had the feeling of being spied upon, even by our Muslim servant. Then when Jews were arbitrarily jailed or expelled from their jobs, or the country, a climate of fear and insecurity shrouded us. Violent pogroms erupted; mobs killed Jews in the street, raped Jewish women, vandalized Jewish shops, and burned Jewish schools and hospitals. All Jewish assets were sequestered, including those of my father. Jews were fired from administrative jobs and liberal professions. We lived with the fear that life could end at any moment.

During WWII, the Jewish Palestinian soldiers in the British army had trained the young Egyptian Jews for self-defense and as Zionists. Hence the Jewish quarter could be defended when attacked and young Zionists could clandestinely reach Palestine.

Gordon: After the Revolt of the Free Officers Movement in 1952 and toppling of the aristocracy under King Farouk I, were restrictions placed on the Egyptian Jewish community?

Bat Ye'or: The restrictions of 1947-48 were never totally removed. Jews could hardly find a job and were under police supervision. The anti-Jewish hatred became customary, especially with the arrivals of numerous German Nazi criminals who organized the anti Jewish policy of the new government. Jews were attacked and humiliated in public places and they could not answer or defend themselves. They found themselves at the mercy of anonymous denunciations. Young people realized they had no future in Egypt and many left for Israel or to study in Europe. The community was already organizing the last phase of its 3.000 years of history.

Gordon: What affect did the Israeli spy scandal, the Lavon Affair of 1954, have on the status of Egypt's Jews and your family?

Bat Ye'or: It increased the animosity against the Jews, their segregation, isolation and close watch by the secret police.

Gordon: What happened to you and your family after the outbreak of the Suez Crisis and First Sinai War in 1956?

Bat Ye'or: The anti-Jewish apartheid system deepened. Jews were expelled from clubs, forbidden to go to restaurants, cinemas and public places. Many were immediately expelled from the country or thrown into jail. The secret police would come at night to arrest them. Others, like my mother, were under house arrest and their bank assets frozen. Their telephones were suppressed. Many Jews were isolated and could not communicate. Many left the country immediately, abandoning everything. I remember seeing their flats and beautiful villas ransacked. Each one was leaving in secret, fearing to be prevented from leaving their country which had become a jail.

Just before my mother was put under house arrest, I accompanied her to the bank where she quickly withdrew her jewels. We sold our flat for nothing since the pillage of Jewish homes had lowered prices. I choose twenty books among the hundreds we had and we sold all the rest. This was heart-breaking, as I always wanted to be a writer. I had accumulated many diaries since an early age, and later essays and literary criticisms. I realized that I was witnessing the agony of the Egyptian

Jewish community and I made notes for a book. One night I burnt them all in the chimney. It was like dying. I knew we could only leave with two cases each and that the censors would read every piece of paper.

Families were dispersed in all directions. One sister went to London with her husband and child, another planned to go to Belgium, cousins went to Brazil, others went to Switzerland and France. As people were leaving secretly, I never knew whether I would be seeing them for the last time. I was living through the death of a world, not knowing if I would survive the next day. While the mob rejoiced in pillaging, I observed closely the inner destruction of family, friendships, bonds, society and the dignity and resolve of the victims.

By then, I had very few friends remaining. For me they belonged to a beloved and disappearing world that was dying with a part of my life, where everything being so transient also became so precious. In the last months preceding our departure, I walked alone throughout Cairo and Alexandria, their old quarters, their museums and every place that now was deserted of friends and family. For years I was fascinated by Egyptology, art and history. I knew I would never see these treasures again.

We left at night in secret. My father and mother could hardly walk. Thanks to a lawyer my father had at last sold a parcel of land. The proceeds from this sale, together with my mother's jewels were sent out of the country through a clandestine channel. The Swiss consulate gave us a Nansen passport since Egyptian Jews were allowed to leave Egypt only on condition that they renounce their nationality and all their belongings in Egypt and never come back. We all signed such a declaration.

We had reservations on a KLM flight. We were kept at the airport for hours, our bodies searched, our cases emptied on the floor, insulted, humiliated and threatened by an Egyptian Sudanese officer who was cracking a whip (curbash) around us. My meager twenty Egyptian pounds were confiscated. Finally, they let us depart. We stopped at Amsterdam where my other sister came from Belgium, with her husband and baby to see us and tell us that money and jewels were safely deposited in a bank.

It was strange to see them in an Amsterdam hotel. We were now refugees, homeless, stateless, in a world where we knew no one. We were full of apprehension on the threshold of a new life, where we would destroy our past to build the future. It was my first night in exile.

Gordon: After your ejection from Egypt in 1957, how were you and your family able to enter the UK as stateless persons?

Bat Ye'or: Being stateless made it difficult to be admitted into another country. Although we were political refugees, it was not easy for my expelled British brother-in-law, to get us into England on a short term resident permit and on his guarantee that we had enough money to live. I wanted to go to Israel; however, my mother decided that we would go to London where my sister, her four year-old son and her British husband lived as refugees. We stayed with them for a month in their small unheated flat.

We started our life as stateless, robbed, homeless refugees in a cold, wet English winter. A life where you hardly had enough to eat and you did not know where you would sleep at night, where time is like an endless dark coldness penetrating soul and body. I had to plan the future of my parents with the little money we saved. My mother had a broken leg and my father had been an invalid since the age of three when he contracted polio. Both never worked, they always had money and servants. They were totally unfit to face such a situation. When we left my sister's home I found a room for my parents with great difficulty. Doors were slammed in my face, no-one wanted to lodge stateless invalids. I started writing a short novel inspired by our situation. I used to go to museums to write because they were heated. Museums were like my home. I spent months walking throughout London, frozen to the bones in the rain and snow, to find a suitable home for my parents, where they would live comfortably but also rent a few rooms. I thought I would then leave for Israel.

Gordon: How did you and your husband David Littman meet in the UK?

Bat Ye'or: Other Jewish refugees put us in contact with a Jewish organization helping Egyptian refugees. They assisted us in every way, advising and providing us with a card allowing us to get warm clothing from Marks & Spencer. When I found a house on London's outskirt, in Ealing Broadway, the Jewish organization gave us small loans. From October when we arrived in London till April, I spent six months walking throughout the London fog and rain or writing in museums. I knew no one and had become a kind of aggressive animal always hungry and cold fighting despair by creating fictional characters totally lost in the fog of life.

The Jewish organization gave me a one year grant to study at the London University, Institute of Archeology. There I met David. He offered me biscuits at the break in the cafeteria. It was often the only thing I ate during the long hours I spent at the Institute. David and I shared a love for archeology, museums, history and art. My teachers were not happy with me because I was writing my novels during their courses, and I was a rebellious student. David immediately felt the need to protect and advise me in spite of my bad character. We met every day at the university and we took the same underground line back home. David's station was Holland Park, less that half mine, but often he stayed with me till I arrived and went back on the same line. At this time we led the life of penniless students, but we were young, both idealists living in the world of ideas, music and art.

Life in London was harsh. With trepidation, I had to adapt constantly to new situations which were often painful. However, I discovered liberty there and a whole new intellectual atmosphere that I missed so much in Egypt. In England, people were polite, welcoming, warm and helpful. Escaping from Egyptian bondage and racist hatred, I discovered on this grey, cold English island, human kindness and the incommensurable world of culture and knowledge. All while going through misery and distress.

Gordon: Following your marriage in 1959, both you and your husband were involved in Operation Mural, the covert effort to help Jewish children emigrate from Morocco to Israel on behalf of the Jewish Agency. Could you tell us about that undertaking and the recent honors bestowed on your family by the State of Israel?

Bat Ye'or: After the birth of my first child, I wanted to do a mitzvah. I felt I had received so much that I had a debt to pay back to the Jewish people. In Egypt, I felt international and rejected religious belonging. However, in England I realized that I was ejected from Egypt because I was Jewish. In my exiled loneliness, foreigners came to help us because we were Jewish. I then understood where my place was and to which people I belonged.

We lived temporarily in Lausanne, my husband was reading William Shirer's book on the genocide of European Jewry, *The Rise and Fall of the Third Reich*. He was shocked and accepted a proposal that came by chance to go to Morocco and secretly rescue Jewish children. Jews were forbidden then to leave Morocco. We went on a voluntary basis without being paid. My husband did not know how dangerous it was to work for a Zionist organization in a Muslim country, but I knew that we risked death or years in jail. I took my daughter with me, in my student straw bag, and was pregnant with my second daughter.

We went undercover as Christians working for a Swiss organization. There we were contacted by a Zionist underground which we didn't know, was Israeli. My husband did a fantastic job and in a few months managed to send from Morocco to Israel, via Switzerland and France, 530 children. Their parents followed by other means. However, having accomplished that, we had to leave in haste. That was Operation Mural, my husband's code name. Recently, a film was done on Operation Mural and shown at the San Francisco Jewish Film Festival in 2009. Israeli President Shimon Peres received us as did the whole Israeli and Moroccan Jewish clandestine network involved in this operation. In 2009 my husband received the "Hero of Silence" Order from the Israel Intelligence Heritage & Commemoration Centre. It was a strong acknowledgment of his total dedication to this operation saving Moroccan Jewish children from bondage to bring them to freedom. We liked the Moroccans we met. However, we rejected the Jewish immigration policy of the King that forced us to act in the way we did.

Gordon: What prompted your life long scholarly investigations into Islamic Jihad and Dhimmitude - the treatment of non-Muslim minorities under Islam?

Bat Ye'or: I never expected I would do such research. I was a novelist writing a long historical novel on the Egyptian Jewish community and while reading hundreds of books and researching for this novel, I discovered the dhimmi condition. This book was refused by a publisher because the historical material was too heavy. I extracted it and wrote a short, factual historical book. I thought then that I would go back to my novel, but I developed the historical book for a Hebrew edition. Then I noticed that the ignorance on these topics were so immense that I decided to publish a book of documents. The French political and academic world was totally opposed to my views. It took me three years to find a publisher. I had to be very careful in writing *Le Dhimmi*. Strangley enough, Christians were more interested than Jews. They requested that I develop and research these same themes and I never went back to my novels. I realized that writing novels on the dhimmi, forced me to examine the documents through other perspectives than just historical, in order to penetrate the humanity, soul, and human experience of dhimmi – a study which I introduced into my writing.

Gordon: What is "dhimmitude" and how did the term originate?

Bat Ye'or: The term originated when, at the request of Lebanese Christian friends, I extended my research from the condition of the Jewish dhimmi to the Christian. I realized then that I had to deal with a total different situation. The impact of Islam on Christianity triggered mechanisms in every sector of the Christian state, demography, culture and society that aimed at transforming a Christian country, population and culture into an Islamic society. The phenomenon started always with a Muslim minority within a Christian majority and ended with a Muslim majority governing a Christian subdued minority on the way to its extinction. I studied the religious, juridical, demographical factors of these evolutions over 13th centuries and called these encompassing well structured mechanisms "dhimmitude." Hence dhimmitude is a complex historical evolution linked to Islam's relations with non-Muslims. It is correlated to the jihad ideology and jurisdiction and integrated into the shariah. It is rooted into the Koran, the Sunnah and the biographies of the Prophet Muhammad. In other words it is within the very core of Islam.

While I was doing my research, I was looking for a term that would contain all those complex interactions of correlated factors. I founded the word dhimmitude and I discussed it with my Lebanese friends without daring to write it in articles since I was so much abused just in using the word dhimmi. My friend spoke about this word to Bashir Gemayel who used it in his last speech before his assassination. Years later a Lebanese Christian told me that because Gemayel spoke of dhimmitude, Christians would then accept it, but that they would never had accepted it from me. I thought then that chance favored me because dhimmitude is the most important concept to understand in order to face the XXI century's challenges.

Gordon: Over four decades you have published seminal works in the study of dhimmitude, beginning in 1971 with *Les Juifs en Egypte* and *The Dhimmi*, translated into English in 1985, that established you as an international scholar. Could you outline the major historical themes of these works on dhimmitude and the controversies they spawned?

Bat Ye'or: The major themes consist in studying the various and different levels of the process of religious, social and political Christian disintegration linked to dhimmitude. I also added the psychological elements which were not considered before. Countless works analyzed or just mentioned among other topics, the condition of Jews and Christians in Islam. My contribution into this domain was to make it into a special discipline and to give it a name. Naming objects or concepts provides the minds with conceptual tools allowing the classification of elements; they can then be recognized and placed into a structure.

I had already done this work with the dhimmi, and I was attacked because I made of the dhimmi condition a special category. For me it enters into a social, religious, legal category among others developed by human societies because it had a legal structure. It is not happening by chance. The dhimmi condition is integrated into a determined policy with its ideological and legal structure like the system of slavery or apartheid. Its constitutive elements can be recognized unchanged throughout the centuries and the lands where Islamic law is implemented.

Other critics were scandalized because I had put Jews and Christians together into the same dhimmi category. This was of course a political and racist view rooted in the conviction that Christians couldn't be in the same category of the devilish Jews. The proponents of this opinion militated for a Christian-Muslim alliance against the Jews, whom they accused of causing conflicts between Muslims and them. My view on the dhimmi, a common condition for Jews and Christians together oppressed by the same Muslim law, followed by my conceptualization of dhimmitude, couldn't be more horrific to them.

I also underlined the fact that the so-called protection granted to the dhimmi was a protection against the threats of jihad: death, slavery or forced conversion imposed by Muslim law on non-Muslims. Hence the toleration came within a condemnation. Such protection does not deserve any admiration or gratitude from its victims, because it belongs to an unjust system that denies to non-Muslims the right to live. It is tolerant only in the Islamic conception of justice. If we say that it is tolerant, it implies that we agree with the first condition: the condemnation.

My discussion on the specificities of Islamic tolerance clarified the fallacies of this notion and its superficiality. This point also brought me many enemies since the belief in the justice of Islamic law and therefore in the justice of the system of dhimmitude is a religious obligation for Muslims and therefore for the cohorts of their supporters in the West. I recognize of course that my researches are far from being perfect and should be improved and corrected, but the controversies were spawned more by politics or antisemitism than by historical arguments.

My books also demonstrated that slavery was not practiced only by the West; Islam practiced it on a much larger and longer scale. Likewise the wars of conquest, colonialism and imperialism were much more pursued by Muslims than by Christians. Those historical facts were acrimoniously opposed by Europeans. My publications on the persecution of Christians in Muslim countries, raised suspicion and hate from Christian pro-palestinian sectors. All in all, my work couldn't be more opposed to the European policy of alliances and integration with the Muslim world, based on a common Euro-Arab hatred of Israel. Europe was involved in the creation of Palestine and the weakening, the demise of Israel.

Gordon: You published an essay in the *National Review* in 2002 that led to a major work, *Eurabia: The Euro–Arab Axis,* published in 2005. Could you tell us the origins of the term, your book's principal thesis and its implications for the future of the EU, UK and even America?

Bat Ye'or: This term Eurabia was created by European politicians and intellectuals that militated from the late 1960s for the Palestinians and a Euro-Arab rapprochement, and even a Euro-Arab symbiosis around the Mediterranean. This movement was antisemitic and anti-American, it gathered many former Nazis and their supporters and collaborators in European countries. It was supported by the French Ministry of Foreign Affairs. In 1973 it became an unofficial but organized policy of the European Community and its executive office, the European Commission, together with the Arab League.

My book examines the numerous official texts, policies and decisions generated by the ideology of Eurabia and their consequences in the countries of the European Community, on their domestic and international affairs. I analyze these transformations within the dhimmitude historical framework since the Muslim world's relations with the non-Muslim world has not changed. The implications for the West are its Islamization and the destruction of the Judeo-Christian civilization, the phenomenon that I have examined in its historical development since the seventh century in its various modalities throughout numerous lands.

Gordon: What do you believe is behind the condonment of Islamic doctrine, adoption of Islamic law, in Western legal systems and the rise of de facto self-governing Muslim areas in the EU and UK?

Bat Ye'or: There are many factors. First, Western demography is weak and our population are aging and rich. Moreover Westerners abhor wars. Two world wars produced genocides, hecatombs and incommensurable sufferings. Our Western leaders know perfectly well the history of jihad and its consequences on non-Muslims. Precisely for this reason, they chose a policy of appeasement and rapprochement with the Muslim world, taking also in consideration the economic and energy factors, as well as tactical alliances against other states. I do not think that the Eurabian project had foreseen the consequences of a massive Muslim presence in the West, but now our leaders cannot conceive another policy than submission, dhimmitude and Islamization of their own countries by multiculturalism and globalization. This policy adheres to materialist and opportunist considerations under the guise of humanitarian aims; it is devoid of any ethic and morality.

Gordon: How dangerous do you believe are those Stealth Jihad threats to the future of Western civilization and Judeo-Christian values?

Bat Ye'or: Stealth jihad exists in every sector of Western society, in law, culture, schools, universities, policies, banking, economics, media. The aim is to destroy the Judeo-Christian values and to Islamize Western societies, following the thousand years of Islamic conquest of Christian lands. They are helped in the West by the promoters of multiculturalism and the Left.

Gordon: Why in your view have EU elites and mainstream media dismissed the threats implied by *Eurabia*?

Bat Ye'or: Some dismissed them by personal political interests and lust; others because they wanted like the Nazis, to destroy the Christian civilization rooted in Judaism and loved Islam. Christian traitors joining and supporting the Muslim forces against their own people represent a permanent and strong current in the Muslim-Christian interactions and wars throughout history. Now, they are deadly afraid of terrorism if they dare change policy. As for the media, I consider that it obeys the orders of the Organization of Islamic Cooperation (OIC) that represents the Ummah, the universal Muslim community. The OIC is working at all levels with European leaders and Western leaders. The blasphemy laws punishing the criticism of Islam are implemented in the West at the request of the OIC. Likewise European countries adopted a recent decision to teach religions in schools because the OIC insisted upon it.

Gordon: Who do you consider allies in the EU and America in furthering your *Eurabia* thesis of the threat of Islamization to the future of the West?

Bat Ye'or: Every European is aware of Europe's transformation under the pressure of massive Muslim immigration. Some Muslims are perfectly integrated and oppose the Islamization of European school teaching, culture, law, society. No European or American well integrated in its Western and Judeo-Christian culture could possibly welcome its replacement by a Koranic shariah society, imposing its religious conception of history which affirms that jihad is just and resistance to jihad is aggression. Nor could he accept the discriminated condition of the women, the denial of the equality of human beings, and the restrictions on knowledge. Hence, to answer your questions, I would say that this problem, that has been obfuscated by our leaders for so long, is not my problem but a worry to all Westerners.

Gordon: You have developed the term "Palestinism." Could you explain that term and why it is at the root of Europe's decline and the isolation of Israel?

Bat Ye'or: Palestinism is a world policy initiated and imposed by the OIC and its Western allies that aims to transfer to Palestinian Muslims the history, and the cultural and religious heritage of the Jewish people. The origin of this belief is in the Koran which states that the Bible is a falsification and that the biblical figures, including Jesus and the apostles were all Muslim prophets who preached Islam. This theory suppresses Jewish and Christian history and legitimacy. Palestinism struggles to eliminate Israel and replace it with a Muslim Palestine since it is based on the Islamization of the Bible.

Palestinism is also a political and theological current working for the Islamization of Christianity by replacing its Jewish biblical roots by the Koranic interpretation of the Bible. The promoter of such theology is the Sabeel Christian Center in Jerusalem that teaches Christians the Islamic interpretation of the Bible.

Palestinism is at the base of the whole Eurabian construct, European dhimmitude and the submission of Western leaders. Palestinism encompasses all Western-Muslim relationships, this is the reason why the West has made the creation of Palestine and the destruction of Israel the most urgent topics of the planet. This is also in obedience to the OIC who made of Palestinism/antisemitism the base of its policy with the West and its subjugation. Support for the Palestinians is the guaranty for Europe's security. Westerners have paid billions of jizya (tribute) to the Palestinians as a protection from terrorism. The OIC obliges the West to deny Israel's rights and adopt the Islamic conception of history where Jewish and Christian rights to their history and culture are denied as we have seen recently with the Islamization of the Hebrew Patriarch tombs in Hebron by UNESCO.

Palestinism makes the destruction of Israel a universal duty.

Gordon: In the United States a grass roots movement has arisen seeking to bar adoption of Shariah law in our American legal system. Three states, Arizona, Louisiana and Tennessee, have enacted anti-Sharia laws. Other State legislatures are considering similar legislation. Do you view that as a positive sign, despite objections raised by Muslim Brotherhood front groups and civil liberties allies in the US?

Bat Ye'or: It is a positive sign because Shariah law follows Koranic values that are opposed to ours and applies the Declaration of Human Rights in Islam which are in many ways contrary to the Universal Declaration of Human Rights.

Gordon: Given the eruption of the Arab Spring in the Middle East, what do you see as the ultimate outcome?

Bat Ye'or: I am quite pessimist. There is no base or structure in any Arab country for democratic governments. The extremists and the Muslim Brotherhood will control the whole area and will work to reestablish the 7th century caliphate and its jihadist ideology of world conquest. Shariah and democracy are antinomic.

Gordon: How imperiled do you believe is America's long term support for Israel in the wake of the Arab Spring?

Bat Ye'or: The enemy Israel is facing is America's enemy, and if

Americans do not understand it, America will disappear.

Gordon: Your new book, *Europe, Globalization, and the Coming Universal Caliphate*, expands upon your original thesis in *Eurabia*. Can that dark prospect somehow be reversed, and defeated?

Bat Ye'or: It can if the West understands the complex and various aspects of this confrontation, but we are far from that.

16
NINA SHEA
NOVEMBER 2011

Apostasy and blasphemy under Islamic Shariah laws have received considerable attention since February 14, 1989 when Ayatollah Khomeini, the founding Supreme Ruler of the Islamic Republic of Iran, issued a death fatwa with a $5.2 million bounty against Indian-born British author, Salman Rushdie for publishing his fourth novel, *The Satanic Verses*. Rushdie's comments the prior day during a CBS Morning News program, were prescient:

> Frankly, I wish I had written a more critical book. I mean, a religion that claims, that is able to behave like this; religious leaders, let's say, who are able to behave like this, and then say that this is a religion which must be above any kind of whisper or criticism, that doesn't add up. It seems to me that Islamic fundamentalists could do with a little bit of criticism right now.

The title of Rushdie's novel was a reference to his spoofing of Mohammed and the controversial Qur'anic verses invoking three goddesses in the pantheon at the Kabah in Mecca which were used by Mohammed to entreat converts to the new monotheist faith (See Q: 19-20, Q.22:52 and Q. 53: 19-23).

What followed in the wake of that ruling by the Shiite Supreme Ruler Khomeini were incidents of book burnings, riots, many deaths and injuries, assassinations and terror bombings in Pakistan, India, Japan, Turkey, the UK and even the US.

That defining episode came at the conclusion of a decade long war between Shiite Iran and Sunni-dominated Iraq in which millions of lives were sacrificed in a contest of wills between the totalitarian Shiite theocracy versus the Sunni Arab autocracy. In the end, Iran capitulated and Khomenei died in June, 1989 within months of issuing the Rushdie fatwa. Iraq became the super-power in the Gulf region. The late Saddam Hussein then fomented the First Gulf War in 1990-1991 by invading Kuwait only to be toppled in the US-led Second Gulf War in 2003.

Closely following the issuance of Khomeini's death fatwa, Salman Rushdie went into 24/7 witness protection provided by the UK Home Secretary, after issuing a formal notice of contrition that he later repudiated. While nominally a Muslim, it was not until much later that Rushdie revealed that he was an apostate, someone who had left Islam by personal choice. As such, Rushdie could be subject to corporeal punishment including death as a political traitor to Islam[1] with or without a formal fatwa.

The 57 member Muslim nation Organization of the Islamic Conference (OIC) (renamed in 2011, the Organization of Islamic Cooperation) issued the Islamic version of the 1948 UN Universal Declaration of Human Rights (UNDHR) in Cairo in 1990. Article 18 of the UNDHR made it an inalienable right for a person to change his or her religious persuasion by personal choice. The First Amendment of the U.S. Constitution mandates protection of the rights of citizens in the exercise of freedom of worship and freedom of speech, including criticism of a religion. Those international and national covenants were clearly in conflict with the blasphemy provisions of Islamic law. The stage was then set for a two decade long effort by the OIC to introduce annual resolutions at the UN General Assembly and the UN Human Rights Council (UNHRC) seeking the criminalization of "blasphemy," the implication being, that Islam was the *prima partes*. The cartoon of Mohammed as a terrorist wearing a bomb-shaped turban drawn by Kurt Westergaard

---

1 See: Ibn Rushd (Averroes), The Distinguished Jurist's Primer, "Chapter on the Hukm of the Murtadd (Apostate)," Volume II, (p. 552), Section 56.10; Ahmad ibn Naqib al-Misri, *Reliance of the Traveller*, translation approved by Al-Azhar Islamic Research Academy and IIIT, 1994 (p. 595); Shaikh Syed Abul A'ala Maududi, Pakistani Islamic authority, The Punishment of the Apostate According to Islamic Law, translation by Syed Silas Husain, 1994 and Louay Safi, the former Executive Director of IIIT and the Executive Director of the Islamic Society of North America (ISNA) Leadership Development Center, Peace and the Limits of War, IIIT publication, 2003 (p. 25).

published in 2005 by the Danish newspaper *Jyllands-Posten* triggered riots across the Muslim world causing wide spread property damage and more than 200 deaths in 2006. The OIC manipulated those riots and brought pressure on the Council of Europe (COE) to review Article 10 of the European Convention on Human Rights governing free speech with regard to blasphemy. A COE information document noted an important change adopted in 2008:

> The European Commission for Democracy through Law (Venice Commission) concluded that in a democracy religious groups must, as any other groups, tolerate criticisms in public statements and debates related to their activities, teachings and beliefs, as long as the criticisms do not constitute deliberate and gratuitous insults or hate speech, an incitement to disturb public order, violence or discrimination towards people who adhere to specific religions.

In March of 2011, the UNHRC passed Resolution 1618 "Combating intolerance, negative stereotyping and stigmatization of, and discrimination, incitement to violence, and violence against persons based on religion or belief."

According to the Washington-based Human Rights First group this would amount to a victory in pushback against OIC efforts endeavoring to impose criminalization of "blasphemy" under Islamic doctrine. Human Rights First has identified scores of cases that provide ample warning of the misuse of blasphemy laws at the national level. The organization's study, *Blasphemy Laws Exposed*, documented over 70 such cases in 15 countries where the enforcement of blasphemy laws have resulted in death sentences and long prison terms as well as arbitrary detentions, and have sparked assaults, murders and mob attacks. In July of 2011, an international meeting was held in Istanbul involving Foreign Ministers from the EU, Members of the Arab League, Representatives of the Vatican, US Secretary Clinton and the Secretary General of the OIC. Conspicuous by its absence was the State of Israel. The objective of the international gathering at the Yildiz Palace in Istanbul was to implement UNHRC resolution 1618. Secretary Clinton said:

> In Europe, we are seeing communities coming together to address both the old scourge of antisemitism and the new strains of anti-Muslim bias that continue to undermine the continent's

democratic ideals. Across the Middle East and Asia, we look to both people and leaders to resist the incitement of extremists who seek to inflame sectarian tensions, and reject the persecution of religious minorities such as the Copts or Ahmadis or Baha'is.

Secretary Clinton then issued an invitation to hold a summit in Washington in December of 2011 with the OIC to discuss implementation of UNHRC Res. 1618. The *Islam Exposed* blog said when the UNHRC resolution was up for a vote in March of 2011:

> The resolution represents a change of tactics, not strategic objectives. It is designed to deceive human rights activists, and it appears to be a success.

Given these developments, we invited Nina Shea, human rights lawyer and advocate, Director of the Washington, DC-based Stonegate Institute Center for Religious Freedom and co-author with Center Senior fellow, Paul Marshall of *Silenced: How Apostasy and Blasphemy Codes are Choking Freedom Worldwide* to discuss these issues. Ms. Shea is also a Commissioner of the Congressionally-chartered US Commission on International Religious Freedom.

Gordon: What are blasphemy and apostasy under doctrinal Islam?

Shea: The traditional formulation of Islam calls for punishment by death for blasphemy and apostasy. These offenses are actually not defined and there is a mixing of the terminology, blending together blasphemy, apostasy, insulting Islam, defaming Islam and heresy. All of these terms are used interchangeably. They are applied differently from country to country and from place to place. They change over time and from jurisdiction to jurisdiction, they expand and contract. What is prevailing Islamic doctrine on both blasphemy and apostasy is extremely subjective depending on who is doing the interpreting. Paul Marshall and I have surveyed several leading Muslim countries in our new book *Silenced*, which shows this. *Silenced* is a survey on the human rights impact of contemporary blasphemy and apostasy codes in leading Muslim counties today; it is not a theological study.

Gordon: When did blasphemy and apostasy laws first gain world attention in the 20th Century?

Shea: It began with the 1989 fatwa by Iran's Ayatollah Khomeini against Salman Rushdie for his novel, *The Satanic Verses*. That was the first time that the world took note in the modern period of a demand by a Muslim power that Western governments coerce compliance within their borders of Islamic rules restricting speech. Few realize that this push started with and is pushed now primarily by governments. It is the governmental promotion of this within the UN and on the level of nation states that has given this movement traction and ensured it could not be marginalized. Soon after Khomeini's fatwa was issued, Sunni powers like Saudi Arabia and Pakistan, while not associating themselves directly with the Iranian Shiite regime's fatwa, also joined in this campaign to force the West to conform to Islamic expectations regarding blasphemy; they worked largely through the Organization of Islamic Cooperation (OIC) – an international body with 56 member states. Horrible events ensued. Rushdie's Japanese translator was murdered. Four other collaborators on the book, including translators throughout Europe were violently attacked. A hotel was blown up killing over a score of people in Turkey because his Turkish publisher was staying there. Two California bookstores carrying *The Satanic Verses* were firebombed. Khomeini's fatwa sent Rushdie into hiding.

Gordon: What is the agenda of the Organization of Islamic Cooperation (OIC) encouraging the global spread of codes opposing blasphemy and apostasy?

Shea: There is a twofold agenda. One is the religious agenda to make the world – especially the West -- comply with Islamic laws on blasphemy and apostasy. The other is a political agenda to draw attention away from the dismal human rights records of leading members of the OIC. We saw that occur in the U.N with both Sudan and Iran who were under scrutiny, criticism and condemnation by human rights bodies for stoning women and girls accused of adultery. Instead the OIC aims to put Western countries in the dock for not regulating speech on behalf of a religious institution, letting their citizens ridicule or criticize Islam. This would turn the international human rights system on its head.

Gordon: Why is this development a threat to religious freedom and free speech, under international human and civil rights laws?

Shea: The OIC has diplomatically pushed for an international blasphemy law for twenty years. It has given respectability to the demands of a mad man like Ayatollah Khomeini or the late Osama bin Laden. It gives authority and financial backing to push this campaign. It is reinforced by violence as we saw in the firebombing of the French satirical magazine *Charlie Hebdo* after it ran a spoof on sharia law in Tunisia with a cartoon of Mohammed. The OIC has made headway particularly in Europe where just a few years ago a so called framework document was adopted by the EU. It calls for the mandatory adoption of criminal hate speech laws to punish citizens in European countries if they criticize, denigrate or stereotype on the basis of religion, particularly when it concerns certain minorities like Muslims. Virtually all 47 member states of the Council of Europe now have hate speech laws, which can be used as proxies for Islamic blasphemy laws.

Gordon: Has the U.S. been complicit in the spread of these codes?

Shea: The U.S. has a strong Constitutional First Amendment. To date we haven't seen the capitulation like in Western Europe, Canada or Australia to this push to have the state regulate speech on behalf of Islam. However, we have seen other very disturbing developments. Mostly because of violence, threats and intimidation, we have seen self-censorship, particularly among establishment institutions and government agencies. For example, the US Department of Homeland Security and the State Department issued speech guidelines or terminology codes to its employees that forbid the use of the terms Salafist, Caliphate or Jihadist. That makes it very difficult for America's policy professionals to analyze world events. Current headlines reveal that Salafi groups are threatening to gain or influence power in Egypt and Libya. How can our foreign policy makers even grasp what is going on if they can't use these terms? Then there are academic institutions, publishing houses, and the press, refusing to take on certain issues regarding Islam or present negative critiques of Islam. Yale University Press refused to publish a page from the Danish newspaper that had cartoons of Mohammed in it. That was for a scholarly book advertised as the "definitive work" on the Danish cartoon crisis. Unfortunately, there are a growing number of such examples.

Gordon: Did the Obama administration join with Egypt in furthering the agenda of the OIC?

Shea: Yes. And that's the second troubling development I had in mind. The Obama Administration has gone down a path of trying to find common ground with the OIC on this issue. One of their efforts was a UN Human Rights Council (UNHRC) hate speech Resolution in 2009 that the US co-sponsored with Egypt, which represented the OIC. That resolution calls for states to implement religious hate speech legislation. It was clearly directed at criticism of Islam. But the problem didn't start there. It started with the June 2009 speech that President Obama gave in Cairo. That speech had a little noticed statement to the effect that Obama understands that it is part of his responsibility as President to do everything he can to fight against "negative stereotyping of Islam" wherever it appears: Note, he was calling for shielding from critical speech the religion of Islam, not Muslims, and not any other religion. What that means we don't quite know yet. However, that speech has been a blueprint for the administration's foreign policy with the Muslim world. One of the things that grew out of it was the UNHRC resolution in 2009. There is now a new step: The Obama Administration has invited the OIC to a conference in Washington in December to discuss how to combat speech that negatively stereotypes Islam. Secretary of State Hillary Clinton announced this when she co-chaired an OIC conference in Istanbul, Turkey, last July. She says that the implementation measures will not include laws limiting speech but the OIC representatives make clear that that is precisely what they aim to achieve at the Washington conference. It is a scandal that the US is partnering on an issue regarding free speech with an organization like the OIC that is committed to undermining free speech.

Gordon: In your book you discuss reformists within the Muslim Ummah. Who are they, what are their general messages and why have they been rejected and their lives threatened?

Shea: The foreword to our new book was written by the late Indonesian President, Abdurrahman Wahid who was also head of the largest Muslim association in the world. He was a respected Islamic scholar. His foreword is entitled, "God Needs No Defense." He makes the case that there is really no Qur'anic authority for punishing sins of blasphemy, apostasy and heresy in this world. Similar arguments are made by two other well known Islamic scholars, Abdullah Saeed from the Maldives and Abu-Zayd from Egypt, both of whom also wrote essays for *Silenced*. We include these three scholars to show - not that they are a dominant or even majority opinion, they're not - but that there is a debate occurring now within Islam and that we should be supporting the pro-freedom side of that debate. These are the very ones needed to reconcile Islam with the modern pluralistic world. Abu-Zayd had to flee Egypt and seek asylum in the Netherlands. He was driven out because of accusations that he was a heretic after he tried to introduce a reformist interpretation of Islam. Egypt was purportedly a secular country at that time, which shows the potency of these charges. Abdullah Saeed is in exile in Australia. He wrote a book against the temporal punishment for apostasy and blasphemy, pointing out that punishment for such offenses in the early Islamic period occurred in a certain context that made them akin to treason today and that it is time to rethink this issue. That did not go over well with some and he was seriously threatened.

There are other Muslims that we write about who are trying to get this conversation underway, but it's extremely difficult because there is a circularity to this issue. For example, in Afghanistan, an editor wrote an article saying that that country's apostasy and blasphemy laws should be repealed so that there can be greater intellectual debate, exploration and discussion about women's rights, and as a result he was arrested and faced the death penalty for blasphemy (he was eventually pardoned). Pakistan offers another example: Punjab Governor Salman Taseer was assassinated this year for blasphemy after he called for the blasphemy law there to be repealed. The assassin was treated as a hero by the lawyers association and many others and when he was convicted of murder, the judge who convicted him had to flee for his life. It is extremely difficult to overturn blasphemy laws when you are punished for being blasphemous by suggesting it. That is another reason, in addition to protecting our own liberties, why it is so important for the West to resist this push. If moderate Muslims are ever going to be heard, they need political space. Europe is already putting its citizens on trial for crimes of insulting, denigrating or vilifying Islam; this means that even in the West the most extreme Muslims will be given a platform within society to exert power. At a minimum, if the US co-sponsors with the OIC of initiatives to stop the negative stereotyping of Islam, it is betraying the victims of blasphemy charges abroad and validating the repressive agenda of that organization.

Gordon: In your book you also pay attention to valiant heroes of freedom of religion, minority Christians particularly in Pakistan who have been murdered by mobs. Is that a reflection of the mob-rule in an Islamic country and is it exemplary of developments elsewhere in the Ummah?

Shea: In the Muslim world, when particular states have policies to punish persons for blasphemy it is often thought that such policies will advance social peace and national harmony. In fact it is just the opposite. It fans the flames of bigotry and hatred. It gives the most radical elements within Islam a platform to exert power from within society. In Pakistan, accusations of blasphemy are hurled like weapons – against business rivals, unpopular teachers, other sects, neighbors. There are false accusations of Qur'an burnings that have triggered pogroms against Christians and minority Muslim sects. The existence of a blasphemy law actually exacerbates extra-judicial mob violence. This year saw the assassination of a friend of mine, Shahbaz Bhatti, the sole Christian member of Pakistan's Cabinet. He was Minister for Minority Affairs, and was calling for the repeal of the blasphemy laws. Christians and minority Ahmadi Muslims are extremely vulnerable. The Ahmadi are banned from worshipping in mosques in Pakistan. They cannot vote or obtain passports without signing a document renouncing their faith. Christians' testimony in court is not given full weight so a simple accusation by a Muslim is enough to convict them when they are accused of blasphemy—no evidence is needed. Blasphemy and apostasy laws fan popular hatreds of non-Muslims and heterodox minority Muslims.

Blasphemy and apostasy laws are manipulated by politicians and religious leaders for political purposes. That was very clear in the Danish cartoon case where the whole Muslim world appeared to rise up at once in outrage over the small Danish paper publishing political caricatures of Mohammed. According to the findings of the Yale University Press book that exhaustively investigated the subject, that violence was an orchestrated political reaction from countries in the Middle East like Iran and Syria who were pushing back against Western sanctions regarding their nuclear weapons development programs. There was also anger from autocratic Arab governments about the Bush freedom agenda at the time, especially from Egypt and Saudi Arabia. So political motives led to manufactured outrage. Polls showed that extraordinary large percentages of people in Egypt and in the West Bank had heard of the Danish cartoons despite the fact that these are very closed systems where censorship is prevalent and they rank very low on freedom of expression indices. They tend to know what their governments want them to know. Another example occurred in Afghanistan last year when riots and murders followed the burning of a Koran by an obscure Florida church; note that no violent protest registered from the heart of the Islamic world, in Arab countries. The violent reaction in Afghanistan alone reflected grievances against the US in Afghanistan more than anything else. The manipulation of the issues of blasphemy and apostasy offences occur to direct violence within Muslim societies, too, not just against foreigners on the international level.

Gordon: With the eruption of the so called Arab Spring, do you think there are diminished prospects for the minority Christian presence in the Middle East?

Shea: I'm quite concerned that the Christians will not be tolerated, even less so than they were prior to the eruption of the Arab Spring. They will be driven out. We are already seeing that take place in Iraq where half the Christian population has already left. I am very concerned about Egypt because that has the largest Christian and largest religious minority population in the entire Middle East - about 10 million Coptic Christians. The next largest contingents of Christians are in Lebanon, and Syra, each having a million or two.

Gordon: What in your view can this country do to alleviate the continuing persecution of Christians not only in the Middle East but elsewhere in the Muslim world?

Shea: I think there are a number of things the United States can do. One is to condition our aid on removing the laws that repress subjugated minorities. Our government needs to raise its voice and assert influence instead of thinking that it can accomplish more by silence or by blaming both sides. Unfortunately it did that recently in Egypt when the Copts were massacred at a demonstration in Maspero in early October. The White House issued a statement calling for both sides to exercise restraint when one side was clearly the victim of the massacre.

Gordon: You have served as a Commissioner of the U.S. Commission on International Religious Freedom (USCIRF) since its founding in 1999 monitoring religious persecution around the world. What do you deem USCIRF's most significant accomplishments?

Shea: USCIRF is the boldest and clearest voice within the government addressing what is actually happening to Christians, Jews and other minorities like the Ahmadi, the Bahai, and Zoroastrians within these Islamist dictatorships and regimes. Perhaps, the USCRIF's greatest accomplishment was its help in reframing the North - South Civil War in Sudan as a religious conflict. That conflict ignited when the Islamist government in Khartoum, the National Islamic Front of General Bashir, tried to forcibly impose Islamic law on the Christian-animist South and the South rebelled. The North prosecuted its side of the conflict with bombings of the civilian population, forcible mass starvation, forced Islamic conversion and even slavery. The South prevailed with the creation of the Republic of South Sudan in July of this year. That was because of the Comprehensive Peace Agreement brokered by the US in 2005.

For many years prior to the conclusion of the CPA, the secular international human rights groups, the press and our government defined this, not as a conflict over religious freedom, but in terms of a struggle over resources. Their understanding was that tribes in the Sudan were simply fighting over water, then it became a struggle over oil after oil came online in the late 1990s in the country's South. The foreign policy establishment believed this even though Bashir himself called it a "jihad." When USCIRF reframed it in religious terms, this led to certain policy steps that were then adopted by the Bush Administration that led in turn to the independence of South Sudan in July this year and religious freedom for its people. I think that was perhaps the greatest achievement of USCIRF as it affected millions of South Sudanese lives - over two million people had been killed in south and central Sudan in the 19 year war over Islamization. Many thousands of southerners more would have been killed, if secession hadn't happened. We are still seeing the same tactics of enforced starvation and aerial bombardment by the Islamist North in the Nuba Mountains and in Darfur. The Northern Islamist government has perpetrated serial genocide. At least we were able to spare the Christian-animist South from possible extinction.

USCIRF has also pointed out the world's worst abusers of religious freedom. We did not hesitate to put countries like Saudi Arabia or China on that list. The State Department eventually did the same upon our recommendation. This year, USCIRF also named Pakistan and Egypt as egregious religious freedom vioilators and put them on the list; so far, the State Department hasn't done so. Under the International Religious

Freedom Act, the US government is to adopt sanctions or other policies in response to such designation.

We also did something that the State Department has been unwilling to acknowledge. USCIRF was the first official body to blow the whistle on the content of Saudi textbooks -- textbooks calling for the killing of Christians, Jews and members of other religions. We put that issue on the map. The State Department is finally after many years commissioning a study of Saudi textbooks to look at what is inside those books. So I think that we have made some unprecedented calls that may have unsettled many in the Washington establishment. Unfortunately, I think the Commission's mandate is at risk because of those important stands.

Gordon: The enabling legislation for USCIRF is up for reauthorization this year. What are the prospects for its reauthorization now pending before the Congress?

Shea: That won't be known until November 18th. The House passed its reauthorization bill, overwhelmingly. It was also considered non-controversial and was expected to pass easily in the Senate. But it is now in danger of being killed in the US Senate. A senator in the Democratic leadership has a secret hold on it, for which he has not explained his reasons or even acknowledged that he has a hold on it. Other senators must persuade him to withdraw that hold on reauthorization if US-CIRF is to continue. Readers should press their senators to ensure the reauthorization of USCIRF. I am a commissioner on USCIRF and want to emphasize that none of the commissioners are compensated and the budget, set for $3 million, is miniscule by government standards, unlike, for example, the US Institute for Peace, which just built a gigantic building designed by an award winning international architect for holding its dialogue sessions. Unlike the USIP, the religious freedom commission doesn't simply engage in dialogue to talk about finding common ground. We consider religious freedom non-negotiable. We meet with Saudi, Chinese, Turkish and other foreign officials and raise complaints and prisoner cases, and challenge them to stop persecuting Christians, Jews, Baha'is, Ahmadis, Koranists and others. We point to the standards of the Universal Declaration of Human Rights – that every person has the right to choose and practice a religion or no religion at all. We're often the only group with official stature doing so. For example, when we were in Saudi Arabia this year, we saw official American delegations in Riyadh representing oil and military interests, which I don't belittle, but we were the only delegation meeting with the Ministers of Justice, Education and Islamic Affairs about the uncomfortable subjects of religious violence and persecution that are official Saudi policies. We were the only ones pleading for the release of Saudi religious prisoners, for the allowance of churches within the kingdom so that its millions of foreign workers from the Philippines, Ethiopia, Lebanon and elsewhere can have houses of worship, and for the reform of its textbooks, which incite high school students to commit violence against Christians and Jews in the name of Islam.

Gordon: What is it that concerned Americans can do to bring attention to the predicament facing USCIRF at the present time?

Shea: USCIRF is an extremely important element within our government. It has an official voice. When it speaks it has a status that non-govenmental groups like my own Center for Religious Freedom, for example, do not have. USCIRF hasn't flinched in taking a hard look at religious persecution and the lack of freedom in Pakistan, Egypt, Iraq, Nigeria and Saudi Arabia. What can Americans do? It is very urgent that they press their senators to reauthorize it. Reauthorizing means renewing its mandate. To preserve this official government voice for bedrock American freedoms of religious and liberty abroad - which serves both our values and our interests in today's globalized world - Americans should email or call their senators and call for the reauthorization of USCIRF.

Gordon: Among your achievements both at the Center for Religious Freedom and USCIRF has been prodding the Saudi Education Ministry to redact the religious study texts that it uses both in the Kingdom and around the globe through a number of private schools like the Islamic Saudi Academy (ISA) in Northern Virginia. What has been your experience dealing directly with the Saudi Ministry and the ISA in Virginia?

Shea: First, a point of clarification: the textbooks used in Saudi Arabia and posted online by the Saudi government have not been redacted or reformed. When earlier this year, I met with the Saudi Minister of Education in Riyadh, I found out that they do not put a priority on textbooks reform at all. The most problematic textbooks are those that glorify and promote militant jihad to spread Islam, which are high school level textbooks. The Saudi monarch and hence his government ministers have not even begun to revise the high school level texts. Instead, they are engaged with establishing technology institutes for college students. I'm concerned because the people that we are worried about will never get to college. They will be influenced as teenagers by these high school texts and will follow the path of other Saudis who became jihadis or assassins. Bin Laden was educated in Saudi Arabia as were most of the 9/11 terrorists. At the height of the insurgency in Iraq, most of the foreign terrorists captured by our troops were Saudis.

Another problem closer to home is the ISA, a private school in Fairfax County, Virginia, sponsored and controlled by the Royal Saudi Embassy in nearby Washington, DC. That school redacted textbooks two years ago, taking out every passage I had cited in my report for the Center for Religious Freedom of the Hudson Institute. However, I remain suspicious of what it is teaching because the currently redacted texts (it uses Saudi Ministry of Education texts with lessons teaching jihad and directing religious-based violence now blacked out.) make no mention of jihad whatsoever. In effect, ISA textbooks went from describing and teaching jihad as the most important pillar of Islam to saying nothing about it at all. Jihad is a central tenet of Islam and it is crucial - as the Saudis' (highly touted by our government) terrorism reeducation program itself states - that there be a responsible explanation of jihad, that it means self-improvement or what have you. Currently the newly redacted ISA textbooks instruct students, if they have any question about this or any other issue, to refer to Ibn Taymiyyah (1262 to 1328 C.E) who is considered the spiritual theologian of jihad. The West Point Counterterrorism Center Study found him to be the most widely cited authority for Islamist terrorists that had been captured by US troops in Iraq and Afghanistan. It isn't acceptable for the ISA in Virginia to just say nothing about one of the biggest threats of our time. It suggests that the teachers are handing out supplemental materials or perhaps directing students to the Saudi Ministry of Education website where the un-redacted texts continue to be posted, or to other dangerous websites. On this basis, I was able to meet with the Southern private school accreditation agency and convince it to withhold its accreditation of the ISA which it did in 2010. It issued a report stating that the ISA was not transparent, or cooperative, and did not meet the group's criteria. The accrediting agency's determination and my own Saudi textbook analyses can be found on the Stonegate website: http://crf. stonegate.org/.

Gordon: We started this conversation discussing a major event that triggered expansion of Islamic blasphemy and apostasy codes worldwide. That was the death fatwa issued against author Salman Rushdie by Khomeini, Supreme leader of the Iranian Islamic Republic in 1989. Then we had the Saudi-sponsored OIC leading the imposition of blasphemy and apostasy codes on the West. Which of these two extremist jihadist tyrannies, a potentially nuclear Iran or Wahhabist Saudi Arabia, do you view as most dangerous?

Shea: Iran and Saudi Arabia are two faces of the same coin. They are competing for power within the Islamic world. They are doing that by spreading their extremist ideas, exerting force and destabilizing each other's allies. They are both extremely dangerous and both of their agendas are inimical to Western interests. We are going to have a very difficult time dealing with them because our political leaders do not understand the Islamic ideology contest we are facing - a totalitarian ideology that seeks to religiously "cleanse" the Middle East and eventually overcome us by intimidation, violence and most of all by manipulating fear. There has been no serious attempt so far by our government to understand this threat from the contesting ideologies that dominate the Muslim world. Instead, we have an administration in Washington reflexively welcoming the "Arab Spring" as inevitably bringing forth a flowering of individual freedoms and good will toward all. The events there – with the dominance of the Muslim Brotherhood, the emergence of Wahhabi/Salafi groups, the massacre of Egypt's Copts, who are the region's largest non-Muslim minority, the rampant antisemitism and the officially stoked intolerance of the Jewish state of Israel – are shaping up to be just the opposite. We're passively witnessing the empowering of an anti-American, anti-Christian, and anti-Jewish region-wide bloc, and a totalitarian theological iron curtain poised to descend on large parts of the Middle East.

* * *

In our interview with Nina Shea, an appeal was made to concerned Americans to contact their Congressional Representatives and Senators to support renewal of the authority and funding for the US Commission on International Religious Freedom (USCIRF). Shortly after we published our interview with Shea, a minor miracle occurred; the USCIRF received a three year reprieve. We noted this encouraging development in an *Iconoclast* article on December 16, 2011:

> Leonard A. Leo, Chair of the US Commission on International Religious Freedom, is one happy man tonight given the US House of Representatives vote that extended the life of the Congressionally-chartered Capitol Hill human rights group for three years. Tens of millions oppressed religious minorities in the Muslim Ummah will have a valued voice in our Nation's capitol to defend their interests in the West. This positive development can be credited to the original author of the 1998 International Religious Freedom Act, Rep. Frank Wolf (R-VA) and the Members of the House who voted to continued this valued program.

On the other hand, Shea and many others were concerned about the outcome of the State Department meetings with representatives of the OIC, EU and NGOs over implementation of UNHRC Resolution 1618 on combating religious intolerance. Shea noted the "bad idea" of the State Department conference on Islamophobia in a *National Review Online* article:

> Legal and security officials of a delegation which will remain unnamed gave a sweeping overview of American founding principles on religious freedom and how they have been breached time and again in American history by attacks against a broad variety of religious minority groups — including now against Muslims. A raft of current cases was mentioned; America's relative exemplary and distinctive achievement in upholding religious freedom in an emphatically pluralistic society was not. That same speaker reassured the audience, which was packed with diplomats from around the world, that the Obama administration is working diligently to prosecute American Islamophobes and is transforming the U.S. Justice Department into the conscience of the nation, though it could no doubt learn a thing or two from the assembled delegates on other ways to stop persistent religious intolerance in America.
>
> Across the room, smirking delegates from some of the world's most repressive and intolerant regimes could be spotted, furiously taking notes.

The US Departments of Justice and Homeland Security have been charged by the Obama White House to produce proposals on how to implement UNHRC resolution 1618 in the US. This is effectively a capitulation to Shariah blasphemy codes in violation of the free speech guarantees of the First Amendment of the US Constitution.

17
ELISABETH SABADITSCH-WOLFF
NOVEMBER 2011

As 2011 drew to a close, a constellation of events, in the Middle East, Europe and the US have thrust certain doctrinal precepts of Islam which endanger basic Western values such as freedom of speech, into public debate. Terms like Shariah, blasphemy and Islamophobia have entered the mainstream largely at the insistence of the Saudi-based 57-member Organization of Islamic Cooperation (OIC). Bat Ye'or has described this organization in her recent book as the focal point of a rising world-wide Caliphate.

Witness these events. On October 28th, The Organization for Security Cooperation in Europe (OSCE) issued new guidelines for combating Islamophobia at a conference in Vienna followed by a two day forum on November 10 and 11th to discuss implementation at the Secretariat Headquarters at the Hofburg. On November 4th, The Federalist Society for Law and Public Policy Studies held an international symposium on Capitol Hill in Washington, DC to address the topic of *Silenced*: "Are Global Trends to Ban Religious Defamation, Religious Insult, and Islamophobia a New Challenge to First Amendment Freedoms?" On November 11th, the first national conference "The Constitution or Shariah: Preserving Freedom," was held in Nashville, Tennessee with scholars and experts from the US, U.K., Australia and Nigeria addressing the issues of Shariah and the Islamization of America.

This debate has arisen in the wake of more than 17,000 Islamic terror attacks perpetrated by jihadis throughout the last decade. Among them were the attacks of September 11, 2001 in New York and Washington DC, Bali on October 12, 2002, Madrid on March 11, 2004, London on July 7, 2005 and Mumbai on November 26, 2008.

The reaction in the West has been to grapple with combating the reality of Islamic terrorism, while avoiding any reference to the underlying totalitarian jihadist principles masquerading behind the thin veneer of religious practices that passes for Islam.

In place of understanding and action to counter the intolerance of Islamic doctrine, what has eventuated has been a series of dialogues between representatives of the OIC and Western officials. These have occurred at different venues such as the UN Alliance of Civilizations in Madrid, the Council of Europe, the OIC Secretariat in Ankara and at the Secretariat of the Organization for Security Co-operation in Europe (OSCE). These dialogues have a singular objective. That is to deny free speech and the right to criticize a religion, thereby subverting national constitutions and universal human rights laws and declarations and to further the adoption of Islamic Shariah law. Another symposium on blasphemy occured at the State Department in Washington, DC Bottom, when US Secretary of State Hillary Clinton hosted a three day conference on December 12-15th of 2011, with representatives of the OIC, EU and concerned NGOs. Secretary Clinton announced in Ankara in July of 2011, that the conference would address the implementation of guidelines against religious intolerance adopted in a resolution at the UN Human Rights Council in March of 2011.

Arrayed against this attack on freedom of speech is an intrepid band of European critics who have been brought to trial for their criticism of Islam. Among them are the Hon. Geert Wilders of The Netherlands, Lars Hedegaard of Denmark and Elisabeth Sabaditsch-Wolff of Austria. While Wilders has been acquitted in an Amsterdam District Court of all charges, Hedegaard and Wolff have been convicted in municipal courts in Copenhagen and Vienna for daring to tell the truth about doctrinal Islam. Under prevailing EU laws, Islam has been granted preferential status as a recognized religion and granted protection under statutes against "hate speech."

Both Hedegaard and Wolff are courageous free speakers active in the counter-jihad movements in their respective countries and the EU. The lower court decisions have not impeded their willingness to speak out in criticism of the spread of Shariah under official auspices in the EU at the insistence of the OIC. Wolff appealed her lower court decision decision which was, unfortunately, affirmed. She attended the OSCE Islamophobia guidelines conference. In the interview, she paints a picture of abject dhimmi-like acquiescence by the OSCE, and the condonment of Shariah in her native Austria. At the conclusion of our interview with her, she warns America of the dangers of adopting Shariah blasphemy guidelines as outlined at the State Department–sponsored conference on combating religious intolerance. Wolff also describes how through NGOs like the *Burgerbewegung Pax Europa* (Citizens' Movement Pax Europa hereafter "Pax Europa") and The International Civil Liberties Alliance (ICLA) she and others have been able to combat the implementation of Islamic doctrine at these international forums.

Gordon: What is the OSCE?

Wolff: The Organization for Security Cooperation in Europe (OSCE) is the largest regional security organization. It puts the political will of its participating states into practice through its field missions. There are 56 states from Europe, Central Asia, and North America who are participating states. The OSCE has a comprehensive approach that encompasses political, military, economic and environmental, as well as, human rights aspects. These are called dimensions. These 56 states span the globe encompassing three continents and more than one billion people. What is important to mention about the human rights dimension is that discussion of human rights had been a long standing taboo in East/West relations and these human rights then became, by virtue of the 1975 Helsinki Final Act, a legitimate subject of dialogue. The COSCE was originally called the Conference for Security and Co-operation prior to the establishment of the OSCE. The Organization has been instrumental in keeping the spotlight on human rights.

Gordon: Who are OSCE participating states?

Wolff: OSCE participating states are all of the countries in Europe, Russia, the former Russian Republics, Kazakhstan, Turkmenistan etc, Canada and the United States.

Gordon: Who are the OSCE co-operating partners in the Middle East, Asia and Oceania?

Wolff: The co-operating partners in the Middle East are Algeria, Egypt, Israel, Jordan, Morocco and Tunisia. There are also co-operating partners in Asia which are Japan, South Korea, Thailand, Afghanistan and Mongolia. Australia became a co-operating partner in 2009.

Gordon: What members of the OIC belong to the OSCE and its cooperating partners?

Wolff: The member states of the OIC that are also partners in the OSCE are Turkey, which is a participating state and the co-operating partners as I mentioned before, Algeria, Egypt, Jordan, Morocco, Tunisia, and Afghanistan.

Gordon: Where is the Secretariat for the OSCE located?

Wolff: The main Secretariat for the OSCE is located right here in Vienna in the Vienna Hofburg which used to be the seat of the former Austro-Hungarian empire, i.e., the Emperor himself resided in the Hofburg. The OSCE Office for Democratic Institutions and Human Rights (ODIHR) has its headquarters in Warsaw, Poland.

Gordon: What is the OSCE ODIHR?

Wolff: The ODIHR is the specialized institution dealing with elections, human rights and democratization, as well as tolerance and non-discrimination. ODIHR has an important role to fulfill in facilitating dialogue among states, governments and very importantly, civil society. Let me also add here that the role of civil society is a very important one especially in the human dimension. One of the most significant features of the human dimension is that it is open to the participation of NGO's. Civil society has a vital function both in combating human rights violations and as a voice in the debate on such issues. The participation of NGO's at Human Dimension meetings are on an equal footing with government representatives. This is crucial as it enriches the debate and makes the exchanges more relevant and constructive. The value placed on NGO participation is one of the things that sets apart the Human Dimension from other high level human rights conferences. The NGO's, from states where civil society is weak and constrained, via the Human Dimension meetings, provide one of the few opportunities where their voices can be heard before an international audience. This is crucial in that it is the only possibility for NGO's like Pax Europa, Act for America, ICLA and others to make their voices heard. The registration process is an easy one at the ODIHR website, ODIHR.pl. One can simply register to attend these sessions. We need as many supporters as possible. It doesn't matter whether or not you agree on every single point that we talk about but we need help from other counter-jihad organizations.

Gordon: What occurred at the OSCE meeting on October 28th?

Wolff: The meeting in Vienna on October 28th was focused on confronting intolerance and discrimination against Muslims in public discourse. This was the third in a series of meetings. The first one held in March, 2011 was on confronting antisemitism in public discourse. The second, which was held in Rome in October, covered intolerance against Christians. What was especially worrisome about this third meeting was that the OSCE and other international institutions are talking about terms that have no legal definition. If there are no legal definitions then what are we actually talking about? Let me give you an example from the agenda that was made available on the website. When ODIHR refers to anti-Muslim prejudices and stereotypes, no example is given. The agenda also asks how it is possible to draw a distinction between acceptable and unacceptable speech? Freedom of speech is an absolute concept. Who decides what is acceptable and unacceptable? Since the OIC was present at this meeting one can only assume that it is Shariah law that draws the distinction between acceptable and unacceptable speech.

Gordon: Did the OIC send representatives to that meeting?

Wolff: Yes, definitely. The OIC was very heavily represented with both a high ranking Ambassador to the OSCE as well as NGO's that are definitely linked in support of the OIC. The other representatives were basically the diplomats who represent states that are also members in the OIC. Let me also add regarding that meeting on October 28th that there was a lot of talk about the phenomenon of Islamophobia and how evil it is and that it needs to be combated. In Austria there is definitely no Islamophobia that can be seen in public discourse. Quite the contrary, as the Ministry of Interior actually supports and helps integration. There is a big fund, an integration fund, which has a budget of a couple of million Euros. There are programs called Mentoring for Migrants. There is a Charter of Diversity. There is a State Secretary for Integration who says that it doesn't matter where a person comes from; rather it is only important what this person can contribute to Austrian society.

There are dialogues in Austria. There are intercultural dialogues. There are conferences like, for instance, "Islam in a pluralistic world." The Secretary General of the OIC had a long talk with the former Austrian Foreign Minister, Plassnik, on the topic of "sharing values and combating intolerance." The Minister of Foreign Affairs has installed a task force for intercultural and inter-religious dialogue. It is a partner in the UN Alliance of Civilizations and just a few weeks ago the International King Abdullah Center for Dialogue was opened here in Vienna. What more can one do? Let me also add here that for all of the dialogue that has been going on and taking place for the last fifty years or more, nothing has ever come from them. There are no results from these dialogues. We are talking and talking and talking without any results.

Gordon: Which NGO's attended the Session of the OSCE Conference on Confronting Intolerance and Discrimination Against Muslims in Public Discourse?

Wolff: You had a number of different NGO's concerned with intolerance against Muslims all over Europe. First and foremost is the Turkish NGO based in France, the Council for Justice, Peace and Equality (COJEP). They work closely together with the OIC. When you have COJEP speaking you actually have the OIC speaking.

Gordon: What was the Pax Europa position on the OSCE Islamophobia Guidelines at the October 28th Meetings?

Wolff: The main position of Pax Europa was that it rejects strongly the notion that criticism of religion, i.e., Islam, constitutes Islamophobia. In addition, Pax Europa does not acknowledge the validity of the premises based on "racism." Arguments using the term "racism" employ invalid premises that are empirically untested and have no scientific basis. Pax Europa firmly believes that it cannot be the state's responsibility to regulate citizen's opinions and in particular that speaking documentable truth must never be punishable under the law.

Gordon: What was the purpose of the two-day supplementary session that ended November 11th?

Wolff: November 11th focused on prevention of racism, xenophobia and hate crimes through educational and awareness raising initiatives. That in itself was already worrisome to us because if you try to change people's opinions through educational and awareness raising initiatives the line between education and indoctrination is a very thin one. Even though I raised this topic during the conference itself, I did not get any response. In the agenda one can read that "awareness raising initiatives on racism [and] xenophobia, aim to bring positive and sustainable change to society by promoting universally respected values." We immediately raised the issue during the plenary session: "What are those values? What are we talking about? Which human rights are we talking about? What is the definition of human rights in the OSCE language?" It was interesting to note that no such definition was given. Pax Europa recommended that the OSCE support the abolition of all hate speech and blasphemy laws in participating states as these laws are not compatible with a free society. On the contrary, during the conference on October 28th as well as the one on November 10th and 11th, the necessity for tightening of hate speech and hate crimes laws was stressed. In the opinions of myself and my colleagues who attended the meeting this is indeed a very troublesome development. We believe that the hate crime laws are in place. We have plenty of laws. They just need to be enforced.

Gordon: Did the same groups of NGO's and the OIC attend that session as well?

Wolff: No, there were different NGOs and OIC members that attended the November 10th and 11th meetings. It was actually very interesting to note that there were very few NGO's on the list of participants. Either the topic is getting tiresome for the NGO's or people are just not interested that much anymore. However, this did have a positive impact on us, the counter-jihad groups, because we were able to interject our views, speaking loudly and more often.

Gordon: What positions did you represent on behalf of Pax Europa at the supplementary session?

Wolff: Well as usual I asked for clarifications of the term, "extremist speech," and I also wanted to know who decides what constitutes hate speech.

Gordon: Is the OSCE Islamophobia Document a furtherance

of the Council of Europe Religious Intolerance Guidelines adopted in 2008?

Wolff: The answer here is "oh definitely." The OSCE Document is a practical application of the Council of Europe guidelines. It goes from general to primary and secondary education. Let me give you an example. According to the Council of Europe documents, school textbooks should not present distorted interpretations of religious and cultural history. Now as usual I have two questions. First of all, what happens with the teaching of the two Turkish sieges of Vienna in 1529 and 1683? Number 2, who decides what is considered "distorted" and according to whom? Another example, "stereotypes that present Islamists contradicting fundamental European values must be avoided." As usual I have two more questions. First, what about the U.N. Universal Declaration of Human Rights, *vis a vis* the Cairo Declaration of Human Rights and Islam? Is the Cairo Declaration perhaps contradictory to fundamental European values and what European values are we talking about? Can we have a definition of these European values? Number 2, what about the responsibility of states to look into the teachings of Islam and its obvious hatred of the "other?" Is this compatible with the Human Dimension of the OSCE? I'm not sure I will get answers to these questions. Nevertheless, I think these questions are absolutely crucial in any dialogue that we want to have.

Gordon: What is the agenda behind the OIC presence at these OSCE meetings?

Wolff: The OIC is demanding that OSCE implement Shariah law violating the right to free speech. This comes as a result of OIC guidelines to insure cooperation with the relevant government and non-government organizations in order to counter Islamophobia, which is extremely worrying. Remember that Islamophobia is a concept that has no legal definition. This is, in effect, an extraterritorial call to submit to Shariah law. Now one wonders how the OSCE with its commitment to human rights can actually follow a call to submit to Shariah law? Hopefully one of these days there will be politicians, Secretaries General and others who will understand the dangers that lie in this call to submit to Shariah law.

Gordon: The U.S. State Department is holding meetings in mid-

December on Religious Tolerance with the OIC and EU based on the Ankara Declaration. Many in the U.S. are concerned that this could be a prelude to adoption of OIC blasphemy guidelines. Given your experience and monitoring of these OSCE developments, should we be concerned and why?

Wolff: I can only tell you that you should be extremely concerned especially in view of the fact that blasphemy laws are being discussed. Now one wonders how these laws can be compatible with the First Amendment of the U.S. Constitution on the right to freedom of speech. It's very concerning that the U.S. Government would even meet with Muslim nations to discuss religious tolerance. One would expect that Secretary Clinton, her office or her advisors, would have looked into the teachings of the Qur'an. Has Mrs. Clinton even read the Qur'an cover to cover? However, looking at the agenda for this meeting I can only surmise that she has not read the Qur'an. In addition, a State Department official, according to Fox News, said that the meeting is meant to combat intolerance while being fully consistent with freedom of expression. I don't think that this will be possible. I think the State Department is trying to square a circle. Shariah law can never be consistent with freedom of expression. If one looks into the doctrine, if one reads *The Reliance of the Traveller: A Classic Manual on Islamic Sacred Law*, one realizes immediately that there is no freedom of expression under Shariah law. Secretary Clinton has also said that nations should not criminalize speech. Why is she allowing the OIC to even discuss that in your country? Look what happened to me here in Austria. I had to stand trial because what I said was deemed criminal.

I think we should start talking to our elected officials. I am very concerned about these changes and believe that hate speech laws should be abolished. There should be universal freedom of expression. One should be allowed to say whatever one wants with very few exceptions. Calls to kill people, calls to violence should be unacceptable. Must be unacceptable. Must be punished. I would also like to remind the readers that criticism of a religion must never be considered hate speech, must never be considered blasphemous, and must never be forbidden under the law. Because otherwise we are losing our freedom of speech and we all know that without freedom of speech there is no democracy. Freedom of speech and conscience is what forms, what shapes our democracy. I am very sorry to say that as Austria has submitted to Shariah law and its provisions, we can no longer be considered a democracy. The

OIC in my opinion can try to silence people like me, people critical of Islam as much as they want to, however, I will never be silenced. I will continue to speak out and I will continue to say that I am deeply concerned about the teachings of Islam.

* * *

Shortly following our interview with Elisabeth Sabaditsch-Wolff on December 20, 2011, she lost her appeal of a municipal Viennese court decision. We noted the outcome in an *Iconoclast* article:

> A Vienna appellate court Judge upheld the lower court decision that Elisabeth Sabaditsch-Wolff "denigrated a religion" - Islam. The appellate court ruling also suggested reduction of the fine, 480 Euros as being excessive and remanded the matter to the lower court for adjudication. *Gates of Vienna* (GOV) noted the Judge's ruling:
>
>> Judge Leo Levnaic-Iwanski upheld the verdict of the lower court, which convicted Elisabeth on the charge of "denigration of religious beliefs of a legally recognized religion."
>>
>> The judge found that the length of time her trial had taken was excessive, and that her fine should be reduced. A new date will be set in the lower court for the announcement of the fine.
>
> While Wolff has a supportive husband and mother, she is also concerned for the future of her daughter Ella and fellow Austrians. If she had to leave her native Austria, where could she and her family possibly go? Given her husband's military career in Austria and her family in Vienna, that would be a wrenching prospect.... Wolff will need to stay the course with private assistance and fight for her and our Free Speech.

Her experience demonstrates that adoption of blasphemy codes trumps free speech.

We understand that arrangements are being made for a speaking tour in the US in 2012 for Wolff. She unstintingly continues to give private lectures about the tyranny of Islamic doctrine in spite of these misguided Austrian courts' decisions.

18
IBN WARRAQ
DECEMBER 2011

Ibn Warraq, a leading apostate from Islam, author of numerous critical works on the subject, is best described as a humanist. Born a Muslim in India at the dawn of the partition of the British Raj into the modern nations of India and Pakistan, his family, like millions of other Muslims, removed themselves to Pakistan. However, unlike others, his family saw fit to send both he and his elder brother to a boarding school in the English Midlands. For that far-seeing act, both Warraq and we are grateful. As a young student assisted by a welcoming environment, he nurtured a life-long appreciation of his new surroundings, culture and the cornerstone Judeo-Christian values that form the basis of the Western Enlightenment. Later at university, his curiosity about his cultural origins led him to begin a professional application of Western critical thinking to an historical examination of the origins of Islam, the Qur'an and Mohammed. That resulted in his rejection of Islam and its replacement with secularism.

He was not unaware of the perilous path he had chosen. That is reflected in the *nom de plume* he chose - that of an early Ninth Century Muslim free thinker, Muhammed Ibn al-Warraq, who was castigated as a heretic for scoffing at Islam in his writings as a "divine faith" revealed by the Prophet Mohammed. Not unlike the original Ibn Warraq, the contemporary Ibn Warraq was aroused by the example of fellow British Indian author Salman Rushdie, who suffered the deprivations from death fatwas issued by Iranian Ayatollahs for his contemporary heterdox beliefs. And like the original Ibn Warraq, our colleague has been unstinting in his criticism of Islam, despite fatwas by Muslim clerics issued against his life, and in emboldening fellow apostates to speak out against the totalitarian creed of Islam and its oppression of human rights, freedom and liberty.

I met Ibn Warraq in 2003 at a presentation he made at the Charles Hotel in Cambridge, Massachusetts entitled, "Apostasy and Apostates under Islam," a reference to the book, *Leaving Islam: Apostates Speak Out*, edited by him. During a visit with Dr. Andrew Bostom at the latter's home in Rhode Island that weekend, I read and commented on an essay Warraq had written critiquing the work of the late Edward Said. Said had created a misleading post-colonial doctrine in his book, *Orientalism*, which maligned the West by falsely accusing it of imposing a racist view via imperialism on the Muslim Ummah. (As if the historical Islam didn't encompass the grand sweep of its own imperialistic conquests. Conquests that left, death, slavery and dhimmitude for those unbelievers who lived in danger of extinction as subjugated minorities in Muslim realms.)

That essay eventuated in a later major work of Warraq's, *Defending the West*, a theme furthered in his latest book, *Why The West is Best*. My next encounter with him occurred in St. Petersburg, Florida in 2007, where he had organized the Secular Islam Summit. There I also met and conferred with his fellow apostates from Islam, Nonie Darwish and Dr. Wafa Sultan. I was present when both he and Darwish launched Former Muslims United – a group devoted to advocating the human and civil rights for apostates - in a hearing room of the Rayburn Office Building in Washington, DC in 2009. The following June in 2010, we met again at a Symposium of the *New English Review* in Nashville. There, he excoriated Western Islamologists for not critically examining the historical origins of Islamic and Qur'anic doctrine, out of fear of offending Muslim clerical authorities. In his paper "Historical Methodology and the Believer" delivered at the symposium, he said:

> Without criticism of Islam, Islam will remain unassailed in its dogmatic, fanatical, medieval fortress; ossified, totalitarian and intolerant. It will continue to stifle thought, human rights, individuality, originality and truth.
>
> Western intellectual Islamologists have totally failed in their duties as intellectuals. They have betrayed their calling by aban-

doning their critical faculties when it comes to Islam.

Given this background we reached out to Ibn Warraq for this interview.

Gordon: Tell us about your family background in Pakistan and why you were sent to boarding school in England.

Warraq: Yes, my family was Muslim; we were from an area of India which is still part of India, the Gujarat. In fact I was born in a town called Rajkot. It's the town where Gandhi grew up although he was not born there. Gandhi's father worked for the Maharajah of the state. I was born there in 1946, one year before partition. When Pakistan came into being in 1947 my family decided to move to the newly created Pakistan. We went to the city of Karachi which was then the capitol. My family were businessmen, dealing in export – import. My grandfather had told my father to go to Karachi buy some property and invest there though my grandfather himself was at that time in Mozambique which was then Portuguese East Africa. I grew up in Karachi until the age of nine when my father decided to send me to a boarding school in England with my brother who is a year older. The main reason was he had no faith in the future of Pakistan. He was a witness to coups d'état, social unrest, riots, insecurity and the terrible educational system. He really saw no hope there and he was not a particularly religious person. He never forced religion down our throats. In fact he once told my grandmother that she was ruining us with her religious mumbo jumbo which really upset her a lot. However, he did bow down to public pressure. In a country like Pakistan, there was an awful lot of conformity. Pressure to conform weighed so heavily on people like my father that he sent my brother and me to a Qur'anic school. One of my earliest memories is going to a Qur'anic school where we learned to recite the parts of the Qur'an by heart without understanding a word because it was in Arabic. At the age of nine I found myself in the rural setting of Worcestershire, England in the Midlands.

Gordon: How did the experience of going to a private school in England transform your thinking about Western versus Islamic values?

Warraq: It did in a very indirect way. I was not conscious of big terms like Western values or Islamic values. What happened was, as I recount in my book called *Virgins, What Virgins and Other Essays*, I slowly started becoming English without realizing it. I was acquiring a taste for English folk songs, for the English countryside, for what the scholar Nikolaus Pevsner called the Englishness of English art. I loved everything about the experience. It was a great period of discovery, awakening and intellectual curiosity. I always have this tendency to form very strong local attachments, so I was very keen to find out about this school I was going to, its history, and the countryside. I was acquiring a kind of English character if you like, Englishness in my attitudes about things.

Gordon: You attended the University of Edinburgh. What were some of the seminal intellectual influences there?

Warraq: I went up there to study the history of art, basically European art. Because of a certain cultural identity crisis, I decided I would study Arabic to find out something about the faith I was born into. I studied Arabic under a very well known Professor, W. Montgomery Watt - a highly revered man who died a few years ago at over 90 years of age. He wrote a very influential biography of Mohammed which was highly respected in the Islamic world. At the same time I was going through all of the classic texts that young people were reading. I remember reading authors like Oscar Wilde, Henry James, and the classic texts of the period: Sartre's *La Nausee*, Camus' *L'Etranger*, Hesse's *Steppenwolf*, and so on. I was very confused and not very well focused. I found most of my fellow students very immature and I was glad to get out of there as soon as I could into the wider world.

Gordon: When did you decide to remain in the West and what career options did you contemplate?

Warraq: That decision was made for me because my mother died when I was one and my father died while I was at Edinburgh. Therefore, I no longer had any connections to Pakistan. I had an uncle in Mozambique but there was no question of my settling there. I had some very vague literary pretensions. Like many of my generation I also had a fascination and passion for the cinema. I wanted to go to the National School in London but I never managed to get in. I was drifting around with a group of hippies at the end of the 1960's and the early 1970's. I decided that I just couldn't lie around because most of my hippie friends were faking it. Most of them came from middle class families, whereas when I said I didn't know where my next meal was coming from I really meant it. I had some rough times and I decided I had to get a job. I decided I would become a teacher and did another degree in teacher training and began teaching in London.

Gordon: How did the death fatwa issued by the late Ayatollah Khomeini against the life of British author Salman Rushdie influence your thinking and writings?

Warraq: Khomeini's fatwa in 1989 had an enormous influence. In fact it worried me that people still refused to take seriously the dangers posed by this theocratic regime. They refused to acknowledge the powerful influence it was having on the resurgence of radical Islam in the entire Middle East. Many people from the subcontinent of India, like me, still revere Salman Rushdie because he was the first successful writer of Indian origin – he was highly feted and regarded. He won the Booker Prize. We really revered him. He was also a skeptic. Moreover, he wrote this scandalous book, *The Satanic Verses,* that criticized Islam. The fatwa was a great shock to me. This event really pushed me to write my first book, *Why I Am Not a Muslim*. It was my wake up call to Western intellectuals. I was a little disappointed to see how many of the Western intellectuals reacted to the fatwa on Rushdie. They blamed him. They blamed the victim. Intellectuals like John Berger, historians like Hugh Trevor-Roper, not to mention John Le Carré, the novelist. They all blamed Rushdie. They didn't take his side at all. That was a great shock to me and I felt that it was time I said something. I was given the opportunity so I was happy to do that.

Gordon: What aspects of doctrinal Islam were critical to your decision to leave Islam?

Warraq: There was not one aspect. The whole thing, the whole construct didn't make any sense to me. It was a dense radical construct. It started with premises which I just couldn't accept. For example that the Qur'an was the word of God, which was not obvious to me. Islam did not encourage free thought, free discussion; it did not encourage free inquiry. These things are very important to me. Islam tried to rule over every single aspect of your life. I really valued my freedoms which I had come to take for granted. It was the fatwa on Rushdie which woke me up, the fact that I had to do something about defending him. Thus the entire construct was so against all the things that I valued; freedom of thought, freedom of action, the equality of women which are denied under Islam.

Gordon: Could you explain the significance of your choice of Ibn Warraq as a *nom de plume*?

Warraq: Yes, it's very simple actually. It was, again, forced on me. I wanted to take the nom de plume of Ibn al-Rawandi. Ibn al-Rawandi was a great free thinker, one of the few prominent free thinkers in Islam. However, his name had been taken by an Englishman who later became a good friend of mine. He died a few years ago. I took the name of Ibn al-Rawandi's teacher who was called Ibn al-Warraq. He was also a free thinker and lived in late Ninth Century and died in early the Tenth Century.

Gordon: What compelled you to go public about your apostasy in writing and publishing, *Why I Am Not a Muslim*?

Warraq: I think it was basically the Rushdie affair which pushed me into it. The way it happened was I was subscribing to a free thought magazine called, *Free Inquiry*. They had been running a series of articles by former Christians of various denominations with the title, "Why I am not a (blank)," and then you would fill in the blank with why I am not a Mormon, why I am not a Unitarian, etc. They couldn't find anyone to write one on "Why I am not a Muslim" so they asked me and I jumped at the idea. I wrote an article first. That was in 1992. Since *Free Inquiry* was in fact edited by a man who also founded and ran a publishing house called Prometheus I asked him whether Prometheus would be interested in a book-length version of the article and he said "yes." That is how the book came about.

Gordon: Your earliest published works focused on the origins of the Qur'an. Did that form the intellectual basis for your criticism of doctrinal Islam?

Warraq: Yes, my work was not a criticism of doctrinal aspects of Islam. Rather, I looked at the origins of Islam and what we knew about Islam which fascinated me. Anyone who is fascinated by history wants to know what really happened. History and a passion for history goes with a passion for truth; to find out what really happened. That is the path that I took as I really wanted to know the origins of the Qur'an. Of course I did not accept the traditional Muslim account which was totally ahistorical. All of my criticism of Islam was contained in my first book, *Why I Am Not a Muslim*. The next book was a scholarly criticism of various theories as to the origins of the Qur'an and the meaning of the Qur'an so they're not quite the same thing. I'll give you an example. Many of my Muslim apostate friends are quite happy to accept the traditional account of the life of Mohammed because it gives them plenty of ammunition to attack him as a pedophile and man with a sword in one hand and the Qur'an in the other. Someone who is intolerant and someone who is antisemitic.

Now all that doesn't interest me whatsoever. What interests me is what do we know about Mohammed, what do we know that is true? How do we know that Mohammed did X, Y and Z? Can we accept the Hadith which are accounts of the acts and sayings of Mohammed? My apostate friends sometimes don't really understand what I'm getting at, they say well it's all there, you know, in black and white. It's there in the history books, it's written by Arab Muslims themselves so it must be true. Whereas I am a skeptic and I have a deeper understanding of historical methodology and point out that no, this cannot have been the case. Thus, I have been engaged in a slightly different kind of intellectual activity. If you read the magnificent works of Jonathan Israel, the Professor at the Institute of Advanced Study, on the history of the Enlightenment, the European Enlightenment, you would realize that it all started with Spinoza and Spinoza's critique of the Christian Bible. I believe this is my mission as well. My eventual goal is to bring about enlightenment, not just a reformation. I think it can only come about with a critique of the Qur'an in a similar fashion.

Gordon: You have taken up the cause of *Defending the West* in your book of the same title, from critics like Edward Said. Why do you consider that an important aspect of your work?

Warraq: We are at this moment in danger of losing freedoms won at great cost over the centuries. These are freedoms I value. Since the Second World War, Western intellectuals have been very reluctant to defend these freedoms, to defend the values of the West. One of the greatest critics of the West was Edward Said. I had to point out that while people were so enthralled with Edward Said's arguments that they hadn't examined them properly. He was no historian and he had no knowledge of Islam. He gave a very contentious account of what happened during the rise of the British Empire. My view was that we were in danger of losing sight of the positive aspects of Western Civilization because we were too afraid to defend the West. Even the notion of just defending the West was considered far too euro-centric and in fact racist and imperialist. People were just too ashamed to claim anything for Western civilization. Extraordinary post-Columbian feelings of guilt were partly responsible. People like Edward Said, Noam Chomsky and others were also responsible for this defensive attitude. I thought it was time to stand up and to show that Said was talking nonsense most of the time.

Gordon: Why do you believe that the prevailing liberal criticism of Western values is dangerous?

Warraq: First of all, it's so biased, it's so one-sided. There isn't an equivalent criticism of Islam especially and secondly it's historically unsound. Take for example their criticism of Western attitudes towards race, slavery and imperialism. If you take all three and compare them to racism or imperialism of the Islamic world, you will see that slavery has existed in every single civilization, in fact, the Arabs have been some of the greatest slave traders of all. Slavery continues to this day in the Islamic world although this is not admitted by them. I know that people like Dr. Charles Jacobs of the American Anti-Slavery Group had made videos of slave markets in Africa well into the 1990's. While slavery has existed in every single civilization, it was the West which first took steps to abolish slavery. In fact, the kings of various African states were absolutely shocked that Britain had abolished slavery. They argued, what were they going to live on? The British couldn't do this. Their people relied on making money from slavery. These African leaders sent people to talk to Queen Victoria and said, you know, come off it. We have lived on slavery for all of these years. Abolitionism did not find positive response in Africa as it did in Western societies and cultures.

Gordon: You are intellectually a secularist. How has that affected your writings and your activism?

Warraq: I think it helps me to be a bit more objective. In my new book, *Why the West is Best*, I give full credit to various aspects of Judaism and Christianity in the making of the West which is something which many of my secularist friends wish to deny. They only want to empathize with the Greco-Roman heritage. Whereas I feel that this is historically not accurate and really unfair. I have always felt that many Christians, deeply sincere Christians, support the idea of separation of State and Church and are secularist in that sense as well. They believe that religion should be very much a private affair and should not be given special treatment. The State should not fund churches for example.

Gordon: You were one of the co-founders of Former Muslims United, launched in September 2009. How important is it that apostates from Islam speak out against violations of their civil and human rights in both the West and the Muslim Ummah?

Warraq: Apostates from Islam, in any Islamic country, would not last very long. They would be very lucky to escape with their lives. There have been a number of cases of apostates who have been murdered, been imprisoned. While many Islamic countries pay lip service to the idea of freedom of religion, they don't put up with conversion from Islam to another religion. This is the case with terrible consequences in Iran. Hundreds of people have died. Western Intellectuals seem to keep quiet on these issues. However, it is very dangerous for an apostate in the Islamic world. Apostates from Islam, even in the West, remain rather terrified which I find very disturbing. I have met many apostates who have come to me and said, "your books have changed our lives but we cannot bring your books home. We have to read them, in secret, in libraries and so on." I find that really appalling. There was a report a few years ago in the *Washington Times*, by the journalist Julia Duin, who wrote a marvelous account of the conversions of many Egyptians to Christianity from Islam. They had to have their meetings in secret as they were threatened. Even despite this, they must learn to speak fearlessly, otherwise their positions will have been in vain. I think if they were to hold their heads up high this would encourage apostates in the Islamic world. We should defend those apostates in the Islamic world as much as possible.

Gordon: Do you consider the current campaign of the Organization of Islamic Cooperation to impose Islamic Sharia blasphemy laws on the West injurious?

Warraq: Absolutely. They are trying to ban any kind of criticism of Islam. It is already labeled Islamophobia to criticize Islam, which is totally absurd. The OIC is trying to pass resolutions at the United Nations which would be legally binding and would make any criticism of Islam liable to legal punishment. That is terrible. Of course that is injurious to Western values. It attacks all values in the First Amendment of the Bill of Rights in the US Constitution, especially freedom of religion, freedom of expression. We cannot hope to win the ideological battle against Islam without criticism of Islam, it is essential that we continue to criticize Islam. These blasphemy laws are designed to silence the critics of Islam.

Gordon: This past year has witnessed declarations by political leaders in the UK, France and Germany about the failure of multi-culturalism. Do you believe that is a signal that Muslim immigrants in the West have failed to integrate with Western values?

Warraq: Yes, that has been the unintended consequence of the vigorously enforced programs of multi-culturalism. I know this first hand because I was teaching in London and I thought it was a great thing. There were some very sound reasons behind this notion of multi-culturalism. However, in fact it all went horribly wrong, because to even criticize values of another culture was considered unacceptable, politically incorrect. From positive attitudes to the cultures of the immigrants we went to denigration of the Western values and acceptance of some of the worst aspects of the cultures of the immigrants. You had de-facto acceptance of polygamy and female genital mutilation, the slow erosion of the rights of women from Muslim countries. It has been a complete disaster and Muslims are the only cultural group in the West who fail to integrate. They want to keep their own values. They want to keep their own marriage laws. They want to keep all their particular taboos and they have no wish to conform to the laws of the host nation. They feel it is the host nation which must change even though they are in the minority. They wish the majority to change. It's quite extraordinarily arrogant. However, unfortunately that is the way it is.

Gordon: What are the principal themes in your latest work, *Why The West is Best*?

Warraq: It is a more focused work than *Defending the West* which critiqued the work of Edward Said. *Why the West is Best* is a more general defense of Western values. I go through the history of the origins of these values starting with the Greeks and the Romans, and highlighting the Judeo-Christian heritage. For example, Christianity introduced the notion of forgiveness. I think forgiveness plays a very important part in Western society and it comes from the Judeo-Christian heritage. I tried to show that some of the usual criticisms of the West just don't hold up. The idea that the West was economically successful because of slavery - it's just nonsense. Slavery had very little to do with the economic success of the West. Just look at the facts and figures and how much slavery actually contributed to development. I tried to debunk some of the notions of the superiority of Eastern spirituality which usually are contrasted with decadent Western materialism which is complete nonsense as well. For example, the greatest number of drug addicts are to be found in Teheran and in Karachi, not in the West. Not in New York believe it or not. It's the same with the roles of slavery, racism and imperialism in the world. These institutions were present in other cultures. However, it was Western civilization which did something about slavery, about racism and voluntarily dissolved its empires leaving behind a very positive legacy of institutions not to mention buildings and roadways. Then I discuss some of the Western values like accepting criticism and irony. Irony, it seems, is a bit incomprehensible to Islamic society. They don't seem to understand irony. The fact that you can actually criticize some of the most basically held beliefs of one's own culture and see the funny side of it, to see the humorous self-criticism or irony is one of the greatest strengths of the West. Then there is the whole notion of objectivity. That is the scientific method which is a gift of the West to the rest of the world which has not been properly appreciated. I end this latest book with some rallying cries as to how we can defend Western civilization.

19
MARK DURIE
FEBRUARY 2012

Dr. Mark Durie is an Australian Anglican minister, human rights activist and theologian. An academic linguist by training, he was honored in 1992 as one of the youngest elected fellows in the Australian Academy of Humanities for his research and development of the first grammar and dictionary of the Acehnese language of Indonesia. He chose in the closing years of the 20th Century to be ordained and enter the Anglican ministry in 1999, abandoning a well-regarded academic career at the University of Melbourne. He is currently Vicar at St. Mary's Anglican Church in Caulfield, Australia, a post he assumed in 2004.

In the mid-1980's he undertook study of Arabic at the University of Leiden in part to become better acquainted with the Islam he encountered while doing research in an Aceh village that lead to his doctorate in linguistics. He was also involved in a 2001 religious vilification case brought by an Islamic group in the State of Victoria against two apostate Muslim Pastors who criticized Islam. He considered the law which was the basis for the case to be ill-conceived and dangerous.

The events of the jihadi atrocities of 9/11 followed by the bombing of a Bali nightspot in October 2002 that killed over 200 fellow Australians propelled Durie to undertake a broad ranging study of Islamic doctrine. In the course of which he made contact with leading scholars, among them Bat Ye'or, Andrew Bostom, Robert Spencer and others. Currently in the midst of completing a second doctorate on Islamic Theology he has published and lectured widely, presenting his view of imperialistic Islam from a theological perspective.

That unique perspective was conveyed in his 2010 book, *The Third Choice: Islam, Dhimmitude and Freedom*.

In our review of Durie's book, "Dhimmitude Dominates," we noted the broad scope of his compact and yet instructive volume.

> He elucidates dhimmitude via discussion of basic Islamic Shariah law contained in the Qu'ranic canon based on the example of Mohammed. What Durie means by the model of Mohammed is captured in an essay by Durie on the impossibility of Islamic reformation:
>
>> . . . Muhammad combined within himself the offices of king, judge, general and religious leader, thus unifying politics, law, the military and religion. To follow his example means creating a theocratic political order, where the laws of the land are controlled by Islamic theology.

Perhaps, his most prescient conclusion in *The Third Choice* concerned the payment of the *jizya*, a critical component of the dhimma of imperialistic Islam, crystallized in the Pact of Umar (Umar Ibn al-Khattab, the Second Caliph) following his conquest of Syria and Jerusalem in 637 C.E. *Jizya*, a form of poll tax under Shariah, was in Durie's view a form of payment by the despised non-believer to avoid beheading, what Durie deemed "ritualized barbarity." Durie described how demeaning and servile this oppressive act was for Christians and Jews, the "protected people" of the dhimma, as codified under Shariah-Islamic law:

> The intended result of the *jizya* ritual is for the dhimmi to lose all sense of his own personhood. In return for this loss, the dhimmi was supposed to feel humility and gratitude towards his Muslim masters. Al-Mawardi said that the *jizya* head tax was either a sign of contempt, because of the dhimmis' unbelief, or a sign of the mildness of Muslims, who granted them quarter (instead of killing or enslaving them) so humble gratitude was the intended response.
>
> The remarks of al-Mawardi and Ibn Ajibah make clear that its true meaning is to be found in psychological attitudes of in-

feriority and indebtedness imposed upon non-Muslims living under Islam, as they willingly and gratefully handed over the *jizya* in service to the Muslim community.

Durie's publication of *The Third Choice* burnished his reputation in the field of Islamic scholarship. That led to a number of international presentations, many in the US, during the past two years. In January 2011, he appeared in Washington, DC at the invitation of Nina Shea, executive director of Stonegate Institute Center for Religious Freedom. He presented on the topic of the Organization of Islamic Cooperation (OIC) and the companion supreme Sunni Shariah legal body, the International Fiqh Academy (IFA). He returned to Washington in November 2011 to present at a forum sponsored by the Federalist Society on the occasion of the publication of Nina Shea and Paul Marshall's book: *Silenced: How Apostasy & Blasphemy Codes are Choking Freedom Worldwide*.

In January of 2012, Durie had a number of engagements in the US. In Atlanta, he spoke at a conference of Christian Islamic scholars where he opposed the view of Miroslav Volf's book *Allah*, which argues that Christians and Muslims worship the same God. In Philadelphia, he spoke at an event sponsored by the Middle East Forum on "Muslims in the West: Loyal to Whom?" during which he explored the legal problems - backed by IFA fatwas - for Muslims who wish to be loyal citizens of Western nations. In Boston, he gave a sermon contrasting Mohammed with Jesus. In suburban Stoughton, Massachusetts, Durie spoke at a luncheon of Christian pastors and Orthodox rabbis endeavoring to explain Islam. At Rabbi Jonathan Hausman's synagogue, Congregation Ahavath Torah, Durie spoke on the issues of Christian and Islamic doctrine that impact on the future of Israel.

Against this background, we were fortunate to have caught up with Dr. Durie and interviewed him at the conclusion of his most recent lecture tour of the US in early 2012.

Gordon: Your doctoral dissertation was on Acehnese language and culture in Indonesia. What was unique about the Acehnese transformation from its Hindu origins to Islam?

Durie: The Acehnese are cousins to the Chams of Vietnam. Historical evidence suggests that after the destruction of the once great Hindu Champa kingdom in southern Vietnam in 1471, some high-born Chams found refuge in Aceh. Disillusioned by the much degraded state of Hinduism in India (memory was perhaps still fresh of the catastrophic massacre of more than 100,000 Hindus by Timur at Delhi in 1398). The Aceh-Chams embraced Islam and spread it in the region. From its first beginnings, the Acehnese sultanate was engaged in jihad against the Portuguese, who conquered Mallaca in 1511. Later they waged jihad against the Dutch.

Gordon: How did the Acehnese experience deepen your interest and study of Qu'ranic Islamic doctrine?

Durie: I must admit that while doing field work in Aceh my focus was very much on the language and culture, not on the Canon of Islam. My engagement with Islam was at the level of my Acehnese friends' understanding. We talked about their pilgrimages to Mecca, their hopes and personal beliefs. I did not attempt a systematic study of Islam from its foundations, although I was curious. I sensed that engaging with Islam at that level could drive a wedge between me and my Acehnese hosts. In any case I did not have the resources to do this while living in an Acehnese village. However there was one area of Acehnese theology which I came to know well, which was the institution of jihad, which had played a major role in the self-understanding of the Acehnese people.

Gordon: What course of formal and informal study into Islamic doctrine did you follow and whose critical scholarship and criticism assisted you in this endeavor?

Durie: I began studying Arabic in Leiden in 1985 with Professor G. W. J. Drewes, who had been a student of Snouck Hurgronje. Snouck Hurgronje had been the leading scholar of Islam in his generation: a pilgrim to Mecca in 1885, he guided the Dutch in overcoming the Acehnese jihad insurgency from around 1890 on. During the 1990's I also apprised myself of Bat Ye'or's writings on the dhimma. I did not commence my systematic study of Islam until after the 9/11 atrocity. At that time I researched through many volumes of hadiths, studies of the Qur'an, revised my Arabic, and engaged in a systematic exploration of what Islam teaches, and how this is changing the world today. For the past three years I have also been undertaking a second doctorate - this time in Islamic Theology. My research focus is on whether the Qur'an can be considered a continuation of Biblical faith, or a clear break from it.

Gordon: What prompted your career change and when did you enter the Anglican Ministry?

Durie: I was leading an academic department at the University of Melbourne when I felt called to pastoral ministry in the early 1990's. Although I loved my academic work, I had a deep sense of the need of the church for guidance and felt that the coming years would be very difficult for people of faith. I resigned my tenured university position in 1998 and was ordained at the start of 1999.

Gordon: When did you assume your position as vicar at St. Mary's Church in Caulfield?

Durie: I have been at St Mary's Caulfield since the start of 2004. I enjoy pastoral work and it is not easy to squeeze in my work on Islam in the midst of other duties, including hatches, matches and dispatches.

Gordon: What prompted your human rights activism in Australia and internationally?

Durie: It was a matter of seeing the need and stepping in to fill the gap. On the one hand I was concerned both by the erosion of freedoms in the West, in an increasingly hostile climate for Christians, and on the other hand by the rise of Muslim radicalism, which was imposing a bitter burden on Christians in Muslim-majority societies. I was quite frankly appalled by what I found when I looked carefully into the teachings of Muslim groups throughout the West. Everywhere I looked I found eulogies for jihad and hopes for establishing a Shariah state. Hardly anyone seemed to care. That woke me up and pushed me to get busy researching, writing and speaking.

Denial can be deadly. I was deep into digesting the Islamic source materials when I heard the news of the October 2002 Bali bombing, in which many Australians were killed. However this attack had been preceded and to my mind greatly overshadowed by on-going jihad militia attacks, forced conversions and massacres of Christians in Eastern Indonesia, resulting in half a million people becoming internally displaced. There was even an active al-Qaeda camp functioning quite openly and providing training for the militias. The current President of Indonesia, Susilo Bambang Yudhoyono, was Minister for Security at the time, and he defended the militias, even though he was aware of the carnage. The

Australian media had been ignoring this "slow-burn" jihad against Indonesia's Christians, yet was shocked when a night club was blown up in "peaceful" Indonesia.

Gordon: In your human rights activism, what aspects of Islamic doctrine and Shariah most concern you and why?

Durie: I am concerned about five main areas. In Islamic societies I am troubled by the status of Muslim women under Shariah, the abuse of people who leave Islam — so-called "apostates," the systematic degradation of non-Muslims, of which Christians form the largest numbers today, and the lack of freedom that ordinary Muslims face if they wish to vary from the received dogmas and practices of their faith. And in Western, non-Muslims societies, I am concerned by the "dhimmitude of the West," including the voluntary surrender of the right to freedom of speech where Islam is concerned.

Gordon: How significant is Australia's Muslim population and what are the prevailing positions of its communal and religious leaders versus those of Australian political leadership regarding integration in the civil polity of the country?

Durie: Australian Muslims are less than 2% of the population. They are not a large component, although more concentrated in some localities where their presence is more noticed. They have very diverse ethnic origins. Many have come from societies which are less strict in Islamic practice, such as Bosnia, Turkey, Indonesia and Fiji. The most prominent single group are comprised of Lebanese living in Sydney, who tend to be more conservative. Australian Muslims differ greatly about the issue of integration: one can find just about every imaginable viewpoint. However some Muslim leaders have spoken out against integration, and reject participation in the Australian political processes. There are also regular requests for Australian Muslims to have distinct legal provisions, such as Shariah family law. Repeated Australian governments have rejected this, insisting that we will not embrace a plurality of legal systems. Australian Muslims attract a lot more media attention - and more anxiety - than any comparable group. I do not expect that will change in the coming years.

Gordon: In 2001, the State of Victoria adopted a Racial and Religious Tolerance Act which became the basis of a legal action brought by the Islamic Council of Victoria against two apostate Pastors of the Catch the Fire Ministry for their criticism of Islam. What can you tell us about this landmark case and its consequences?

Durie: This complaint, made against Pastors Daniel Scot and Daniel Nalliah was initially successful. The judge found the pastors guilty of "vilifying" Muslims, and ordered them to take out expensive advertisements announcing that they had been found guilty. He also forbad them from expressing their views about Islam in Australia. However the Supreme Court in Victoria threw out this judgment. Eventually the two sides settled. The process was enormously expensive for the Christians, costing several hundred thousand dollars: the Muslims were represented pro bono by a leading law firm. The Christians contended that they had not been vilifying Muslims, but had a right to criticize Islam. They said that much of the Muslims' complaint was about accurate quotes from the Qur'an. "Does the Qur'an vilify Muslims?" they asked. The Muslims contended that to attack Islam is to attack Muslims, and their lawyers repeatedly argued that speaking the truth should not be considered a defense for vilification charges.

Many Australians were deeply concerned about this case, and as a result of it other states across the nation did not proceed with introducing similar laws. Victoria modified the law, but it still remains on the statute books. It is a bad law, ill-conceived and poorly drafted.

One of the consequences of the case is that it made it easier for Australians to debate Islam in public forums.

The case has also had global ramifications: it seems that Tony Blair's desire to introduce hate-speech laws in Britain could not be fully realized because of the impact of this case in Australia.

Gordon: What are the major themes of your books on Islam, *Liberty to the Captives*, *Revelation: Do We Worship the Same God?* and *The Third Choice: Islam, Dhimmitude and Freedom*?

Durie: My first book, *Revelation: Do We Worship the Same God?* considers the question of whether Muslims and Christians worship the same God; whether we honour the same Jesus, and whether the Islamic 'Holy Spirit' (Ruh Al-Qudus) is the same Holy Spirit as in the Bible. In all three cases I found that the differences are very considerable.

The Third Choice: Islam, Dhimmitude and Freedom is above all an account of Islam as a faith. It has useful discussions of topics as diverse as *taqiyya* (lawful deception) and female circumcision. It also explores the meaning of the dhimma pact and its implications for non-Muslims living under Islam. *Liberty to the Captives* is a supplement to *The Third Choice* specifically written for Christians. It explains how the contrast between the response to rejection in Jesus' and Mohammed's life provides a key to a spiritual response for Christians, enabling them to stand against and reject the odious claims of the dhimma system.

Gordon: What is the significance of your interpretation of dhimmitude?

Durie: I can mention three points.
I delved deeply into the life of Mohammed to explain the spiritual origins of dhimmitude, and especially the concept of *fitna* or "trial, persecution" (of Muslims), and the motif of imposing humiliation upon those who reject Islam. I regard the dhimma laws as an elaborate system designed to minimize obstacles for Islam by humiliating non-Muslims. The 'success' of non-Muslims is a theological offense which the dhimma system is designed to remove.

I also provided a deep and path-breaking analysis of the meaning of the *jizya* payment ritual, for which around 30 Islamic commentaries were consulted, most of which had not been translated from the Arabic. I established that the tax payment ritual is an enactment of the dhimmi's decapitation, with powerful symbolic significance. The concept of redeeming one's life by simultaneously enacting one's death and handing over a blood-price is key to understanding dhimmi status.

I also argued that where Christians are persecuted by Muslims under Shariah conditions, it tracks Shariah law's discriminatory provisions. For example, modern-day restrictions on building and repairing churches is grounded in the principles of Shariah law. In other words actual persecution of non-Muslims by Muslims is thoroughly theological in its motivations.

Gordon: How do you differentiate your criticism of Islam with the works of Bat Ye'or, Andrew Bostom, Robert Spencer and other scholars and authors?

Durie: My writings are more theological and focused on world view transformation. I lay out theological principles as a whole system, linking them up to history and canonical texts. For example, I explain the importance of the concepts of "guidance" and "success" in Islam, showing how these shape aspects of Shariah law. My writings also tend to be more concise and easier to digest than those of Bat Ye'or and Andrew Bostom. This is partly a matter of style – after all Bat Ye'or's writings are translated from academic French – but I work hard to elucidate the transformative belief system which underpins the dhimma. I explain how the whole system makes sense from the inside, from the perspective of a true believer. That is why *The Third Choice* is not just about dhimmitude: it is also an explanation of Islam itself, in which I clarify issues which often cause confusion, such as the doctrine of *taqiyya* "deception." I discuss whether reform of Islam is possible, by examining disputes among Muslims about the Shariah practice of female circumcision. There is also a pastoral perspective which runs through my writings. Robert Spencer's writings are more polemical. I am not just concerned to win the argument about Islam, but to count the cost to the human soul exacted by Islamic teachings, and how this damage could be healed, both for non-Muslims and Muslims alike. I want to win and heal hearts, not just win minds.

Gordon: There have been several trials in the EU regarding criticism of Islam: Geert Wilders in The Netherlands, Lars Hedegaard in Denmark and Elisabeth Sabaditsch-Wolff in Austria. Wilders has been acquitted, but both Hedegaard and Wolff have been convicted and fined. What are your views on these free speech cases?

Durie: These cases represent the failure of Western legal systems to chart their way through the difficult waters of resurgent Islamic demands to control infidel speech about Islam. A fundamental error of the West has been to look to established ideas about racism and multiculturalism to interpret issues of religious freedom. People in the West don't understand - and prefer to discount - religion so they think of Islam as a kind of culture or ethnicity, which is a mistake. Criticism of Islam is not hate-speech against Muslims. Bad ideas deserve to be criticized. The sooner Western states come to their senses the better.

Gordon: What concerns you about threats to human rights from the Organization of Islamic Cooperation, the political arm of the Muslim Ummah, and fatwas of the International Fiqh Academy?

Durie: The OIC is trying to impose Shariah principles upon the legal system of the whole world. They are using the UN to stop infidels from criticizing Islam, in any jurisdiction. It is part of their religion to insist that no-one speaks ill of Islam or Mohammed. Non-Muslim states need to realize that this is an imperialistic attempt to impose Islamic sensibilities upon non-believers.

The International Fiqh Academy was set up as a kind of global supreme legal authority for the Islamic world. It is very significant, yet often overlooked. Its rulings on topics such as citizenship and coexistence, freedom of speech, freedom of religion and women's rights are a blast from the past, an attempt to weld medieval Islamic theological perspectives onto modern life.

Non-Muslims need to pay attention, and to say, in the clearest possible language to the OIC: "No, not in my back yard."

Gordon: How troubling are the threats to the human rights of minority Christian populations and apostates in major Muslim countries embroiled in the Arab Spring?

Durie: The situation for Christians in the Middle East, with the exception of Israel and Lebanon, is dire. Hundreds of thousands of Christians have fled their homes in Iraq. Many of them have ended up in Syria, which is now also looking insecure and unsafe. In essence, Christians in the Middle East are being gradually, inexorably, squeezed back into the dhimma straightjacket of a few centuries ago by age-old processes motivated by Shariah. How far this journey - which can be tracked by a grisly trail of blood throughout the 20th Century - will progress remains unclear. The most likely outcome is a continued demographic draining of Christians from the Middle East.

Gordon: What should world Christian bodies do to defend the rights of beleaguered Christian minorities in Muslim lands?

Durie: They should pay attention, report accurately what is happening, grieve the martyrs, lobby politicians, pray for their brothers and sisters in the faith, provide material support, and where needed offer sanctuary. The biggest problem is a culture of denial. To deal with the present we must acknowledge and come to terms with the Islamic doctrines which drive the institution of dhimmitude. We need to acknowledge what Islam is if we are to adequately address and counter its imperialistic demands upon non-Muslims. Otherwise we will only come up with band aid measures which fall hopelessly short of what is required. Stop-gap measures cannot withstand consistent ideological pressure.

Gordon: Who should assist in resettlement of these threatened Christian minorities in their diasporas?

Durie: Majority Christian nations should lead the way in welcoming and resettling Christian minorities fleeing Islamic states. It's so obvious that people need to look after their own families, yet our secular principle of non-discrimination makes it very hard for us to selectively offer shelter to Christians. Christians are often discriminated against in resettlement processes, especially when Western governments have employed Muslims in their embassies and immigration departments. Muslim nations would not have such scruples at helping their co-religionists.

Gordon: In a recent essay you have proposed several rules for dealing with "sensitive subjects." What are they?

Durie: This essay was very much influenced by my involvement in the vilification case in Victoria. As talk about Islam becomes more heated, we need the best-informed voices to also be the most persuasive.
I offered ten principles:

State your purpose and stay on topic.
Check your facts.
Don't say things you don't have adequate evidence for.
Take your information from the most authoritative and original source you can.
If your source has limitations be aware of this and acknowledge it.
Be dispassionate and avoid emotive judgments.
Avoid stereotyping.
Refer people to original sources, so people can check things for themselves.
Take appropriate responsibility for inferences others may come to from what you are saying.
Be clear.

Gordon: In your most recent Calvin Seminary Conference Lectures in Michigan, you presented on how the colonial Dutch at the turn of the 20th Century conducted a successful counter-insurgency campaign in Aceh. What role was played by a Dutch academic expert on Islam?

Durie: Snouck Hurgronje's proposals were considered to have turned the tide of a decades-long and very costly jihad insurgency. It had been a political nightmare for the Dutch. Some of Snouck Hurgronje's key points were that the Dutch had to finally grasp that they were fighting a religious war. This meant that the power and influence of the ulamas had been raised to new heights by jihad conditions. They had to support traditional non-Islamic authority structures in Acehnese culture, specifically the traditional rulers whose interests balanced those of religious leaders. They had to stop brutalizing and punishing the general population, and they needed to pursue and eliminate hostile religious leaders who were stoking the jihad dogma among the people. Snouck Hurgronje argued that key Islamic leaders who were driving the insurgency could never be "converted" to the Dutch cause.

To implement this policy the Dutch used lightly armed groups of soldiers to pursue the Islamic teachers through the jungles. After a decade of following this policy the jihad insurgency war was essentially won.

Gordon: How do you view the prospects for preserving Western human rights in the face of demands for Shariah compliance by the rising Caliphate of the OIC?

Durie: The West appears to have little capacity for containing the rise of Shariah across the Muslim world. We are caught flat-footed without a clue about what is happening, and are standing confused by all the voices coming from the Muslim world, not knowing which way to turn. The issue is ultimately not our lack of influence. It is our lack of will, and widespread denial. We do not know even how to recognize, let alone support the voices of moderation. We refuse to admit the real nature of the problem, namely its theological roots. We have shown little capacity for befriending those who are struggling for human rights in Islamic states. Our elites are grotesquely relieved to partner with ideologues who sooth them with deceptive words, while all the time these ill-found partners oppose essential principles of universal human rights.

We show no capacity to promote the values which have made our nations great. We are well launched into a pattern of cultural decline and are spiritually exhausted. We find that we have little energy to resist the demands of determined Shariah ideologues. Things may get better, but they may need to get worse first. I remain mainly optimistic about the future, but by no means naive about the struggles facing us, and the losses we will have to endure.

EPILOGUE

In this collection of interviews we have endeavored to present the imporant contributions of several contemporary watchers on the ramparts who are often in physical danger. They have toiled endlessly in a daunting struggle combating the spread of what Dr. Mark Durie has aptly called, "imperialist Islam." An Islam which is a totalitarian doctrine posing as a theology, propelled by what Bat Ye'or calls a "rising Caliphate" - the 57 member OIC, the second largest international body at the UN. The OIC represents the agenda of the world wide community of Muslim believers, the ummah, and is backed by the vast treasury of petro-dollars from its sponsor, Saudi Arabia. The OIC's agenda is a Grand Jihad whose ultimate objective is Islamization of the West. It seeks to achieve this goal by endeavoring to snuff out basic constitutional freedoms guaranteeing free speech, unfettered thought, and the political liberties grounded in Western Judeo-Christian values. The OIC and its Muslim Brotherhood supporters in the West have invented terms like "Islamophobia" and have manipulated our laws, infiltrated our governments and intimidated lawful authorities. They have used fear to stifle criticism of the violent hatred directed at unbelievers and Muslim apostates who have fled to the West hoping for sanctuary. The OIC has successfully insinuated itself in the councils of law in the EU, effectively fostering compliance with Islamic Shariah doctrine. The OIC Cairo Declaration of 1990 decreed that human rights must comply with Shariah. The OIC has furthered this agenda in the US with the State Department Conference in December 2011 seeking implementation of UNHRC Res. 1618 on Combating Religious Intolerance. In reality, this would entail adoption of Shariah blasphemy codes. Disturbingly, the

Obama Administration has abetted the insinuation of Shariah blasphemy codes that Nina Shea notes will suborn the US Constitutional guarantees of free speech, under the First Amendment, including the right to criticize religion. Pushing back against Shariah compliance is what motivated the development of the uniform "American Law for American Courts" by its architect David Yerushalmi, Esq. and his colleagues at the newly formed pro bono law firm, the American Freedom Law Center.

Resistance to the OIC agenda of Shariah compliance was reflected in the successful acquittal of the Honorable Geert Wilders, leader of the Freedom Party (PVV) in the Netherlands at the conclusion of a long show trial in Amsterdam. However, given the convictions for "hate speech" by both Lars Hedegaard in Denmark and Elisabeth Sabaditsch-Wolff in Austria and others, a number of EU countries have capitulated to the OIC's Shariah compliance agenda. Moreover, the continued threats to the lives of free thinkers like Danish editorial cartoonist Kurt Westergaard and Swedish artist Lars Vilks clearly indicate that capitulation to Shariah has resulted from the threat of jihadist violence to achieve its ends in the West.

In conclusion, the successful onslaught of the rising OIC Caliphate and its Grand Jihad has blinded the West as to how to combat the spread of its agenda. By recognizing the courageous actions of these free thinkers and advocates, we might follow their example thereby informing and emboldening others to rise up and avert the severe decree of Islamic conquest via Grand Jihad.

Jerry Gordon, 2011

CPSIA information can be obtained at www.ICGtesting.com
Printed in the USA
LVOW102224220212

270026LV00002B/5/P

9 780578 099934